Hyperspace
and the Spiritual Realm

Hyperspace and the Spiritual Realm

Building of the Scriptural Case that the Spiritual Realm is located in the Higher Dimensions of our Space Time Continuum (Hyperspace)

Dr. Gary Sutliff

Hyperspace Chief Publications

Gilbert Arizona

Copyright © 2011 by Dr. Gary Sutliff

All rights reserved

First Edition: March 2013

Published by Hyperspace Chief; Gilbert, Arizona

Printed in the United States of America

Cover Photo: The cover photo is an artistic rendering using photo warping techniques designed to elicit the sense of warping space and time. It was done Rebekah Bell, a talented artist who works in many mediums and is also my first daughter. She brings great honor to her father.

"I pity the man who never thinks about heaven" [1] *J.C. Ryle*

---

[1] J.C. Ryle, *Heaven* (Ross-shire, UK: Christian Focus Pub., 1969), 19.

Table of Contents

Acknowledgements .... *xiii*

1 Introduction 1
2 Stepping Through the Veil 7
    2.1 The Story and Drama: Jesus Magically Appears 7
    2.2 Hyperspace Overview: 10
    2.3 Analysis: What is Going On? 12
    2.4 Explanation and Full Story: Road to Emmaus 19
    2.5 Summary of Jesus' Appearances: 23
3 Poking Through the Veil 25
    3.1 Story and Drama 26
    3.2 Hyperspace Overview 31
    3.3 Analysis of the Floating Hand 32
    3.4 Explanation for the Floating Hand 34
    3.5 Summary of Angel's Hand 35
4 Seeing Through the Veil 37
    4.1 Peeking into Hyperspace: The Story 37
    4.2 Hyperspace Overview 40
    4.3 Analysis of Behind the Veil 41
    4.4 Summary of Elisha's Servant Event 53
5 Journey in Hyperspace 55
    5.1 Background to a Journey in Hyperspace 55
    5.2 Story and Drama 60
    5.3 Hyperspace Overview: Hyperspace Journey 61
    5.4 Analysis of Hyperspace Journey 62
    5.5 Summary of Hyperspace Journey 74
6 The Great City in Hyperspace (Map of Heaven) 77
    6.1 Introduction to Heaven and It's Location 77
    6.2 Background and Definitions 79
    6.3 Heaven and the Spiritual Realm 82
    6.4 Spiritual Mt. Zion: City of the Living God 84

	6.5	Analogies for Hyperspace 102
	6.6	God: Creator Beyond Time and Space 106
	6.7	Summary of Heavenly Jerusalem 110
7	Hyperspace Underworld (Map of Hades) 113
	7.1	Introduction to the Underworld 113
	7.2	Grave: 116
	7.3	Hades or Sheol 117
	7.4	Bottomless Pit (Abyss - *abyssos*) 124
	7.5	Lake of Fire: Gehenna 129
	7.6	Summary of the Underworld 134
8	Hyperspace Universe 137
	8.1	Introduction: 137
	8.2	Rolled Up Thin Universe 138
	8.3	Tearing the Fabric of Space 142
	8.4	Creation Cosmology & Big Bang 142
	8.5	Beginning of Time 148
	8.6	Christ's Love is Hyperdimensional 154
	8.7	Summary of Biblical Cosmology: 156
9	History of Hyperspace Thought 161
	9.1	Birth of Higher Dimensional Thought 164
	9.2	Quantum Mechanics, String Theory and M-Theory 167
	9.3	Connecting Hyperspace and the Spiritual Realm 170
	9.4	Summary of Higher Dimensional History 173
10	Visualizing Hyperspace 175
	10.1	The Hyperspace You Have Always Known 176
	10.2	Spatial Dimensions 177
	10.3	Attempts at Visualization 180
	10.4	Summary of Visualizing Higher Dimensions 183
11	Big Picture & Summary 185
	11.1	General Summary 185
	11.2	Summary of the Case for Hyperspace and Heaven 186
	11.3	Summary of Scientific and Spiritual Findings and Discoveries 189
	11.4	Value of Hyperspace Research 192
	11.5	Thank You 193
12	Appendix I 195

13 Appendix II 199

Acknowledgements

The study and researching of hyperspace has been an incredible journey for me. It has led to an amazing and expanded appreciation of God's fantastic creation. Insights gained have brought me to times of exciting and great worship and praise as the majesty of what the Lord has established comes into focus. It is my greatest prayer and purpose of this book is for you to experience this same thing.

God has used many people to help shape me throughout the course of my life and several deserve special noting here. From an early age I learned a love of Scripture from my Mom, a great servant of the Lord. From my dad, I learned a love of science, engineering and technical things. Dad was a great father; I look forward to seeing him again. My 3 brothers Ron, David and Michael toughened me for persistent and diligent study; they are all real and true men of God.

All of my three children, their families and six grandkids bring great joy to my life (Rebekah, Chad and sons Daniel, Nathan and Isaac; Alyson, Casey and sons Hadon and Noah; Will, Erin, daughter Avery and soon to be another).

I first learned of Hyperspace through the teachings of the incredible leader and teacher, Dr. Chuck Missler. What an amazing man of spiritual and scientific insights. I owe him a great deal. This book is an outgrowth of my doctoral dissertation done for Louisiana Baptist University (LBU) and I am very grateful to the support of them and my advisor David Keeny.

It was my pastor, Mark Connelly, lead pastor of Mission Community Church, who encouraged me to dig deeper into this subject, noting that there wasn't a lot of material available. Mark is a great man with a strong heart for justice and he is being mightily used by God for exciting kingdom purposes. It is a privilege to be working with him.

Very special recognition should be given to Jim Wes, a great physicist and research industry leader who gave a lot of personal time to this work. He made significant contributions of ideas and suggestions. He vetted much of the basic research and conclusions both for the dissertation and this book as well. I am deeply indebted to this very technically talented and spiritually focused man. Through this project he has become a great friend to me: a blessing from God.

Lastly, I shudder to think where in life I would have ended up if it weren't for my loving wife Kay. She continues to love and be patient with a husband who is not easy to be with. In any objective review of my life accomplishments, she will certainly deserve most all the credit. Thank you my love.

May God richly bless you and reward you for spending time looking into this seldom examined but most unveiling subject..

Gary Sutliff

Bond Servant of Jesus Christ

1 Introduction

Job 38:33: *"Do you know the ordinances of the heavens, Or fix their rule over the earth?"*

In the very beginning God made the heaven<u>s</u>; plural meaning more than one (Gen 1:1). Our Lord created a vast unseen world where angels are busy at work and dark forces of wickedness are contending with them (Eph 6:12). Some people view the mysterious unseen world with a misty, vaporish ethereal type dominion. However, scripture indicates that Heaven is a place of substance; in fact much more substance than even what our world has. Heaven is where Jesus is now dwelling, sitting at the right hand of the Father (Acts 7:55). There is a great purpose for heaven and the activities that take place there. The Bible indicates that Jesus, now resurrected, has a solid tangible body that can be touched (Luke 24:39). Surprisingly, He ate food in their presence on several occasions (Luke 24:41-43; John 21:12-15). A ghost doesn't eat food. Also something that many don't realize is that angels also eat food (Psalm 78:23-25, Gen 18:8; 19:1). Other residents of the spiritual realm include horses of some kind (2 Kings 6:16-17) and chariots of fire, what ever they are (2 Kings 6:16-17). There is a tremendous amount of activity in the spiritual realm. The unseen world is truly a place of very tangible and solid things and important events occur there that impact our world.

But, if heaven is real, then where is it?

Personal Observations: For years I backpacked and mountain climbed on the peaks of the California Sierra Mountains. We would spend months looking over topographical maps, reading accounts of others who had been there and planning our routes. It built great excitement and I couldn't wait to begin the adventure. Reading the maps was fun and helped

Hyperspace in Scripture

with my understanding but it never compared to real views you got once you started up the trail.

I have spent many years developing a Biblical understanding of the physical aspects spiritual realm. This study has resulted in a type of "map" which relates areas and places in the spiritual realm with our seen world. Looking these "maps" over, seeing where our families who have gone before us are, and knowing where Jesus rules from encourages us and builds our faith. I'm not planning on going there soon, there is still lots to do, but without a doubt, I am looking forward to the trip.

Each of us has a day, when our life here is over and we are called "home." On that day, we cross the veil to the other side and are met there by two angels. Our first journey begins as we travel across Hyperspace heading to our destination, the City of the Living God. The journey will be fantastic. We will see things we can scarcely imagine but that will pale in significance to what we will see and experience once we arrive. We're going to meet our savior face to face. We will be reunited with family and friends who have gone before us. It will be other worldly. Today we are working diligently to be faithful servants of our Lord and Master. Today we also enjoy the blessing of being Children of the King. But to go home; that is something to live for. The really grand adventure awaits us there.

Where is Heaven?: Heaven is not a state of mind, Jesus and many other creatures call it home. So, if the spiritual realm is filled with tangible things, it must be located somewhere. That seems pretty obvious however as it turns out, there are only a few possible solutions to Heaven's location. Throughout history, only 4 possible locations for heaven have been suggested. (1) Heaven and the spiritual realm may be out there beyond some distant star. Interesting but this idea conflicts with some of the scriptures that indicate that the spiritual realm is around us (Daniel 10:10-14). (2) Some think that Heaven is perhaps separated out and away from us in some parallel type universe. As with the other concept, this idea also seems to conflict with scripture which describes a closeness. (3) Some simply express confidence in the reality of Heaven but it is just unclear where it is. For a great many years this is the approach most people have had. However, I am suggesting here that scripture actually does give us sufficient insight to understand where Heaven actually is which leads us to the last idea. (4)

Introduction

Heaven is located in the higher dimensions of our space-time continuum or what is sometimes referred to as Hyperspace. This concept at first is a little tough to grasp but as will be shown in this book, it is exactly what the Bible teaches. I don't ask you to understand this concept or accept it right yet but this does brings us to the purpose of this book.

Objectives: This book is written with the objective that everyone may come to (1) fully appreciate the reality of Heaven, (2) understand where God located it and (3) grasp the impact that this has on our personal lives. The bold claim up front is that the spiritual realm is a very real tangible place immediately adjacent to our seen world. Further, the spiritual realm is a fully integrated part of our universe. In fact Heaven is the permanent part of our universe whereas our seen world is temporal and will pass away (2 Cor 4:18).

Good News: So, there is some really good news here. Many are already aware of the first piece of good news which is that Heaven is a very real place. Very few are aware of this second piece of good news which is that Scripture actually tells us where our Lord placed heaven and how it is physically located in relation to our earth. Not many know or understand that but it is my prayer that you will by the time you are done reading the book. But wait, there's more. The third piece of good news is that we even know where the soul/spirits of the dead now reside. There have been many wicked people throughout history who rejected God. We will identify where the underworld is where their souls reside. You may know people or have family or friends who placed their lives in the hands of Jesus asking for Him to be their Lord and Savior but have died. We know where their soul/spirits are. They are with Jesus in the City of the Living God and its location will probably be a surprise to most. These are some very big claims and boldly made only because, as you will see, they are based on a very solid case that has been developed from Scripture.

Importance & Insights: But some have asked; "Come on! Really? Is this even important anyway?" The Holy Spirit seems to think so. Do you think the Holy Spirit told us that resurrected Jesus in His physical touchable body suddenly appeared in the middle of a room with closed doors just to confuse us? The Holy Spirit even records this fact 3 times in the Bible. Do you think that the Holy Spirit gave us that information for no apparent reason? Why didn't Jesus just walk through the door? Perhaps the Holy Spirit is actually telling those who take the Scriptures seriously some important tidbits to facilitate our understanding, not create confusion. Do you think that the angel who traveled across the spiritual realm for 3 long weeks, fighting with adversaries who prevented him for accomplishing what God told him to do and then related all this information to Daniel simply felt like chatting? Why in the world would the Holy Spirit bother to record this lengthy conversation if it wasn't somehow very important?

Everything in Scripture means something. The Holy Spirit has crafted without question the greatest written masterpiece of all time. For those who chose to take the Scriptures seriously, accept them as if Jesus Himself was standing directly in front of them and speaking to them personally, there is a wealth of knowledge and understanding to be gained. There is much wisdom to be learned. So, because the Bible speaks on the subject of Heaven, giving us information, we listen very carefully. We meditate on the subtle things the Holy Spirit whispers to us through the pages of Scripture knowing it has value; knowing that He doesn't waste His time or discuss trivia for trivia's sake. Everything the Holy Spirit says means something.

Science & Scripture: There is one more important item that we need to cover before we start. It is the very core of our approach to this study. Their have been occasions when people have come to some understanding through scientific pursuit and then have attempted to force that understanding back into the Scriptures. On many of these occasions, what is being asserted is incorrect (surprisingly science is often flawed and constantly changes their opinions) and as a result, peoples' asserted declarations of what Scriptures says become false. That is not the approach taken here. This is extremely important point worthy of repetition. We have not adopted the approach of taking some new purported scientific truth and then forced it back into the scriptures. A key tenant of Modern Science is its denial and rejection of the supernatural. For this reason, the scientific community will never lead us to and understanding of the physical aspects of heaven. But the good news is that the Scriptures not only can, but do lead us into a detailed understanding. So, the approach used here was to first objectively examine what the scriptures say on the subject of Heaven and higher dimensions. Based on this examination of the Bible alone, then

Introduction

secondly conclusions are drawn that are firmly grounded in Scripture. Once that is accomplished however, it is actually surprising to find out that modern day physics actually confirms these understandings of higher dimensions. But, please recognize that the problem wasn't worked backwards by forcing a popular scientific insight back into scripture. Instead, a very solid case is built from Scripture and Scripture alone. But it is fascinating how modern physics is confirming many of these Biblical scientific insights. [2]

---

[2] The author has a book that explores many wonderful scientific insights gleaned from the pages of scripture. Gary Sutliff, *God Speaks Science* (Gilbert AZ, Hyperspace Pub., 2007).

Hyperspace in Scripture

2 Stepping Through the Veil

"Unfamiliarity with heaven makes a dull and worldly Christian." [3]
John MacArthur

2.1 THE STORY AND DRAMA: JESUS MAGICALLY APPEARS

John 20:19: *"So when it was evening on that day, the first day of the week, and when the **doors were shut** where the disciples were, for fear of the Jews, **Jesus came and stood in their midst** and *said to them, 'Peace be with you.'"* (emphasis author)

John 20:26: *"After eight days His disciples were again inside, and Thomas with them. **Jesus came, the doors having been shut, and stood in their midst** and said, 'Peace be with you.'"* (emphasis author)

This stunning story where Jesus appears 'magically' in a closed room occurs in John 20:19 (also in Luke 24:36-39) and the event reoccurs in John 20:26.

This day was to be the most astounding and memorable day of their entire lives. It is the events of this day that will begin the disciples' transformation from confusion, fear and despondency to understanding, hope

---

[3] John F. MacArthur, *The Glory of Heaven* (Wheaton, Illinois: Crossway Books, 1995), 64.

Hyperspace in Scripture

and courage. This day becomes perhaps the most celebrated day in all of Christianity. The story of this day would be told and re-told over and over for the next 2,000 years. It is the cornerstone of the gospel, the story of Easter. At the time, however, they thought they just discovered the lowest ebb of life possible. Throughout most of the day, they could not have conceived a reason to celebrate, rather depression was the battle they were fighting. No hope of restoration seemed even possible. It was a lost cause. All of their hopes and dreams had been dashed. Everything they thought they would gain was now lost. It appeared that everything they had labored so hard for so long had in such a short period of time completely vaporized.

At 6:00am a few days earlier things took an ugly turn and by 3:00pm that afternoon, their world was pulverized. For three years they had been riding a challenging wave that they thought would land them on a beautiful island shore in a place of prominence and blessing. Instead, here they were; hiding away in an upstairs room; hiding from the tentacles of the government that they knew was seeking to destroy them. On top of that, they were confused and bewildered over rather bizarre events that had occurred earlier that day. Some of the women in emotional hysteria had made non-sensical claims and Peter and John saw things that defied explanation. But most of all, they were hiding in fear.

Their fear was neither unfounded, nor over inflated. Indeed, the religious leaders had teamed up with the government to fulfill their plot of evil which had successfully resulted in the execution of their leader. This was the very leader that they had all placed their hopes and dreams into. They had faithfully followed him over these years, anticipating both religious and political success but achieving neither. Death had overtaken him and his shattered and tortured body had been placed hastily and not fully prepared in the grave.

One brave member of team had even watched the gruesome execution process designed and perfected long ago to extract maximum pain from its victims. And in this case, it certainly did not disappoint the blood thirsty. In contrast to their hopes, now they had neither religious honor nor political influence. In fact, to the ruling religious, they were heretics and outcasts; and to the government, they were enemies of the state. At the moment before the change, it was indeed a very depressing, dark and fearful situation.

But, as often happens in the deepest bleakness and darkest moments of our lives, the powerful presence of God can burst forth in the strongest of overpowering light. On this what seemed as the most tragic of days, the light of God's protection, care and salvation did indeed come flooding on to the scene. The form that the intense spiritual light took was that of a man, and because it was a man, in the beginning, they just saw something unexplainable. The supernatural, the unexplainable actually caused them to become even more afraid. More truthfully, what they saw further terrified them. It was unexpected, unnatural, and unexplainable and therefore it became unnerving.

Just prior to everything changing, one more thing did happen which put the team off guard. Two of their associates, who had supported their cause had recently arrived and had come into the room. They described a series of events that had just taken place and to them were most remarkable. Perhaps unbelievable would be a better word. They claimed to have seen the executed leader and he was now alive!

Oddly, some of the women associated with the group and two of the group leaders themselves had had similar experiences that day. Naturally, everyone was struggling to comprehend the situation. Believing that their tortured and executed leader was now somehow alive was beyond any level of credibility. A few seemed to believe in something they could not comprehend; most remained in unbelief. As they discussed and debated these things they remained hidden, in a room, behind locked doors. Certainly the threats still remained, and they were very real. They were still in a state of fear after dinner, somewhere just after 8:00pm.[4] In just a moment, rather than simply being afraid, they were about to become terrified.

---

[4] Commentator John Phillips notes from John 20:19a and reasonably deduces from the two on the road to Emmaus were eating the evening meal but then ran back to Jerusalem, some 7 miles: John Phillips *The Gospel of John* (Grand Rapids: Kregel Pub., 1989), 380.

Hyperspace in Scripture

In the middle of the room, behind the closed and locked doors, their leader appeared out of nowhere. The fact that someone would appear out of nowhere would cause anyone to become very afraid. To see what appeared to be their dead leader led them to assume they were probably staring at a ghost or something which then brought on terror. Knowing their state, the leader speaks calming words. He tells them it is him. He tells them he is not a ghost but is real. He invites them to touch him validating that he was in a real tangible and touchable body.

To further demonstrate the reality of the body he possessed, he then asks for some food! Imagine that, the Messiah, the Son of God, the Creator of the Entire Universe who has been crucified, was dead, buried and then on the third day rose bodily in resurrection form victorious from the grave, would like something to eat. It is my guess that as the terror began to subside, it was perhaps replaced by bewilderment. They gave Him some fish. Perhaps it was Thomas's portion since he had already left earlier in the day.

2.2 HYPERSPACE OVERVIEW:

We are still challenged today to fully comprehend the staggering events of this passage even though we look back on it in remote contemplation some 2,000 years later. We are struck by several seemly unexplainable things which, we will find, when viewed from a higher dimensional or Hyperspace perspective, become understandable. These are:

- Jesus appeared out of nowhere into a closed room and subsequently disappears.
- Jesus' resurrected body was material, or tangible (you could touch it and feel it). He wasn't a spirit or ghost.
- His resurrected body could eat (which supports the fact that it was a material or tangible body)

Of high interest to us in this study is the first two. The third one, the fact that resurrected bodies (like the ones we will receive when we are raised up) can eat, is absolutely fascinating and will be developed in a subsequent book as we look further into hyperspace and its implications. But, for our purposes in this study, the key points are that Jesus' resurrected body is a tangible, material real body and that it can appear and disappear from our visible world are key to developing our understanding of where the spiritual realm and heaven really are.

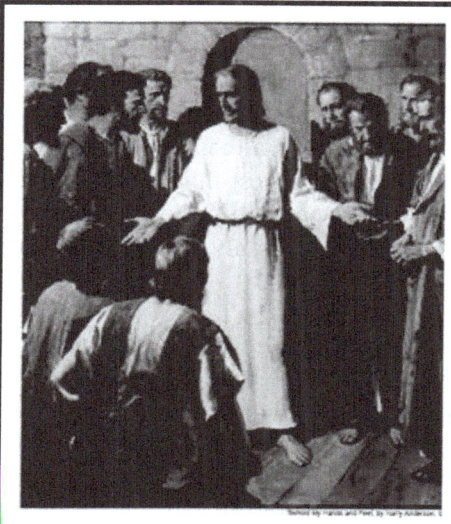 

Figure 1 Resurrected Christ: *Left*, appeared to crowd; *right*, appeared to Mary.[5]

The implications of these observations are also staggering to consider. We find that this passage implies some very profound insights that is not generally recognized. On the basis of the disciple's observations of the event and the Holy Spirit's communication of them, we note three implications:

1) This serves as a clear proof that multi-dimensional hyperspace exists being that it is the only really plausible explanation;
2) Jesus was not just raised from the dead (like Lazarus was), but was resurrected, a significant difference; and

---

[5]"Jesus Showing Hands" and "Jesus with Mary", Gospel Art, http://www.lds.org/library/display/0,4945,8555-1-4779-4,00.html (accessed December 30, 2009).

Hyperspace in Scripture

    3) Jesus, now has a hyperspace body and is capable of moving between our 3D world (the world that we see or what is called the "visible world" (Col 1:16) and the spiritual realm (what is called the unseen world (2 Cor 4:18) located in hyperspace

Jesus could certainly have come up to, knocked on and entered the room through the door. But he didn't. That fact that He didn't becomes important as we recognize that the Holy Spirit has gone to the trouble of recording this detail in scripture. He tells us this for a reason. He is giving us information that He considers important. I'll suggest that it is extremely important and that when we examine the various possibilities of answers that would explain this, a clear picture will emerge and only one real solution will remain.

And there is more good news. As that solution is considered, it becomes the key that the Holy Spirit has given us to unlock the mystery of where heaven and the spiritual realm are. This simple passage even by itself is sufficient to prove that heaven and the spiritual realm are in hyperspace, or otherwise stated, the higher dimensions of our space-time continuum. But, I am getting ahead of myself. Let's do some analysis of this passage.

2.3   ANALYSIS: WHAT IS GOING ON?

Resurrected Body: Lazarus was brought back to life, physical life (as noted in John 11). Jesus was resurrected from the dead. Lazarus was given back normal physical life and would continue to grow old and eventually he would die and be buried again. Jesus was resurrected and the first person to receive a resurrected body. Colossians 1:18 and Revelation 1:5 note that Jesus was the "First born from the dead. According to 1 Corinthians 15:17-54, a resurrected body is "everlasting" or "imperishable" and "does not decay" (1 Cor 15:42, 52-53). Also, a resurrected body is glorified (1 Cor 15:43) and powerful (1 Cor 15:43) as compared to our currently earthly bodies. So, bottom line, Jesus is in a resurrected body and is demonstrating what a resurrected body can do.

Appears and Vanishes: In order to better comprehend the event, we will consider first what Jesus is doing. Luke uses the descriptive term "vanished" as he described the coming and going of the resurrected Christ. Luke 24:31: *"And their eyes were opened, and they knew him; and he*

Jesus Disappears

vanished out of their sight." Vanished is from two Greek words, *ginomai* meaning "to cause to be" or "to become" and *aphantos* meaning "invisible"[6]. This gives a pretty clear indication that Jesus is not just sneaking off while no one is looking. This is also very true in the two John accounts (John 20:19; 20:26). John makes a very specific point of noting in both instances that the doors were closed and Jesus appeared. Jesus was all of a sudden, just there. Factually, He was not there one moment, and then a moment later, He was there. From these observations, scripture clearly tells us that the resurrected Jesus appeared in the middle of a closed room and then subsequently vanished. And He did this on multiple occasions. By taking the disciples accounts seriously, we can glean some excellent information about hyperspace.

Options for how Jesus "Appeared" and "Vanished": Now that it is established that Jesus did much more than just come to life, the major question that arises is: "Where did He go when he disappeared?" Through these passages, the Holy Spirit has given us insight into the capabilities of Jesus and His "resurrected" body. Turns out it can do some pretty amazing things. Also of interest to us, we too (those who have been "born again" – John 3:3, 7; 1Peter 1:3, 23) will one day receive our resurrected body and it will possess the same amazing and exciting characteristics that Christ's body does (more on this in section 5.5.1 - Transfiguration).

As stated before, resurrected Jesus demonstrated hyperspace capability. There are some other options as to what was going on here, but none of these become viable upon consideration.

1) **Invisible Man**: He became "transparent" to us like glass. You can see through Him and don't know he is there unless you reach out and touch Him (you could touch Him: Luke 24:39). This concept seems unlikely, because the passage seems to indicate that He left, not that He was there and you couldn't see Him. He doesn't start talking while no one sees Him. VERY UNLIKELY

---

[6]Luke 24:31, Blueletterbible,
http://www.blueletterbible.org/Bible.cfm?b=Luk&c=24&v=1&t=KJV#conc/31
(accessed January 22, 2010), Strong's #1096 and #855.

Hyperspace in Scripture

2) **Beamed Up**: It could be conceived that, like in the "Star Trek" series, there is a "transporter" which basically breaks down all your molecules, shoots them across space, and then recombines them again. Vincent Price went through this in the 1950's science thriller "The Fly" where he is transported over the phone lines to another location. One problem. Fly went into the transporter. Bummer. Price comes out at the other end with a man's body but with the head of a fly (how the fly's head got big really isn't explained) but what I thought was really cool was the fly's body that got Price's human head. Little fly buzzing around with a miniature human head talking in a squeaky high voice. Now that was cool, too bad he got stuck in that spiders web, real bummer. Anyway, I got side tracked. There seems to be no indication in the Scriptural text of a transporter so I'll leave this as less likely as well. This is in the realm of what I will call "Theo-Magic." It implies that God doesn't act according to His own established laws but just basically makes things happen by "Magic" just because He is God and can do it. Certainly God can do anything He wants and I fully believe in miracles that Jesus and God do, but I don't consider it magic. I think scripture teaches us that God acts according to his own laws and is consistent with them. The great miracles like the Flood of Noah, destruction of Sodom and Gomorrah and even the raising of Lazarus are somehow consistent with God's laws. They are miraculous in nature and only the God of the Universe could make them happen. However, I don't see magic, but God working through His laws to cause something very majestic to happen in a very precise manner at a very precise moment in time. It is something that only a Creator in control of His creation could do. So, "beamed up" is "Theo-Magic" and VERY UNLIKELY.

3) **Ghost**: It's Casper the friendly ghost! He has shown up, but because he is a spirit, sometimes you see him and sometimes you don't. I don't think this is consistent with what the text is saying, because they tell us that the people could "touch" Him (Luke 24:39). A spirit or ghost can't be touched, you would pass your hand right through it. VERY UNLIKELY

4) **Hyperspace**: Potentially Jesus just "moved" in a direction we can't see. He simply stepped into hyperspace or the spiritual realm. It is exactly what physicists tell us that a person who has hyperspace travel capability can do. We will go further into this

explanation but it is worthy of note that this view is consistent with what the passage describes and is a very natural fit to the scriptural text. Moving into hyperspace is the only real plausible option to what is being described. Hyperspace activity is a VERY LIKELY and therefore the preferred answer.

What does it mean to "move into hyperspace"?: A medical doctor of the late 20th Century, A.T. Schofield, recognized that heaven is located in higher dimensions of the universe. One of his key reasons of suggesting this came from his observations that scripture records several events of appearances and disappearances of people. These appearances make a lot of sense if these people are moving in and out of higher dimensions and there is no real other possible solution. Schofield in 1888: "Not only are mysterious appearances and disappearances constantly recorded [in scripture], but very definitely in the case of our Lord, as entering a room in a body 'with flesh and bones,' though all entrance to it was barred. Also, at another time, when sitting at supper, He vanished out of their sight, though in a body and capable of eating and drinking."[7] This same thought about movement into higher dimensions of the space-time continuum is noted by modern Theoretical Physicist Dr Michio Kaku. He said: "Imagine being able to disappear or reappear at will…What being could possess such God-like power? The answer: a being from a higher-dimensional world."[8]

2D to 3D Analogy: Let me suggest an example to help visualize what is taking place. Imagine a world that is flat; a 2D world. In this flat world are some very special people that are also flat. These are the Goombas and Goombas are flat 2 dimensional (2D) little creatures. A Goomba is kind of like a paper doll. Goombas live in a flat surface, what is technically called a plane. In some sense, it is like an ant farm. Goombas move about traveling in their 2D ant farm type world.

---

[7]A.T. Schofield, M.D., *Another World: or The Fourth Dimension* (Blomsbury, England: Swan Sonnenschein & Co., Lim., 1888), 74

[8]Michio Kaku, *Hyperspace* (New York: Anchor Books, 1995), 46.

Hyperspace in Scripture

Now imagine (as shown in Figure 2) that one of these little Goomba creatures has a house. In order for the Goomba to enter into his house, he would first have to open the door and then he could go in. Remember, the Goomba can only move on the flat surface or in a sense, in the ant farm. If a Goomba friend was in the house, they would see the door open and the other Goomba little fellow enter into the house.

Now for the fun part. We'll suggest a different method for the Goomba to get into his house. Suppose we lifter the Goomba off the flat surface, moving him through 3D space and then placed him back onto the flat surface but in the house. This would be fantastic. The Goomba would move to a higher dimension and then re-insert himself inside the home. If there was another Goomba in his house, to him, it would seem like his Goomba friend just appeared out of nowhere.

This analogy uses 2 dimensional people, but takes them through a higher dimension (the 3D) and then puts them back into 2D space. The net affect in the 2D flat plate world is that the Goomba would seem to disappear and then re-appear in a different place (in this case inside the house). This is analogous to Jesus. Jesus, a solid real tangible 3D resurrected being steps into our world from a higher dimension (4D) and then back out again. He can step in at any location, seemingly appearing out of nowhere and then step back out, seemingly disappearing.

Jesus Disappears

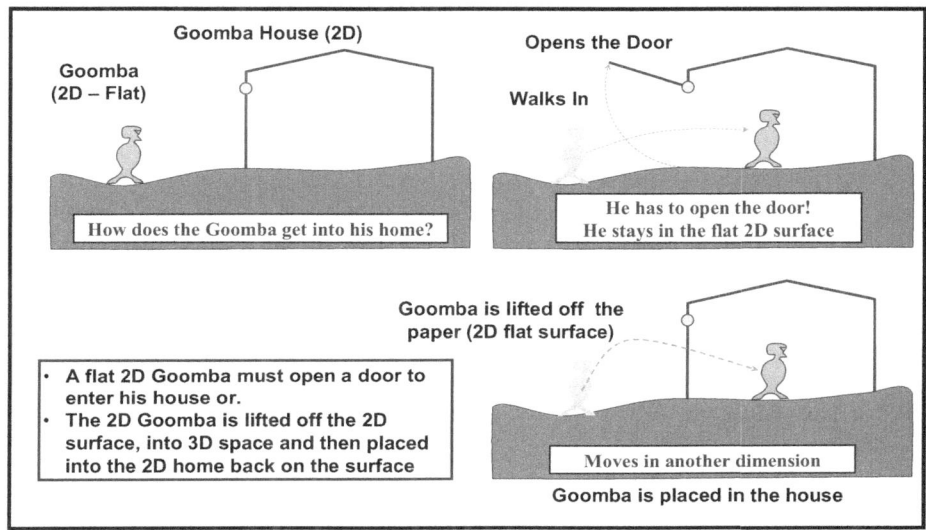

Figure 2. Illustration of using higher dimensions to "appear" and "disappear"

Although we are making our case for heaven in higher dimensions based on the Bible, it is worth noting that the concept of using the additional spatial dimension to travel around or "through" barriers in lower dimensions is exactly what modern physics and the study of higher dimensional hyperspace tells us. As noted physicist Dr. Michio Kaku comments: "Imagine being able to walk through walls. You wouldn't even have to bother with opening doors; you could pass right through them. You wouldn't have to go around buildings; you could enter them through their walls and pillars and out through the back wall. You wouldn't have to detour around mountains; you could step right into them."[9]

Angles and Resurrected Jesus: Now that we are beginning to see how traveling in and out of higher dimensions works, it helps explain to us how things can appear and disappear, lets consider the angels. Imagine that there are angels present with us in a room. Perhaps angels join us at church while we worship. But we can't see them. Where are they? I'll suggest that they are really there, but just standing back slightly in Hyperspace. We can't

---

[9]Michio Kaku, *Hyperspace* (New York: Anchor Books, 1995), 45.

see them, because we can't see in that "direction." I'll call this the spiritual direction. We can't see into the spiritual direction, the direction of the spiritual realm or unseen world because it is located in higher dimensions, in Hyperspace.

The spiritual dimension is not a place of the mind or thought; it is a real place, a tangible place of substance with 4 or more directional dimensions. Given the ability to travel into that dimension, you would find it truer, clearer, and of more substance than our three dimensional world we understand. Consider the example we just discussed. The 2D Goomba has a very limited understanding of his 2D flat world, but there is a bigger reality. In this example, there is a 3D world around him and in comparison, he is just like a flat paper cut-out doll and in the 3D world around him, there are possibly real 3D dolls.

Connectedness between the Spiritual Realm (unseen) and the physical realm (seen): As we are considering the relationship between the seen and unseen worlds another insight begins to develop. Where is the world of the unseen? It is not off far far away. It is not way out there behind some distant star. In actuality, it is all around us. In fact, it is we who are embedded into the full picture of a time-space continuum containing higher dimensions (Hyperspace). An analogy is kind of like altitude. You can go anywhere on the Earth but from every spot; you can jump up in the "up" direction. From every point on Earth, you can still always move "up". It is like that with the spiritual direction. From any point on earth, you can step in the direction of the spiritual realm. The spiritual realm is all everywhere.

As the spiritual realm comes into focus, our own 3D world seems to become dimmer. If we use the 2D / 3D analogy, our world would be like a 2D paper doll world, and in contrast, the spiritual realm in hyperspace becomes the 3D world, the one of true solids and substance. Christian and noted physicists Dr. Lambert Dolphin comments on this point:

> *The Bible depicts the spiritual realm as more solid, more substantial, more permanent than the present, observable, material world. When God created the universe he created it 'two-storied.' The spiritual realm is where the angels dwell. It is a so much more solid and substantial and permanent than our fading material*

world, that we can best describe ourselves as ghosts in a shadow-like world surrounded and embedded in the more substantial world of the spirit. [10]

The spiritual realm is in higher dimensions with more solidness, more vibrancy, more dimension and just plain more of everything. We will see light in a whole new way, a higher dimensional way and colors will be more brilliant and vibrant that we can ever imagine. Sound also will be different with more content that we can imagine. Perhaps this is why Paul, who somehow got a glimpse of the magnificent place commented as follows in 2 Corinthians 12:3-4: *"And I know how such a man--whether in the body or apart from the body I do not know, God knows-- was caught up into Paradise and heard inexpressible words, which a man is not permitted to speak."* (NAS) "Inexpressible words" gives us the insight that it is nearly impossible to describe, and thus we would think so because how can a 2D creature describe the 3D world? How can 3D Paul visit the 4D heaven and describe it to us? Truly, it is difficult but through the scriptures, we anticipate that the unseen world is a very grand place indeed.

2.4   EXPLANATION AND FULL STORY: ROAD TO EMMAUS

We have focused in this chapter on a very special event in the life of the disciples and Jesus. This was when resurrected Jesus first appears to the entire group of disciples (Judas is gone and Thomas who was there for part of the day, for reasons undisclosed, decided to skip the evening "prayer meeting"). Luke notes that there are some other followers there as well; perhaps this was Mary and some of the other women. The day that all this occurred is truly a historic day. It is Sunday, and sometime in the morning just before daylight, Jesus was resurrected and the stone was rolled away from the tomb. Luke also records some other very fascinating events that occurred on this day which include 5 appearances of the resurrected Jesus. Let's link them together chronologically. They are listed out here in order, and then examined from a hyperspace perspective.

---

[10] Dr. Lambert Dolphin, "Is Empty Space Empty?", posted February 1997, http://ldolphin.org/update.html   (accessed January 11, 2010)

Hyperspace in Scripture

1) Luke 24:1-12 (Matt 28:1-10): Jesus is resurrected. Two Mary's and Joanna go to the tomb early in the morning to finish preparing Jesus' body for burial. They find the tomb empty and have an encounter with two angels. They go to the room where the 11 disciples are and tell them the news but are not believed. Peter and John, ("the disciple whom Jesus loved" –John 20:2) go to the tomb and encounter the 2 angels. Subsequently, Mary (Magdalene) has an encounter with resurrected Jesus (Appearance #1: Mark 16:9; John 20:14). Other women have an encounter with resurrected Jesus (Appearance #2: Matt 28:9-10). Peter also has an encounter with resurrected Jesus (it is not clear exactly when on this day that it occurred: Appearance #3: Luke 24:34; 1 Cor 15:5). Peter subsequently returns to the room where the disciples are. Everyone is amazed, confused and for the most part, not believing. For reasons not stated, but apparently in unbelief of the stories, Thomas leaves, probably before dinner (John 20:24).

2) Luke 24:13-33 (also noted in Mark 16:12): On this day, somewhere around 3:00 pm or 4:00 pm Cleopas and another follower of Jesus leave the disciples at Jerusalem headed on a 7 mile trip to Emmaus. They are very disappointed thinking that Jesus was going to become king but was instead crucified. Resurrected Jesus joins them in their travel but they do not recognize Him (Appearance #4). Jesus has a challenging discussion with the two travelers. Jesus asks questions of them stating that: "hadn't the events that had recently happened (Messiah's presentation and crucifixion) been prophesied in the scriptures?" Jesus goes on to show how all of the scripture is linked to the Messiah and that indeed, the rejection and crucifixion had been prophesied. They are really struggling and can't accept the information. When they get to their destination, they have a meal and while Jesus is passing them bread, they realize that it is Jesus (Dr. Chuck Missler suggests that this might have happened because while passing the bread, they saw the wounds on his hands). Jesus disappears from their sight. *"Then their eyes were opened and they recognized him, and he disappeared from their sight."* Luke 24:31 (NIV)

3) Luke 24:33-35 (Mark 16:13): The two travelers, Cleopas and his friend, now in Emmaus, hurry back to Jerusalem and meet the disciples who are still in the room. Presumably, as it is now past

supper time, that crowd has already had dinner. Cleopas and his friend arrive and tell their story and the disciples relate back that Jesus had also appeared to Peter (Simon). There is still general unbelief in the room.

4) Luke 24:36-49 (John 20:19-23; Mark 16:14-18?): Later that evening, the disciples, other followers, probably the women and Cleopas with his friend are there hiding in the room at Jerusalem for fear of the Jews. Resurrected Jesus, appears out of nowhere (Appearance #5). Jesus criticizes them for their lack of belief (Mark 16:14) and after allowing Himself to be touched to demonstrate that He had a real, physical body, He asks for something to eat. They give him a broiled fish which He enjoys while they look on (does anyone else think that this part of the story is kind of strange?).

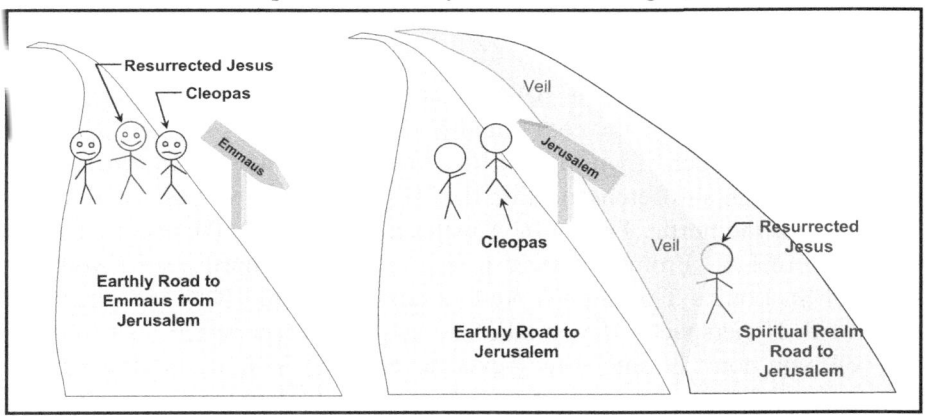

Figure 3 – On the way to Emmaus and the return trip to Jerusalem

So, what is going on here? I'll suggest that if we examine this day from a hyperspace perspective, it can help us understand several things.

First: When you move into or out of higher dimensions (Hyperspace), it is like stepping through an invisible veil or curtain. I think it is helpful to think of moving into Hyperspace as moving behind the veil or curtain. Kind of like when a curtain is drawn across the stage of a theater. An announcer on stage could be telling us about the play before the curtain goes up. When he is done, rather than going off the side of the stage, he could step back through the curtain and disappear. The announcer didn't

Hyperspace in Scripture

magically disappear; he just stepped back through the curtain which is in a direction that we can see through. For this reason, to help our understanding, at times we will use the phrase to "step through the veil."

Second: When you enter Hyperspace, you still have a location. Using the example of the announcer on the stage, when he first steps back through the veil, he really is still on stage, he didn't just disappear. He has a location, he is just on the other side of the curtain, we just can't see him, but he really is right there. Additionally, every place in Hyperspace is not the same, there are many different places. Taking the stage example further, once the announcer steps behind the curtain, he is in the middle of the stage, just behind the curtain. But, he could continue further back on the stage or he could then travel to the left or right on the stage. Once he is behind the curtain, there are many places to go from there. Hyperspace isn't just a single point in space.

Another example; a person can take a step to the north (one direction), or a step to the east (another, 2nd direction), or a step up (a 3rd direction). However, if you live in Los Angeles and take a step towards the north, you are in a different location than if you lived in St. Louis and took a step towards the north. From Los Angeles a step towards the north puts you just north of LA. From St. Louis, a step towards the north leaves you just north of St. Louis. This sounds pretty straight forward. Now it is the same thing with Hyperspace. If you take one step into Hyperspace, just through the veil, you don't go into some never-never land. You are in Hyperspace, just one step from where you entered. You are just the other side of the veil.

The point is that when someone goes into the spiritual realm, into Hyperspace, when they first step through the veil, they are still close to us. However, they are just in the realm that is invisible to us, so we can't see them but they could be very close to us, just on the other side of the veil (or curtain).

Third: After Jesus left the disciples at Emmaus, by going through the veil and entering Hyperspace, He still needed to travel to Jerusalem; which He did through Hyperspace. Because of what we just stated, when Jesus just stepped through the veil, He was in Hyperspace next to Emmaus. He came into the part of Hyperspace that is adjacent to Emmaus. So, if He wanted to meet the disciples in Jerusalem, some 7 miles away, Jesus needed to travel in hyperspace to get to the point that was adjacent to Jerusalem. Cleopas and his buddy wanted to talk with the disciples back in Jerusalem, so they had to travel back the 7 miles to get there. In the same way, even though Jesus is now in Hyperspace, He would have to travel the 7 miles in Hyperspace to get to Jerusalem Hyperspace.

Fourth: When Jesus arrived at Jerusalem Hyperspace, He stepped back through the veil and appeared in the room with the disciples. So, Jesus had to travel in Hyperspace to get to the Jerusalem Hyperspace location from the Emmaus Hyperspace location. Once Jesus arrived to the Hyperspace location adjacent to the Jerusalem room where the disciples were, He could just step back through the veil and enter the room. To the disciples it would have appeared that Jesus just appeared out of nowhere. However, what He really did was step in from Hyperspace.

2.5   SUMMARY OF JESUS' APPEARANCES:

Oh, my dear reader, consider the wonder of these passages of scripture. Jesus, in His resurrected body demonstrates the ability to effortlessly step into and out of our seen 3D world. One of the key reasons that the Holy Spirit tells us this story is so we can know about hyperspace. Everything in scripture means something. The most natural understanding of this passage is to recognize that the unseen world, the spiritual realm is in the higher dimensions (Hyperspace) of our space-time continuum. Jesus is simply stepping into and out of our 3D world by stepping out of and into Hyperspace. All other solutions are basically Theo-magic making Jesus appear and disappear leaving us with innumerable questions like; "What happened to all the atoms and the real material in His body?" In contrast, the concept or solution of higher dimensions fits naturally with the text and reveals to us further insight. It would seem that the Holy Spirit has given us this insight specifically so we can understand that the spiritual realm, the unseen world is higher dimensional. Additionally, we have seen the close connectedness between the seen and unseen realms and recognize that the spiritual realm actually surrounds us completely.

Hyperspace in Scripture

Key take-aways from this chapter are:

- ✓ The unseen Spiritual Realm is located in the higher dimensions of our space-time continuum referred to as Hyperspace

- ✓ Jesus appeared into a closed room because He stepped into (or moved into) our 3D seen world from the higher order 4D unseen world (spiritual realm); as we will refer to it, Jesus stepped through the veil.

- ✓ Resurrected Jesus (and the angels) can move easily in and out of our 3D world by stepping out of and into the 4D spiritual realm. It appears to us that they are magically appearing and disappearing but what is happening, is that they are just moving out of and into Hyperspace by going through the veil.

- ✓ The seen 3D world in actually embedded into or is a part of the larger higher dimensional space-time continuum; we are of the lower order

- ✓ Hyperspace (the spiritual realm) is a very large place and when someone enters it, they are only at one place in it. They are at one point only. Angels in the spiritual realm adjacent to a church in Gilbert Arizona are a thousand miles away from angels in a church in St. Louis Missouri.

3 Poking Through the Veil

"Man is a strange animal. He generally cannot read the handwriting on the wall until his back is up against it." [11] Adlai E. Stevenson: US Ambassador to the United Nations

"This intervention came without trumpet blasts, thundering voices from heaven or earthquakes. Suddenly the finger of a hand appeared on the palace wall and before the wine-reddened eyes of the king, began writing just four words, the first two of them identical. Then, just as suddenly as it had appeared, the hand vanished, leaving only the blazing letters on the wall." [12] Gleason Archer Jr.

"No flash of supernatural light, nor deafening peal of thunder, startled the drunken revelers, thus announcing the interference of God in their impious carousal. But out of the 'sleeve of the night' the Hand of God appeared, and with its finger silently wrote, in mystic characters, on the wall over against the lighted Candlestick, where it could be readily seen by all the assembled guests, the doom of Babylon. The fact that the writing remained indelibly fixed on the wall showed that it was no hallucination of an intoxicated man's fancy. It sobered the King, and filled him with fear, and he at once called for the 'Wise Men' of Babylon to interpret its meaning." [13] Rev. Clarence Larkin

---

[11] Adlai E. Stevenson, "Adlai E. Stevenson Quotes," Thinkexist.com, http://thinkexist.com/quotation/man_is_a_strange_animal-he_generally_cannot_read/221251.html (accessed October 12, 2010).

[12] Frank E. Gaebelein gen. ed., The Expositor's Bible Comentary (Grand Rapids: Zondervan, 1985), Vol. 7: page 70

[13] Rev. Clarence Larkin, The Book of Daniel (Glenside PA: The Clarence Larkin Estate, 1929), 84.

Hyperspace in Scripture

3.1 STORY AND DRAMA

Daniel 5:5-6: *"Suddenly the fingers of a man's hand emerged and began writing opposite the lampstand on the plaster of the wall of the king's palace, and the king saw the back of the hand that did the writing. Then the king's face grew pale and his thoughts alarmed him, and his hip joints went slack and his knees began knocking together."*

When people who don't believe in God or the spiritual realm encounter something overtly supernatural it causes great alarm. When anyone encounters an angel that is in his full display of glory, commonly the person's reaction is one of extreme terror.

Belshazzar is such an example. Belshazzar was leader of the Babylonian World Empire, which at that time was beginning to crumble. He really was only 2nd in command, but he was sitting in the top chair at the time of this event because his father was out of country. Belshazzar had great influence and resources because of his exalted position. In Daniel 5 we find that his empire is being threatened by the up and coming Meads and Persians and they have surrounded Belshazzar's capital city, Babylon. Belshazzar is so confident in the capability of his Babylonian empire that his response is to throw a party, which turns out to be a foolish thing to do.

The party starts off as a super extravaganza for 1,000 of the highest ranking people, and all their wives and concubines. In total there were probably well over 2,000 people present. This was a huge party with the best of foods and an impressive display of wealth. When the party is in full swing, and in an effort to further impress his guests, Belshazzar orders that the gold temple articles (cups, goblets and the like) from Israel's Jerusalem temple be brought in to the party. Many years before, Nebuchadnezzar, Belshazzar's grandfather, had plundered these articles from the great Temple of Solomon which had stood for nearly 400 years until Nebuchadnezzar had destroyed it in 586 B.C.. [14] [15] The Temple articles were in the storage house on display.

Making a mockery of God and the Temple articles, Belshazzar has them brought into the drunken party. This turns out to be a fatal move. Party goers begin to praise the gods of gold, silver and material things, typically a pretty bad strategic move. God takes action. An event occurs that is beyond imagination and so startling that it causes Belshazzar, the host, to soil his pants.[16] What they experience is obviously supernatural and extremely disturbing to everyone in attendance.

Even though this event took place over 2,500 years ago, it's impact is still measured today by the often used quotes which come from this event. Phrases like "the handwriting on the wall" "weighed in the balance" and "come up short" all have their origin to this supernatural interaction between Hyperspace and our world.

While the party of all time is in full swing, it is abruptly interrupted by a wild supernatural display. In the grand ballroom of the great palace, what appears to be a disembodied hand appears out of nowhere and proceeds to write a message on the wall. Four simple words are written on the plaster wall for all to see and read, however, it is a coded message and no one has a clue as to the meaning of the message (see Figure 4).

---

[14] Solomon's Temple was dedicated and opened in 959 B.C.; Dr. Chuck Missler, *The Books of I & II Chronicles*, (Couer D'Alene Idaho: Koinonia House Inc., 2006), 118.

[15] Dr. Chuck Missler, *The Book of Ezekiel* (Couer D'Alene Idaho: Koinonia House Inc., 2008), 7.

[16] Surprisingly, God gave Isaiah a prophecy about this. Isaiah 45:1 records this prophecy about 150 years before it happens and actually foretells the coming world leader by name. It further states that this coming world leader, Cyrus, will "loose the loins of kings," which is the polite way of the King James Version stating that they will soil their pants. Additionally, Cyrus, who did not know the Lord prior to conquering Babylon and the world, because of this prophecy will release the Jews and support their return to Israel to re-build the temple there.

Hyperspace in Scripture

Rembrant's "Belshazzar's Feast"

Palace of Nebuchanezzar where Belshazzar's encounter with the "handwriting on the wall" took place. Rebuilt by Saddam Hussein in the 1980's.

Figure 4 Belchazzar's Feast: *Left*, Rembrant[17]; *right*, Palace[18]

Terror, panic and confusion breaks out among the party guests. Imagine for a moment this bewildering scene. A hand that isn't attached to anything is gouging out a message on the palace wall as the stunned party goers watch in terrifying amazement. Belshazzar "loose his loins"[19] soiling his pants and the party thrills quickly become party chills. Everyone is amazed by the hand from nowhere and the encrypted message it wrote. Belshazzar is traumatized by the event and is further distraught by not being able to read the cryptic message brought in such a supernatural way. He has all the top diviners and conjurers brought in.

---

[17]Rembrandt, "Belshazzar's Feast", http://www.nationalgallery.org.uk/paintings/rembrandt-belshazzars-feast (accessed December 26, 2009).

[18]Photo by Daniel O'Connell, Gunnery Sergeant USMC, "Saddam's Babylonian Palace", About.com, http://architecture.about.com/cs/countriescultures/a/saddamspalace.htm (accessed December 26, 2009).

[19] "Loose his loins" is from the King James Version and literally means that Belshazzar "soiled his pants." Surprisingly, this was prophesied through the great prophet Isaiah who noted in Isaiah 45:1 that Cyrus (who hadn't even been born at the time) would be a great conqueror and would "loose the loins of kings."

One Hand In

Promising great riches, he searches for anyone who can interpret the handwriting on the wall. However, even with all these great promised rewards, no one can provide an explanation of the meaning of the writing. In the mean time, Belshazzar's grandmother, who was the wife of the great King Nebuchadnezzar, founder of the Babylonian Empire, enters the scene and seems not to be all that impressed with the party and Belshazzar.[20] She suggests that Belshazzar call on Daniel, a great man of God and former second in command of the empire. Daniel is now retired, and the queen suggests that Daniel can possibly unravel the mystery writing on the wall.

Daniel, as a captured young slave, had been used by God in a very dramatic way to not only interpret a disturbing dream that Nebuchadnezzar, the former king had many years earlier, but remarkably, he was able to state what the dream was, what it was all about, with no prior information.

Here, Daniel is briefed on the situation and is brought into the grand hall. Daniel, a man of great faith tested and proved, is not pleased with what he sees. He in essence dresses down Belshazzar in front of his guests for his arrogance, ignorance and foolishness. Imagine Daniel's courage and faith that gave him the strength to speak down to the Emperor of the entire world.

Daniel points out that long ago Nebuchadnezzar had learned about the God of Israel. Nebuchadnezzar had lifted himself up in great pride, but was subsequently humbled by God in a dramatic and unusual way. God struck Nebuchadnezzar's mind making him act like an animal living on grass. Years later, God restored Nebuchadnezzar's mind and Nebuchadnezzar then gave credit to the God of Israel for all he had. Nebuchadnezzar even wrote his amazing testimony pledging his faith to the

---

[20]In scripture, Nebuchadnezzar is referred to as Belshazzar's father, however Hebrew does not have a word for grandfather and it is generally believed that Nabondius was Nebuchadnezzar son but was away during this time for reasons that are not stated and Belshazzar, his son is now in charge. This is why Belshazzar can only offer as the best reward, the position of third in the kingdom. Nabondius, who is away, is the first in the kingdom leaving his son Belshazzar, the second in the kingdom in charge. This is noted by Chuck Missler in *The Book of Daniel*, (Coeur d'Alene, Id; Koinonia House Pub., 2004), 41-42.

Hyperspace in Scripture

God of Israel and circulated it to the whole world. It is recorded in Daniel 4 and is perhaps the only part of the Old Testament written by a gentile. Daniel points out that Nebuchadnezzar was corrected from his pride and arrogance and Belshazzar, his grandson, should have not only known this, but learned this lesson. In contrast, Belshazzar has belittled God even to the point of desecrating temple articles. However, Daniel tells Belshazzar that he will interpret the handwriting on the wall.

The writing on the wall consisted of four coded words. According to Hebrew tradition the coding was a transposition method of encryption referred to as an Atbash.[21] Daniel either was given this understanding by God prior to entering the hall or it is quite possible that he recognized the code and interpreted it on the spot. Either way, Daniel reads the message and its interpretation to Belshazzar, and it isn't good news.

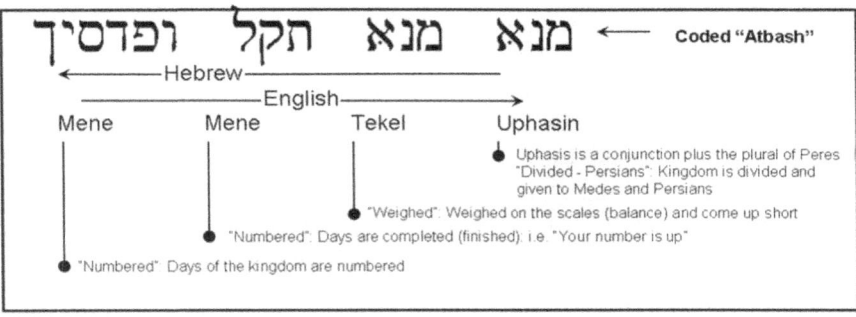

Figure 5 Handwriting on the wall of Daniel

Shown in Figure 5 are the transposed words and their given meaning. As it turns out, Belshazzar's days are numbered and his number is up. He has been weighed in the balance and he is found short or deficient. His kingdom will be divided between the Medes and the Persians. God had marked the arrogant little king Belshazzar for death and as it turned out, he was dead by morning.

---

[21]Dr. Chuck Missler, *Cosmic Codes* (Coeur d'Alene, ID: Koinonia House Pub., 1999), 48, 61.

One Hand In

By a move of military genius, the great, impenetrable and doubled walled city of Babylon that was thought that it could never be captured, will be taken over in one night without any serious fighting. Cyrus the Great, and his general Darius, have diverted some of the River Euphrates thereby lowering it sufficiently for a small group of specially trained soldiers to sneak at night under the city wall. In a quick raid, the special operations soldiers killed King Belshazzar and Babylon's upper echelon. They end up capturing the city so quickly and quietly that it was several days before all the citizens realized that they had been overthrown. Belshazzar, the arrogant little king was now dead as the handwriting on the wall had foretold.

3.2 HYPERSPACE OVERVIEW

The story of a hand appearing out of nowhere which subsequently then writes a message on Belshazzar's palace wall is perhaps nearly as shocking and perplexing to us today as it was those who experienced it. It is difficult to understand anything about how this happened if we view it from our limited 3D perspective. A summary of observations that indicate Hyperspace activity in this incident are noted below:

- A hand appears in a room, apparently out of nowhere and is visible to all

- The hand is visible and likely material (because it either holds a writing instrument and writes physically on the plaster wall or the fingers themselves gouge out the words)

- The hand materially interacts with the wall as it proceeds to write a message then subsequently disappears

This is another fascinating story that the Holy Spirit uses to communicate important information to us. God could have simply have had a prophet like Daniel walk in and give Belshazzar the message. God could have had an angel come walking into the room, deliver the message and walk out. There are many ways that God could have delivered this vital message but He chose to do it with this method. Further, the Holy Spirit records this not to confuse us with mysteries, but to reveal information to us.

It is my opinion that God did this supernatural display to send a message to Belshazzar and the entire world. Belshazzar and his guests were materialists, serving gold and silver. God blows open this scene, so similar to many today, where people who deny God and the supernatural are gathered in celebration of the material world and its all its alluring treasures. To those who deny the supernatural, God does a marvelous demonstration of the supernatural. God does this specifically to let them know that there is more to life that material things, there is a spiritual realm. Further, the Holy Spirit records this story giving us who believe in the spiritual realm specific information as to how the seen and unseen worlds are tied together. As we analyze this story, our objective is to gain this understanding.

3.3 ANALYSIS OF THE FLOATING HAND

What is going on with the hand that appears out of nowhere to write the message? When you consider this problem from a 3D world perspective, it becomes extremely difficult to provide some sort of explanation. However, if a higher dimensional order (Hyperspace) is considered, this bizarre story actually becomes rather simple. If another physical dimension, a higher dimension called the fourth dimension or 4D, is considered, a very straight forward explanation results from this passage. The explanation is that someone who is in the 4th D, reached into our 3D world. Because this person (presumably an angel) only reached in with their hand/arm, that then is all we will see. What is seen is only that portion of the person that reached into the 3D space. Because we can't see into the unseen world in higher dimensions, all we see is the hand/arm that is extended into our 3D space by the person standing in 4D Hyperspace.

I find it uncanny that when modern physicists give examples to describe how people from a higher dimension could interact with us in our 3D world, they relate situations almost exactly like what happened in the Biblical story to Belshazzar. An example that illustrates this is that of a hat. Say a person with a hat is standing one step back in the 4th dimension. If his hat blows off and falls into 3D space, someone else who is standing in the 3D space would all of a sudden see the hat appear seemingly out of nowhere. If the person in Hyperspace who had the hat, reached into the 3D space to retrieve their hat, what the 3D space person would see would be an arm appearing out of nowhere, it picks up the hat and then disappears again taking the hat with it.

This example is illustrated in Figure 6. Secular physicist Dr. Michio Kaku remarks on this example commenting on the fact that as the Hyperspace person reached through the veil to retrieve his hat, the people on the "other side" (the 3D people) would: "see a disembodied hand reaching out the window [veil], desperately groping for the hat."[22]

Figure 6 - Example of hat blowing from 4D space into 3D space showing what happened and how it would look from the 3D world

Another analogy used by Dr. Michio Kaku which describes this type of action is that of a fish pond. The fish, as examples of the 3D world only see what is going on in the water.[23] If a person was standing and looking at the fish, and then drops something in the water and subsequently goes to retrieve it, the fish would experience something like this. The fish would see something all of a sudden appear into their water space and fall to the bottom

---

[22]Michio KaKu, *Hyperspace* (New York: Anchor Books – Random House, 1995), 229.

[23]Michio KaKu, "Hyperspace and the Theory of Everything", http://mkaku.org/home/?page_id=258 (accessed December 23, 2009).

of the pond. Then they would see this arm appear out of nowhere, extend to the bottom of the pond, pick up the object and then disappear again. What is common to us would appear as extraordinary to the fish in their little 3D world below the surface of the water.

The word translated hand is from *etsba* which is an Aramaic word for finger or toes. [24] It is similar to our use of the word digit.

3.4 EXPLANATION FOR THE FLOATING HAND

The best and only really reasonable explanation for this perplexing event comes from viewing it from a Hyperspace perspective. Although it would certainly be shocking and very disturbing for any of us to see a hand appear out of nowhere, write on a wall and then disappear, when viewed from a 4D perspective, it is actually very straightforward. Most logically, an angel standing in Hyperspace, operating under the direction of God, poked his hand/arm through the veil separating the 4D unseen world from the 3D seen world and then proceeded to write on the palace wall. Other explanations like God having an active hand materialize out of nothing although possible, because God can do anything, seem more like "Theo-magic" (God magic) rather than plausible.

Only one question remains, who's hand was it? More than likely it was probably that of an angel, however, it could have been that of the Lord's. Either way, it was a spiritual being, residing in the 4D hyperspace world known as the spiritual realm, who pokes through the fabric of our space-time continuum and leaves a mark in our little 3D world. It was a notable supernatural event. This amazing story of the supernatural continues to impact people today and we occasionally will hear people refer to "the handwriting on the wall".

---

[24] *Etsba*, Blueletterbible, http://www.blueletterbible.org/lang/lexicon/lexicon.cfm?Strongs=H677&t=KJV (accessed August 11, 2011), Strong's #677.

3.5 SUMMARY OF ANGEL'S HAND

When first encountered, it is quite surprising to hear modern physicist describe Hyperspace activity using an example that is virtually identical to and seems like it comes right out of Scripture. All things considered, Hyperspace activity is the most reasonable explanation for understanding this rather bizarre and perplexing event. By considering higher dimension, a very natural explanation is provided for the otherwise unexplainable events that Belshazzar and his guests experienced at the Babylonian Palace. Key take-aways from this chapter are:

- ✓ Real material beings in the unseen world (angels), can penetrate or poke part of themselves into our 3D seen world
- ✓ This story is consistent with Jesus appearing and disappearing only in this case, the angel or whoever it was, just poked their hand into our seen world
- ✓ Hyperspace and the Spiritual Realm is actually right next to and adjacent to our 3D seen world.

Hyperspace in Scripture

4 Seeing Through the Veil

"Ordinarily the human eye cannot see the spiritual forces that are arrayed in the invisible realm. The eye of faith can look into the Word of God and know the truth of the power of the Lord we serve, and can be sure that nothing can ever touch us unless it has passed through the will of God." Donald Grey Barnhouse [25]

4.1 PEEKING INTO HYPERSPACE: THE STORY

2 Kings 6:16-17: *"So he [Elisha] answered, "Do not fear, for those who are with us are more than those who are with them." Then Elisha prayed and said, "O LORD, I pray, open his eyes that he may see." And the LORD opened the servant's eyes and he saw; and behold, the mountain was full of horses and chariots of fire all around Elisha."*

Evil often creeps up on us while we are sleeping and are unaware of its actions. That is what happened to Elisha and his servant. While they were peacefully sleeping one night, in the darkness outside, the enemy was silently making their way surrounding them. The servant had no idea of the trouble that was gathering together just outside. But the servant also was completely unaware that at the same time, the Lord's mighty protection was being put in place. Completely oblivious to both these things, the servant woke up on what he thought was just a normal day. He stepped outside to fetch water and to wash up following his normal routine that he had done so many times before. But this day was to be different; much different.

---

[25] Donald Grey Barnhouse, *The Invisible War* (Grand Rapids: Zondervan, 1965), 134

Hyperspace in Scripture

When the servant steps out on the walk in front of the home, and as he is adjusting to the brightness of the day, he takes note of a frightening action that is occurring around him. In the hills immediately surrounding him there is a very large enemy army. Making up this terrifying sight are numerous mounted troops on horses, horse drawn chariots and a very large army of foot soldiers. The servant's response is perhaps what most of us do when we are caught in surprise and unprepared for battle, he panics. He is not a soldier, has no fighting equipment and clearly, he is very "out gunned" (pardon my use of an old western phrase). So he runs. Running back inside, he cries out to his master. Fear and panic are in his voice and on his face.

"What will we do? What will we do?" cries the servant who is now consumed by terror, giving in to the evil and fear. Evil seeks to control and create panic and is very handily succeeding with the servant. Elisha, however, has quite a different response. Whether he was warned ahead of time by God (he was a prophet after all), or whether he was just normally cool under fire, or if (which is probably more the case) he just had the faith and confidence that God was in control. Perhaps Elisha's faith in God allowed him to exhibit to the servant a confident air. Elisha was not confident in himself to control the situation, but he was confident in God knowing that God had called him and would see to it that his ministry was completed. So, unrattled and unshaken, Elisha steps out onto the porch to see this mighty enemy army, and he makes a very surprising statement.

Elisha, unlike most of us when encountering difficulties, immediately sees the big picture. Elisha knows that all things are really spiritual. He has learned what the Apostle Paul will say many years later; *"For our struggle is not against flesh and blood, but against the rulers, against the powers, against the world forces of this darkness, against the spiritual forces of wickedness in the heavenly places."* (Eph 6:12). The situation is never really about the evil that we see, it is always about God and His forces which we don't see. Knowing this, Elisha makes such a memorable statement that it is often repeated today: *"Do not fear, for those who are with us are more than those who are with them."* (2 Kings 6:16). Wow; what an insight from a man of great faith. The servant was about to find that out the truth of Elisha's proclamation. Elisha knew that there was much more there than what could be seen. Elisha was aware of the spiritual realm and the forces operating there. He had seen his mentor, Elijah, taken

On the Other Side

directly into the spiritual realm not all that many years before. His insight was about to be dramatically revealed to the servant. The one who couldn't comprehend Hyperspace and the spiritual realm was about to be educated.

Elisha, desiring to arrest the fears of his faithful servant asks a favor from God. The poor servant is petrified by the sight of the enemy army and Elisha knows that his panic would subside if he could only see the situation for what it truly was. So Elisha prays. Elisha prays to God that He would open the eyes of the servant in a very special way so he could see what is going on in Hyperspace. Graciously, God grants Elisha's request and the Holy Spirit records this event as an example for all of us to recall when we are in a moment of panic. Miraculously the eyes of the servant are opened so that he can see into the spiritual realm.

Peering into Hyperspace, the servant becomes even more shocked at what he sees there. Right there, just one step back in the higher dimension that we don't normally see are also hills right next to them. The servant sees in the direction of Hyperspace which completely surrounds us although we are typically unaware of it. What the servant sees is perhaps best described in the words of Gulf War leader, US Army General Norman Schwarzkopf as "Shock and awe." Although initially terrified by the enemy human army, the servant now sees a massive spiritual army surrounding them which includes horses and chariots of fire. The servant's heart is lifted as he sees God's mighty display of strength and power. Help has been sent, it is already there in mass.

How cool would it have been to peer into the spiritual realm. How exciting it would be if at times when we are afraid that we could just look into Hyperspace and see the chariots of fire that God has sent there on our behalf making sure that His will is carried out. This is truly a very remarkable story which gives us a unique glimpse into the interaction between forces acting in Hyperspace and our physical world.

Hyperspace in Scripture

4.2 HYPERSPACE OVERVIEW

This wild story further builds our understanding that the spiritual realm is truly located in higher dimensions of our space-time continuum. In fact, the concept that the spiritual realm is in Hyperspace is the only reasonable understanding that we can draw from what is being described. Somehow and in a way we don't know or understand, God really opened the Elisha's servant's eyes so that he could actually see into the spiritual realm. Scripture certainly seems to indicate this is true and the passage really cries out Hyperspace as the solution for understanding.

On top of the amazing insight of just understanding the Hyperspace relationship, we also find some further insightful understandings about what is going on there in Hyperspace (the spiritual realm). As example, the long and often asked question of: "Are there animals in heaven?" appears to be answered. The Holy Spirit responds to the questions with a resounding "Yes!" Key Hyperspace insights are noted below:

- The spiritual realm (unseen world), located in Hyperspace, is directly adjacent to our earthly realm (seen world)

- There are spiritual creatures living and active in the spiritual realm

- The activity in the spiritual realm is directly linked with that activity going on in our earthly realm

- Astonishingly, there are horses and some sort of chariots in the spiritual realm

Once again, we find it fascinating that the Holy Spirit gives us such a meaningful glimpse into the spiritual realm. Far from being text book drama or an analytical exercise, we discover through this story further confirmation that the spiritual realm is in Hyperspace. Additionally, we also gain the important knowledge that even as we are facing difficulties here on earth, God is actively dealing with the situation in the spiritual realm and is in the process of bringing us that solution. This story speaks to us on many levels. It is certainly encouraging us personally and additionally, it gives us a very unique technical insight into the workings of higher dimensional space-time.

4.3 ANALYSIS OF BEHIND THE VEIL

Opened Eyes: There are many instances in scripture where angels make themselves visible to humans (examples include: Lot: (Gen 19:1-3); Daniel (Dan 8:16-19) Shepherds (Luke 2:8-14); Mary (Luke 1:26-37); Zacharias (Luke 1:5-20). Although commentators have a tendency to say that angels can make themselves visible and invisible, what is suggested here something different. I'll suggest that angels don't create a body out of nothing so they can be seen, instead, they have bodies, real tangible bodies, and they just step from the invisible world, through the veil, into our visible world.

If angels are tangible and real, as scripture indicates, how can they appear and disappear? Similar to what we saw with Jesus in His resurrected body, a tangible, touchable body couldn't typically just disappear. If it did, what happened to all the matter that made up the body? What happened to the bones and atoms? To think that they just "disappeared" would suggest some sort of magic, like pulling a rabbit out of a magicians hat. That would be what I'm calling, "Theo-magic." Theo-magic would be God not working through His own laws that He has established, but just doing something almost nonsensical, like magic. I'll suggest that God, although certainly capable of any type of miracle, even magical, typically operates by working within His established laws. In this I don't suggest that God doesn't do miracles, because clearly He does. But, what I do suggest is that God will typically work through His own established laws of physics and the like using the characteristics that only He as God possessed to accomplish His will.

In this case, I'll suggest that the miracle which we clearly don't understand is the opening of the servant's eyes. It doesn't appear that the angels became visible by stepping into the seen world from Hyperspace. Instead, the Lord "opened the eyes" of the young man and he "saw" into Hyperspace, into the spiritual realm. The Hebrew word translated into *look* is *paquach* which is used only 20 times in scripture, and mostly concerning

Hyperspace in Scripture

the eyes and is slightly different than the more common word for *open*, *pathach* which is used 144 times in scripture.[26] Further in this passage, we will find that God somehow miraculously blinds the earthly enemy army. This is temporary because He then later "opens their eyes" as well. 2 Kings 6 uses the same words and phrase for restoring the earthly enemy armies eyes and it does for opening the servant's eyes to Hyperspace. "...LORD opened [*paquach*] their eyes..." (2 Kings 6:20c) Because of this, I'll suggest that some physical or miraculous action took place in the eyes of the servant which enabled him to see into the spiritual realm. This wasn't some sort of dream or vision. What the servant saw was very real, tangible and material.

Elisha's servant's glimpse into Hyperspace is very revealing and a search of scripture for similar events reveals two other stories. The first is in the Old Testament and it gives us some good technical information (the case of Jacob). The second one is in the New Testament and it is a very moving story (the case of Stephen the first Christian martyr).

Jacob – Another Example: Jacob (who was also called Israel) was the grandson of Abraham. Jacob, while running away from his brother fearing the he would kill him, had a surprising vision of the spiritual realm (recorded in Genesis 28). This had all come about because Jacob, with the aid of his mother Rebekah, had stolen the family blessing from his father Isaac. This was done through trickery.

Jacob had a slightly older twin brother named Esau who was actually the first born. Esau, the older, was entitled to special blessings and benefits associated with being the first born. Jacob had disguises himself as Esau and tricked his father Isaac into giving him the blessing. This was aided by Isaac's old age and eyesight difficulties. Immediately after this, Jacob, in fear for his life and knowing that his ruse and deception would soon be exposed fled. He feared that his brother Esau would hunt him down and kill him so Jacob fled the area.

---

[26]"*Paqach*" and "*Paquach*", Blueletterbible.org;
http://www.blueletterbible.org/lang/lexicon/lexicon.cfm?Strongs=H6491&t=KJV and
http://www.blueletterbible.org/lang/lexicon/lexicon.cfm?Strongs=H6605&t=KJV
(accessed December 30, 2009)

On the Other Side

In his flight, Jacob has covered some 50 miles, going through the land that would eventually become Israel. He eventually arrives at a place called Luz. He is tired, it's dark and he lays down trying to make himself comfortable using a stone for a pillow.

That evening, God gives Jacob a vision and Jacob is blessed with a glimpse of what is going on just behind the veil there in Bethel. Jacob sees into the spiritual realm. What he sees are angels going up and coming down this side of a hill or mountain.

Figure 7. Illustrations of Jacobs Ladder: Left, Jim Somerville[27]; *right*, Makaveli Bone[28]

---

[27]Jim Somerville, " We Are Climbing Jacob's Ladder", posted Novenber 16, 2009, http://jimsomerville.wordpress.com/2009/11/16/we-are-climbing-jacobs-ladder/ (accessed February 14, 2010).

[28]MakaveliBone, " Jacob's Ladder", http://media.photobucket.com/image/jacob%252527s%20ladder/MakaveliBone/Jacobs20ladder.jpg (accessed February 14, 2010).

Hyperspace in Scripture

I'm suggesting that what he sees is like a set of switchbacks. Switchbacks is a set of steps or a hiking trail that goes up the side of a hill or mountain (some artist's other interpretations of this are shown in Figure 7). Jacob is so impressed with the sight of this intense angelic activity that he names the place Bethel, meaning "House of God." Scripture states in verse 17 that the place is a "gate of heaven." Fascinating! Evidently, God's heavenly temple must have been close by and Jacob sees a lot of angles going up and coming down the mountain side.

Bible teacher and commentator John Phillips makes an astute observation on this story. He states: "Note, for instance, the statement about the angels 'ascending and descending.' It is not the other way 'round, as we would think. The angels are not coming down to this world from that world and then going back up there again. Exactly the opposite. They are already here. They are down here and are seen as going up to Heaven from Earth and then coming back down to Earth again. That is important. God has already established beachheads on this rebel planet. God has his angels already here, permanently based in enemy territory, so to speak. Nor can Satan expel them. They are here for a variety of reasons and they have constant communication with Heaven." [29]

Stephen – Another Example: Another example of people getting a glimpse of Heaven is the disciple of Jesus, Stephen. Just prior to him being stoned to death for his faith in Jesus, the Christ (Acts 7) he sees into the actual Throne Room of God (the Throne Room of God is further discussed in section 6.4 - Spiritual Mount Zion). What had happened was that Stephen had given a very bold and condemning summary of Israel's history to the Jewish leaders. His point is that throughout their entire history, they always killed the one God sends to them. He builds the case beginning with the rejection of young Joseph by his brothers. Further Stephen notes that Moses was initially rejected by all of Israel. Then he refers to all the prophets that Israel always killed. He then makes the point that the pattern is repeated with Jesus. Israel had rejected Jesus. Then, the Holy Spirit enables Stephen to see directly into the Throne Room of God where he sees Jesus at the right hand of the Father. Well, this is all too much for the Jews and at this the

---

[29] John Phillips, *Exploring the Gospel of John* (Grand Rapids: Kregel Pub., 1989), 50.

On the Other Side

crowd drives Stephen outside the city where they proceed to stone him to death.

Insight of Spiritual Warfare: This are very intriguing cases involving a glimpse into the spiritual realm, hyperspace. From these verses we see not only another documentation of the existence of the spiritual realm and it's location in Hyperspace, but also an insight into the activity taking place in the spiritual realm. Ephesians 6:12 indicates the nature of our true struggles in life which are all connected to the spiritual realm: *"For we wrestle not against flesh and blood, but against principalities, against powers, against the rulers of the darkness of this world, against spiritual wickedness in high places."* We can see that there is a constant battle going on in the spiritual realm around us.

Often it is difficult for us to get an understanding or picture of what is really going on in the spiritual realm. Elisha's encounter, although rare, gives us insight into what is actually common and every day. We have a tendency to see all our encounters, at work, with neighbors and even in our family as just people dealing with people. In reality it is so much more. Every encounter we have with people is an opportunity to demonstrate faith and obedience.

At the same time and while we are doing this, just adjacent to us in the spiritual realm angelic forces are constantly battling. With us it seems that our struggles are only in this realm, in the physical that we see. In actuality, the struggle is spiritual and intense activity is taking place there which is directly linked with our activity. Additionally, the outcomes, whether successful or not is seen the same in both realms.

As we saw in our initial story, Elisha came against the Syrian army and he did so in faith and prayer. Because of this, God brought spiritual forces, an angelic army, together to engage the conflict in the spiritual realm. Elisha had the confidence that God would deal with the situation and he knew that the real battle would be in the spiritual realm. Elisha had faith that God would adequately provision him for the encounter. Elisha, in an effort to help train his new young servant wants him to see and understand this vital principle. So, Elisha prays that the young man will be able to see the angelic army that he knew that God was bringing together for the battle.

Hyperspace in Scripture

God granted this request and the young man peers into the spiritual realm and sees what few other humans, this side of the veil, ever get to see. It is a magnificent display consisting of a great host of horses and chariots of fire.

Connectedness Between the Visible and Invisible Realms: Another observation that can be made from this passage is the closeness between the spiritual realm and that of our 3D space-time continuum. Angels are active and involved all around us. An example would be at church during a service. Believers and angels gather together for church service. They are therefore present during our service. But, where are they? They are actually very near, very close however, just a step back in the 4th dimensional direction so we don't see them. In this case with Elisha, we can see that they are in close proximity as well. They are just one step back in the spiritual realm and not visible to the servant, until God opened his eyes enabling him to see.

Horses in Heaven?: Here is something surprising. This was actually shocking to me when I first considered what the servant saw and then I remember, the Holy Spirit is telling us this story. Just seeing angels with swords prepared for battle, is surprising enough. However, what the young man sees is horses and chariots of fire. The Hebrew word used in this passage for horses is found else where in Scripture some 140 times. Similarly, the word translated as chariot is used some 120 times and fire is used 379 times. All of these are indeed common words in the bible with natural meanings. The servant describes what he sees using these common words which suggest that what he sees is much like what we seen in this world, however, these are obviously spiritual creatures.

This is unexpected. It is kind of natural to anticipate seeing angelic warriors, but to see them in horse driven chariots with fire is surprising. In fact I am going to confess that I really don't know what a "chariot of fire" is.

We draw from this story the following logical conclusions: (1) angelic weaponry includes some special type of chariot and (2) there are real horses in the spiritual realm. It could be further speculated that if horses are present, perhaps other hyperspace creatures are there as well. Although a logical conclusion we'll recognize this as speculation because it is not specifically stated in the verses.

On the Other Side

In addition to the story of Elisha's servant, there is another Biblical passage where horses from the spiritual realm appear. This had occurred several years prior and was witnessed by Elisha. Perhaps this partially explains Elisha's insight that the chariots were there, just on the other side in the unseen world.

The story is found in 2 Kings 2. In this event, Elijah and at the time his younger protégé Elisha, have a supernatural encounter. God has called Elijah directly to heaven and will do so in a very dramatic way. God sends chariots of fire and horses of fire to the earth. They separate Elisha from Elijah so Elijah can be taken directly into Heaven. God didn't want Elisha to follow. [This is a wild story full of Hyperspace activity and will be discussed in detail in a planned 2nd Hyperspace book.]

This event takes place several years before Elisha's servant's event that we have been discussing here. The point worth noting it is that in this encounter, Elisha gets his first glimpse of chariots of fire and horses of fire. 2 Kings 2:11: *"As they were going along and talking, behold, there appeared a **chariot of fire** and **horses of fire** which separated the two of them. And Elijah went up by a whirlwind to heaven."* (emphasis author) Perhaps it is because Elisha had seen a "chariot of fire" before that now years later, he is confident that they are right there in the spiritual realm.

The servants encounter with horses in heaven and Elijah's encounter with horses of fire from heaven shed light on a passage in Revelation concerning the return of Jesus to earth. In the future, as the present age is nearing its final demise, Jesus, the King of Kings will come forth out of Heaven riding to fight the epic battle of Armageddon, and surprisingly, He is riding a white horse.

Some suggest that the horse is not literal. I'll suggest that everything else in the passage is literal and there is nothing to indicate that Jesus is not literally riding a horse as well. Revelation 19:11: *"And I saw heaven opened, and behold a white horse; and he that sat upon him was called Faithful and True, and in righteousness he doth judge and make war."* Did Elisha's young servant see horses in hyperspace? For sure. Will Jesus actually be riding on a hyperspace white horse? It would appear so.

Hyperspace in Scripture

Figure 8 View into Hyperspace: *Left*, Jesus returns on a white horse[30]; *right*, Stephen sees into the spiritual realm just prior to death[31]

Chariots of Fire: The phrase "chariots of fire" is not used anywhere else in scripture and even though many people depict pictures of Elisha being caught into heaven riding in a chariot of fire that is really not what the Bible says. What the Bible says is that he was taken to heaven by a whirlwind. Because the word chariots is the common Hebrew word for chariot, it would seem that this is a reasonable description of what the servant saw, only it is in the spiritual realm. Fire is an interesting

---

[30]"Revelations on Heaven", Divine Revelations, http://www.divinerevelations.info/Documents/7_Jovenes/English_7_Jovenes_Heaven .htm (accessed December 30, 2009).

[31]"Stephen Sees Jesus on the Right Hand of God", Gospel Art, http://www.lds.org/library/display/0,4945,8555-1-4779-4,00.html (accessed December 30, 2009).

observation and very possibly speaks of glowing bright light which is often also associated with an angelic presence.

Allegorical Example of Seeing Behind the Veil: As stated before, it is really impossible for us to visualize higher dimensions or hyperspace. However, an examination of 2D to 3D analogy can help provide insight into 3D to 4D problems. In the story of Elisha's servant, we find that he sees into hyperspace, in a different direction from our 3D world. It is certainly challenging for us to understand how this works. If we relate a 2D to a 3D example, perhaps that will help us understand what is taking place.

We will use our flat 2D Goomba to help us understand. Let's imagine a flat, 2D world that is complete with a ground and a sky. The Goombas live comfortably in this 2 dimensional flat plate type world. They travel along the land, they can dig down into the dirt or they can jump into the 2D sky. We could visualize this world kind of like a giant ant farm. Figure 9 is an illustration of this ant farm 2D like world of the Goombas.

Hyperspace in Scripture

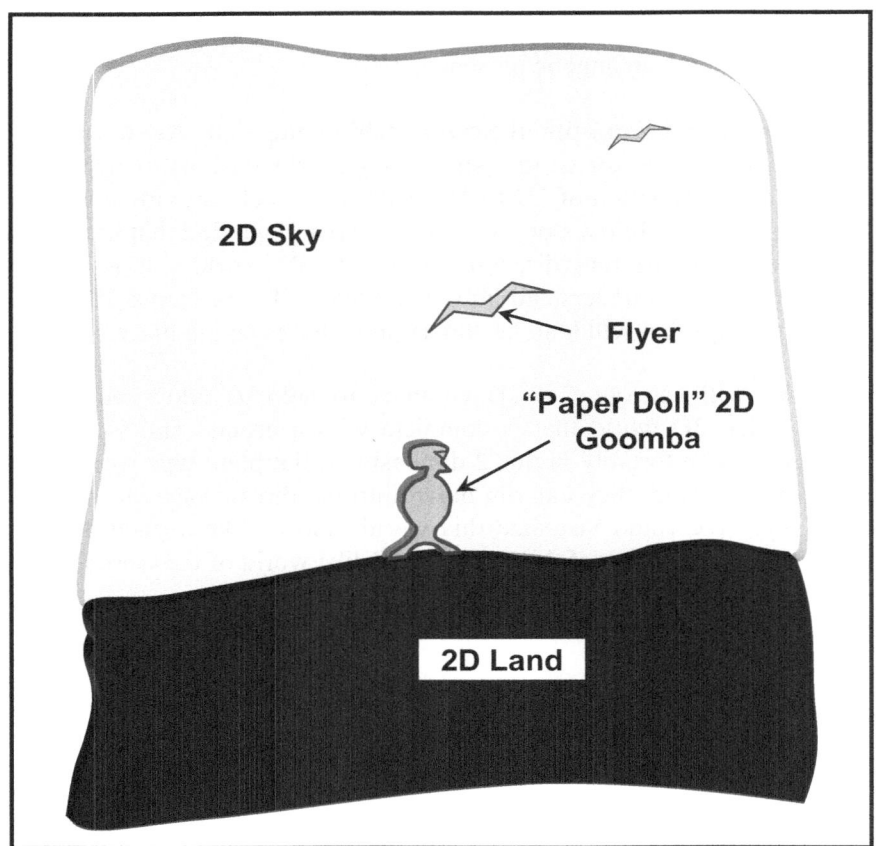

Figure 9 – 2D "Ant Farm" type world of the Goombas

So far, this is pretty straight forward, but now we will make the illustration a little more challenging. What if the Goomba 2D ant farm type world had a higher dimensional spiritual realm? The spiritual realm would be in the third dimension or in 3D. This 3D unseen world would be right next to the 2D ant farm world of the Goombas.

Let's further imagine that in the 3D world are spiritual creatures such as angels. Because the Goombas are only 2D (flat – like paper doll) beings, they can only see inside their "ant farm" so to speak. They won't be able to see into the higher dimensional spiritual realm right next to them. They can only see and know of their fellow Goombas in the 2D world. They

On the Other Side

can't see out into the 3D direction of the unseen world even though they are right there next to them. However, the spiritual creatures (angels) which roam the 3D world can see into the adjacent 2D world of the Goombas. Figure 10 depicts the 3D spiritual realm adjacent to the flat world of the Goombas.

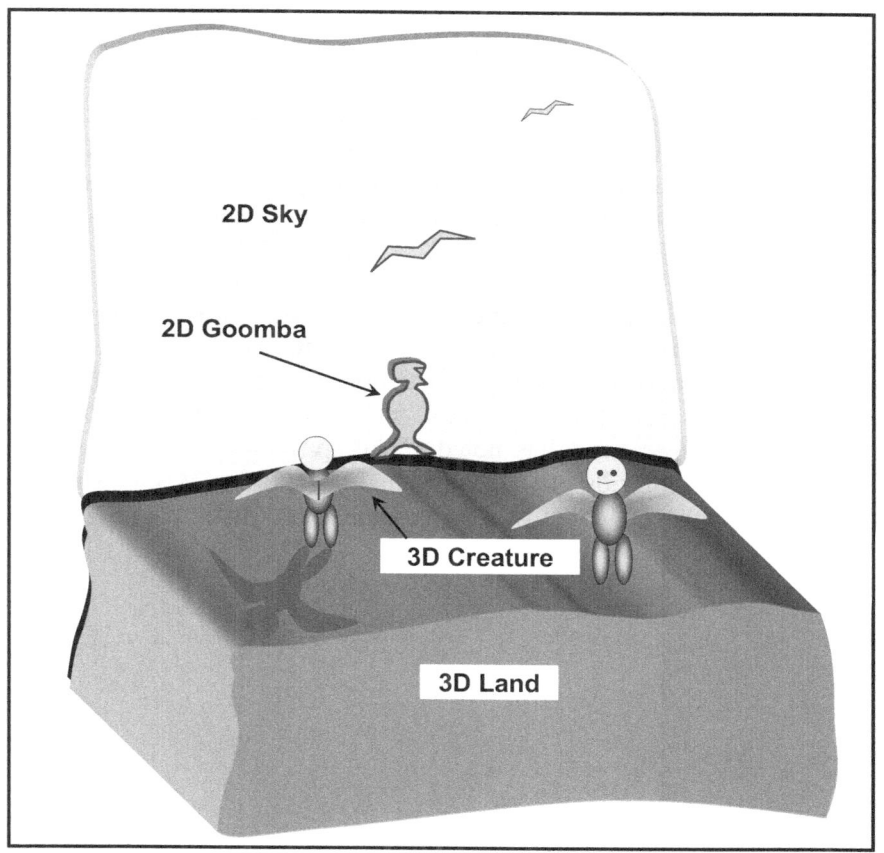

Figure 10 – 3D Spiritual Realm adjacent to the 2D Goomba world

This is a 2D to 3D analogy of the 3D to 4D story of Elisha's servant. The Goombas are 2D flat paper doll type beings that can't see into the higher dimensional world next to them.

Hyperspace in Scripture

In the same way, we are only 3D creatures and can not see into the higher dimensional world that is next to us. Being that Elisha's servant is a 3D person, he can not see into the higher dimensional unseen spiritual realm. However in this Biblical story, God, in some miraculous fashion, "opens the eyes" of the servant so he can see into this unseen realm. When he does, he sees the "Chariots of Fire" and the angels that are already present there. These angels have been right next to the servant the whole time but until God "opened his eyes" he couldn't see them.

This analogy also helps us understand the connectedness between the higher dimensional spiritual realm and our limited world that we know. A spiritual realm in a higher dimension has a connectedness to our world. A specific location in our world would correspond to a specific location in the spiritual realm.

Further, the spiritual beings that are in the spiritual realm can be right adjacent to us and we would not be able to see them. We have no capacity for vision into the higher dimensional spiritual realm. However, their presence is none the less a real reality. As Lambert Dolphin, a believing research scientist has noted: "The spiritual is not, however, far from the earth and outside of space and time beyond the stars. It surrounds us within and without. In fact we are immersed in spirit, and God Himself is a Spirit."[32]

---

[32]Lambert T. Dolphin, *Jesus: Lord of Time and Space* (Green Forest, Arkansas: New Leaf Press., 1988), 14.

4.4 SUMMARY OF ELISHA'S SERVANT EVENT

Elijah's servant certainly experienced an incredible event. He gets a rare glimpse into Hyperspace and the information he passes to us is indeed challenging but very insightful. Some key take-aways from this momentous story are as follows:

- ✓ We Humans can't see into the spiritual realm without God somehow opening our eyes
- ✓ The spiritual realm is connected to our seen world and is directly adjacent to it (also seen in our two prior stories but even more clearly here)
- ✓ Actions in the spiritual realm (Hyperspace) are linked to our earthly realm; we are not only connected physically (dimensionally) but also in activity
- ✓ In addition to angels, there are horses and "chariots of fire" in the spiritual realm

Hyperspace in Scripture

5 Journey in Hyperspace

"Now let us turn to the extraordinary or supernatural things. First the appearance of the angel. Luke does not go aside to argue for the existence of angels. He writes it down with perfect naturalness. The supernatural is written down as being natural. The extraordinary is recorded as ordinary…The angel standing there was supernatural to men, but natural to God." [33] Pastor & Bible Teacher G. Campbell Morgan D.D. speaking of Gabriel's visit to John the Baptist's father, Zacharias (Luke 1)

5.1 BACKGROUND TO A JOURNEY IN HYPERSPACE

Aside from Christ Himself, the prophet Daniel is perhaps the most remarkable and capable person in scripture as well as of all humanity. Taken as a young captive from Israel, he rises to become the second in command of the extremely powerful and world-ruling Babylonian Empire (see Figure 11). Although a select few others have risen to such a position of great prominence, Daniel rises not only once, but a second time, with a second completely different empire to become the second in command of the conquering Medo-Persian World Empire.

His superb administrative and leadership abilities are perhaps only matched by his pure and faithful devotion to serve the God of Israel. It is my opinion that Daniel is possibly the greatest intellect to ever walk the planet and he was wholly devoted to serving God. When he was in his 80's he walked into the great Babylonian palace and translated on the spot a coded message that was written by an angel on the wall and then immediately

---

[33] G. Campbell Morgan, D.D., *The Gospel According to Luke* (Old Tappan, New Jersey: Fleming Revell Co., 1931), 17.

Hyperspace in Scripture

provided the interpretation of its meaning (see Chapter 3). Not a soul among the senior leaders of the world could even do the former, let alone the latter.

Figure 11. Daniel: *Left*, Young Daniel[34]; *middle*, Babylon[35]; *right*, Daniel and Angel[36]

Three times Daniel was told by angels that he was "greatly beloved" by God (Dan 9:23; Dan 10:11; Dan 10:19).[37] However, it was to this great man who: (1) led two world empires; (2) survived a night in the lion's den; (3) was caretaker to Nebuchadnezzar during his 7 year animal period; (4) interpreted dreams from God; (5) was given what is arguably the most

---

[34]"Young Daniel", La Vista Church of Christ, http://lavistachurchofchrist.org/Pictures/Standard%20Bible%20Story%20Readers,%20Book%20Four/target21.html (accessed February 20, 2010).

[35]Malcolm Jack, "Hanging Gardens of Babylon", Heritage Key Christ, http://heritage-key.com/world/hanging-gardens-babylon (accessed February 20, 2010).

[36]Last Call, http://calvarylastcall.blogspot.com/2009/12/daniel-91-111-1-john-218-36-psalm-1211.html, (accessed January 11, 2010).

[37] Daniel speaks great messianic prophecies and is called "beloved of God" three times (Dan 9:23; 10:11; 10:19). The Apostle John, who also provided us the book of Revelation and great future insights into the Messiah, is called the disciple "whom Jesus loved" five times (John 13:23; 19:26; 20:2; 21:7; 21:20).

Journey in Hyperspace

staggering prophecy in the entire Bible which stated over 500 years in advance, the exact day that the Messiah would present himself to Israel; (6) faithfully followed God through unbelievably extreme difficulties; that (7) God chose to give what is possibly the most shocking insight into the spiritual realm man has ever had. It is one of the most transparent insights into hyperspace from which several key principles of the ordinances of Heaven are derived.

This chapter will unpack several of these amazing understandings which provide a strong framework upon which to build a tower of understanding.

After 70 years in captivity in Babylon, the conquered nation of Israel was finally allowed to return to their homeland. Cyrus, had built the Medo-Persian Empire into the largest world empire that had ever existed. Through a dramatic series of events Cyrus becomes a believer in the God of Heaven who declares the future in advanced. In fulfillment of a 150 year old Biblical prophecy, one year after conquering the Babylon, he allows Israel to return to the Holy Land (Ezra 1:1-4). Over 40,000 men and their families, funded by the citizens of what is now Persia, leave the land of Babylon, their home for the past 70 years, and return to Israel.

However a few years later, we find that things weren't going all that well down in Israel. The returning Jews were struggling badly. Daniel, worried about the progress of restoration had taken the matter up in prayer to God (see Figure 12). On a self-imposed modified fast, Daniel spends 21 days in fervent prayer on behalf of his struggling brothers. On the 21st day, Daniel is on the banks of the great river Tigris when he has a close encounter of the angelic kind.

A supernatural entity, from Hyperspace, enters our 3D world. The sight of this being dressed in radiating white, eyes blazing fire, face like lightning, and with a golden belt causes the blood to drain from Daniel's head, making him pale and light-headed. Then, as the being speaks with a voice like the deep roar of a thundering waterfall, Daniel passes out and falls face down on the ground. Such is the reaction of many people who encounter a being who has just arrived from Hyperspace.

Hyperspace in Scripture

Figure 12. Daniel: *Left*, Tigris River[38]; *middle*, In Prayer[39]; *right*, In Prayer[40]

Subsequently, Daniel is touched by an angel, given strength and lifted first to his hands and knees trembling and then to his feet although he continues to shake. The angel addresses Daniel with great honor, as he is called "highly beloved." The angel then informs him that he will be given an important message in response to his prayers. However, prior to being given the answer to his question, Daniel hears a very bizarre story.

The angel tells Daniel why it took 21 days for him to arrive with his answer. The excuse is as shocking as it is informative. Daniel is informed of ranks of angelic warriors and conflicts taking place in the invisible world of the spiritual realm. Further, Daniel discovers that this warfare directly affects him. Once again, Daniel passes out. His reaction is certainly understandable. It is this chapter, and this portion of scripture that we will mine. We will discover that it produces some brilliant high quality gems of insight into activities in higher dimensions.

---

[38]"Tigris River", Treehugger, http://www.treehugger.com/2009/07/12-week/ (accessed Feb 20, 2010).

[39]"Daniel Prays", Well Sphere, http://stanford.wellsphere.com/general-medicine-article/prelude-to-the-lion-s-den/571635 (accessed February 20, 2010).

[40]Dr. Ralph Wilson, "Daniel in Prayer", Jesus Walk, http://www.jesuswalk.com/greatprayers/8_daniel_confession.htm (accessed Feb 20, 2010).

Journey in Hyperspace

Various commentaries express different opinions as to whether the bright shining being is an angel or perhaps a pre-incarnate visitation by the Lord Jesus Himself. Those who support the pre-incarnate view see the angel that touches Daniel and converses with him as a different person from the being that Daniel first sees in the encounter.[41] Personally I am inclined to agree with this. I see the radiating being as Jesus and see a separate being, an angel, as the one who talks with Daniel. As one of the very insightful commentator comments: "The evidence that we have here an appearing of God the Son before His incarnation, in the form of a Man, a great Christophany, is very convincing."[42] This is consistent with other pre-incarnate appearances.

As an example: To Abraham the wanderer, Jesus appeared as a traveler (Gen 18). To Jacob the schemer, Jesus came as a wrestler (Gen 32). To Joshua, the brilliant military leader, Jesus appeared as the top ranking general, the Captain of the Lord's Host (Josh 5:13-15). To Isaiah the great prophet of the coming Messiah, Jesus revealed Himself as the King on the Throne (Isa 6; John 12:37-41). However, to the prophets, Daniel in exile in Babylon and John the apostle in exile on Patamos, Jesus appears as the glorified King-Priest (Dan 10 & Rev 1:12-17).[43] Further insight into pre-incarnate visitations will be discussed in detail in a subsequent book on the subject of hyperspace.

It is important to note however, that for the purpose of this analysis, we are really just interested in the message that the angel gives. For this reason, the question of who that first radiating supernatural being is that Daniel sees is not directly germane to this particular study.

---

[41]The reason for this view is primarily because he (the angel) is unable to defeat an evil angel: this is discussed in the following paragraphs.

[42]A. C. Gaebelein, *"Daniel"* (New York: Our Hope Pub., 1911), 155

[43]Insights from: Warren Wiersbe, *"The Bible Exposition Commentary"* (Colorado Springs: Victor, Cook Communications, 2002), Old Testament: The Prophets: 297.

As to the second being (the angel) that shows up, the one that talks with Daniel, many people seem to think it was the angel Gabriel, because of his prior visit to Daniel. I am inclined to think that as well, but scripture doesn't state this explicitly.

5.2 STORY AND DRAMA

Have you ever had a friend arrive late for a meeting with you? He comes in several minutes late and looking rather disheveled says, "Wow! You won't believe what happened to me as I was trying to get to the meeting." He is so preoccupied with what he has just been through that he is anxious to tell the story. He will end up telling you about traffic or family or something a little out of the norm that caused him to be late. Well, in the linty of excuses, the one given here to Daniel clearly qualifies for the all time "Hall of Fame of Great Excuses" and could be perhaps the winner of all history.

To summarize the tardy angel basically says: "Wow Daniel! I started to come 21 days ago when you first prayed, but I got in a fight with this fallen angel who is the top dog over all the evil forces of the nation of Persia. I was in battle with this guy for 21 days, but couldn't seem to get the upper hand. Finally, God sent the Archangel Michael who was able to push him back and let me through. I then had to fight through some of the lower leaders of the evil ranks, but Wow! I finally made it here with you." The angels specific words are shown in Figure 13.

It is at this point in the narrative that Daniel understandably passes out for the 2nd time. Although Daniel has an unbelievable intellect and has dealt with angels and world leaders, I think he went into overload. This encounter with Gabriel's explanation provides a shocking insight into the actions of the spiritual realm and their effect on us here in the seen world. These thoughts are unpackaged in the next several sections.

Journey in Hyperspace

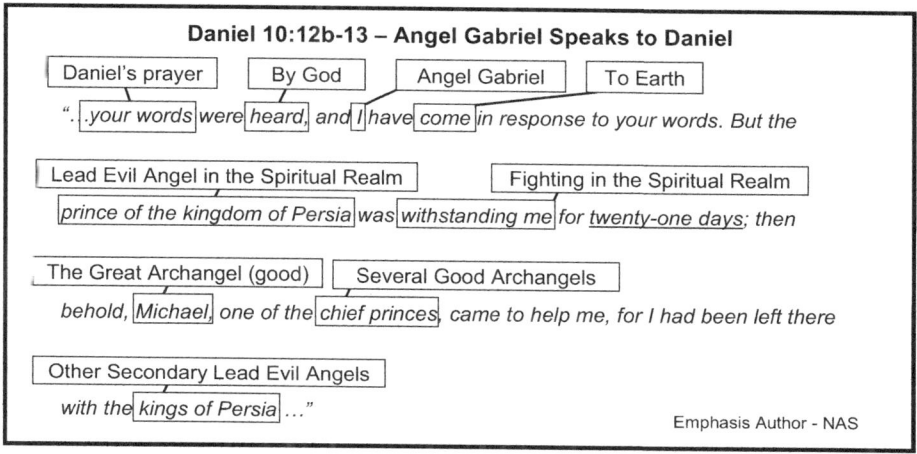

Figure 13 Angel Gabriel gives Daniel an explanation for being late

5.3   HYPERSPACE OVERVIEW: HYPERSPACE JOURNEY

Perhaps this story is the most spectacular scriptural narrative that we have which explains what is going on in the unseen world and how it relates to us. Additionally, from a Hyperspace perspective, it solidifies for us an understanding of the higher dimensional nature of the spiritual realm and its adjacency to us in the lower dimensional visible world. Portrayed to us from the pages of Scripture we see: (1) an angel being dispatched and having to make a journey across some part of Hyperspace; (2) An evil leader in the spiritual realm which parallels that on earth; (3) we see a dominion in the spiritual realm which is the same as on earth; and (4) a battle occurring in the spiritual realm. Combined, this creates a very remarkable glimpse into Hyperspace. Key insights and observations into the nature of Hyperspace are summarized here:

- Just as there are various locations and places in this earth, there are various locations in Hyperspace (example: we have countries and territories and the spiritual realm has territories)

- A territory in the spiritual realm is related to its corresponding territory in the earthly realm (example: Earthly Persia is directly adjacent to, or more accurately, actually embedded in the Persia in the spiritual realm)

- Even though God directed the angel to bring a message to Daniel, the angel still had to carry that task out and it took time to accomplish (as God does with us when He asks us to do things, it takes us time to complete the action – things have to get done)

- As anticipated, there is land or space associated with the spiritual realm. Gabriel was dispatched from some specific location (presumably the Throne of God) and sent on a journey across some part of the spiritual realm to reach Persia.

- In the spiritual realm, creatures have different capabilities and strengths. Gabriel was incapable, with his limited forces, to defeat the evil Prince of Persia. Gabriel needed the help of Michael to win the battle and "break through the lines" (so to speak)

- The warfare taking place in the spiritual realm affected Daniel here on earth

- Time passage in the spiritual realm is the same as on earth (this event took 21 days in both realms)

5.4 ANALYSIS OF HYPERSPACE JOURNEY

Angelic Ranks and Dominions: Much can be garnered from Gabriel's description of what has been going on in the spiritual realm. Angels and other beings of the spiritual realm appear to be organized in ranks similar to a military structure (see Dan 10:13). The Angel Gabriel has been fighting with an evil angel whom is apparently titled the "Prince of Persia." His dominion is that of Persia and other entities are noted who are only "kings of Persia" being lesser and subservient to the Prince.

On the good side it is noted that the angel Michael is titled as a "chief prince," a very high ranking angel. Michael is noted three times in Daniel (10:13; 10:21; 12:1) and we learn that he is in charge over Israel. Jude 9 refers to him as an Archangel and it is seen in Revelation 12:7 that he appears to be the head over all the godly angelic forces. Revelation describes a future and final battle that will occur in the spiritual realm. Michael is the leader of God's forces. This battle will end the warfare that has been going on in the spiritual realm for thousands of years. It will occur during what is described as the Tribulation, which is a 7 year period of time when the earth experiences great trial. Michael and his army will be successful and the net result of the battle is the elimination of evil from the spiritual realm. Satan and all his evil forces are cast from Heaven and become limited to operations only on Earth. Certainly, there will be much celebration in heaven on that day.

Spiritual Realm – Earthly Realm Activity Connectedness: Ephesians 6:12 illuminates the connectedness of the evil spiritual forces that operate in the spiritual realm effecting what goes on here on Earth: *"For we wrestle not against flesh and blood, but against principalities, against powers, against the rulers of the darkness of this world, against spiritual wickedness in high places."*

Identified here are principalities, powers and rulers, all of which are evil and wicked. These evil forces have dominion and effect what is taking place on Earth. The Holy Spirit informs us of the surprising understanding that the struggles and difficulties we face in our life are actually driven by or affected by forces of the unseen world. Colossians 1:6 gives further insight on this describing that these spiritual forces and entities have dominions and are set up much like nations are on this Earth.

Further, as seen here, the dominion of the evil forces parallel that which is on the earth. The evil Prince of Persia has a dominion in the spiritual realm which is connected with the Persia here on Earth. What we can ascertain from this is that a strong parallel exists between nations on Earth and dominions linked to them in the invisible world. A strong connectedness exists at the national level between hyperspace, the spiritual realm and our 3D world. This has staggering implications as we examine both history and current events from a national standpoint.

Spiritual Realm – Earthly Realm Physical Connectedness: We also see a physical connectedness between the "land" of the angels in hyperspace and the "land" of Daniel and us on our Earth. The evil angel is

Hyperspace in Scripture

called the "Prince of Persia." Persia is the country where Daniel is on this Earth at that time.

In the good angel's description of his ordeal, he is dispatched from some unstated location in the spiritual realm (it is presumably the Throne of God). However, in order to reach Daniel who lives in earthly Persia, the angel must travel through the land of spiritual Persia. In spiritual Persia, the good angel encounters the "Prince of Persia," the evil angel whose dominion or territory is that of spiritual Persia. There is a physical link between these two Persia's. This is clearly implied because if they were not, the good angel could have easily traveled around the evil angel. However, because the evil angel's territory is physically connected to the earthly territory, it is impossible to go around; the good angel must go past the evil angel to reach Daniel.

This is exciting news as it confirms for us an insight into how Hyperspace in higher dimensions interplays with our 3D world. Recognizing the Hyperspace is higher dimensional, we would actually anticipate a story just like this. The angel confirms to us the fact that the spiritual realm is indeed part of and connected to our space-time continuum. It is just a higher dimension away from our 3D world.

When this insight is applied to what we see in our physical world, it becomes very illuminating. All areas on this Earth have their connected regions in the spiritual realm. Each of these regions or dominions is controlled by spiritual forces. In some cases we see evil forces controlling areas and in some cases we see where godly forces are in control.

One example is many of the college campuses in America. Many are under the direct control of evil forces that are pushing their evil agendas on our society. All departments from the sciences, who continue to promote an evolutionary thought without any rational reason and deny God as creator, through the philosophy department that promotes a world view that is completely anti-god and devoid of the moral teachings that God has ordained for society's own protection and preservation. At times, just walking on the campus you can sense the presence of evil control, well hidden behind what projects itself as sophisticated elite intellectualism.

Journey in Hyperspace

In another example I have a friend who was on business travel in New Orleans. He is a good Christian man and he passed by a witchcraft and voodoo shop. He decided to go in just to take a look and see what it was all about. He said that all he did was enter and begin to walk in and the sense of evil and foreboding was so strong he was compelled to immediately turn around and walk out.

The exciting news is that even if you are in a city that is dominated by evil you can establish a Godly dominion. Just by pulling a group of believers together who are devoted to carrying out the Lord's objectives, a spiritual beach head is established. The influence of this Godly dominion can grow to become a stronghold for God.

From Daniel's story and Ephesians we learn that there is an actual dominion in the spiritual world, an area of land so to speak, that is connected to our world. Evil spiritual forces can control this land but the good news is that they can be ousted. Controlling positions and high grounds can be established in the spiritual realm. These positions shine God's light into this dark world. But in order to be successful, recognition that the war is spiritual is vital, and our primary weapon is prayer.

Real Battle: So we see that as we seek to accomplish what God has called us to do, we struggle not really against anything physical on this earth, our struggle is really a fight in the spiritual realm. We are connected. A vital key for success is shown in this story and is also highlighted in Ephesians 6 which describes the armor of God. That key is prayer. Because the battle is spiritual and not physical, it needs to be won first in the spiritual realm in order to see success here on Earth.

As shown in Daniel, mentioned by the good angel, as soon as Daniel begins to pray, God directed angelic activity. Prayer is the key for success of any and every endeavor for the Christian's life. We often wonder why our prayers aren't answered quickly and at times we get discouraged because it seems like God isn't listening. What we are clearly taught here is that of course God is listening. Of course God is at work for our best interest; however, because it is first a spiritual battle, it may take awhile for us to see the answer manifest itself. Faith and patience is required when important things are in the balance.

As the great pastor Warren Wiersbe notes: "Here he [Daniel] had been involved in a cosmic spiritual conflict and didn't even know it, and the Lord was using some of His highest angels to answer his prayers! This certainly lifts prayer out of the level of a humdrum religious exercise and shows it to be one of our strongest and most important spiritual weapons."[44] Jesus comments on prayer with a very insightful statement in Matthew 18:18. In context Jesus is discussing dealing with an unrepentant brother, but it leads him to make the following comment: *"Verily I say unto you, Whatsoever ye shall bind on earth shall be bound in heaven: and whatsoever ye shall loose on earth shall be loosed in heaven."* (NAS) Jesus clearly affirms the connectedness between the unseen spiritual world and that of our visible world and notes that prayer is THE effective tool for being successful.

2D-3D Goomba Analogy: 2D-3D Goomba Analogy: A 2D to 3D analogy or comparison may be helpful in understanding what is going on here so we will return to Goomba land for an example. Illustrated in Figure 14 is the 2D Flat Plate (or ant farm) world where the Goombas live. In this illustration on the left, we have the flat 2D Goomba Daniel who lives on a yellow line which represents Persia. In Goomba Daniel's 2D world, he is dwelling in Persia which to him is only a line.

The fuller 3D world (spiritual realm) that encompasses the Goomba's 2D flat plate world includes a spiritual Persia which is an area represented by a yellow patch (in the right of the figure). The yellow patch represents Persia in the spiritual world. There is a physical connectedness between the yellow line Persia of the 2D world and the yellow patch of the 3D world.

A good angel is shown in a position just off the yellow patch, coming from where he was initially dispatched. But as can be seen, in order

---

[44]Warren Wiersbe, *"The Bible Exposition Commentary"* (Colorado Springs: Victor, Cook Communications, 2002), Old Testament: The Prophets: 299.

Journey in Hyperspace

to reach Goomba Daniel, the good angel must cross the yellow patch (or spiritual realm Persia). In spiritual Persia (the yellow patch) is the evil angel, the Prince of Persia who fights with the good angel keeping him from reaching Goomba Daniel.

This is a 2D to 3D example that hopefully sheds some light of understanding on the real problem of our 3D world being encompassed with a higher dimensional 4D world (Hyperspace) where the spiritual realm is. This amazing angelic encounter provides us with important insight into the link or physical connectedness between our Earth and that of the spiritual realm in hyperspace.

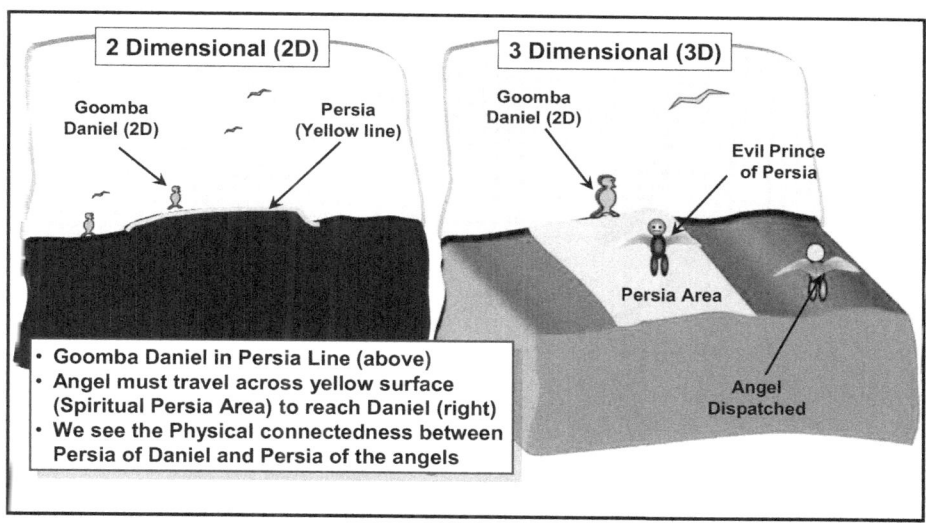

Figure 14. 2D-3D Analogy of the physical connectedness between Persia of Daniels world and the Persia of the Angel's world

2D – 3D World Analogy: If we carry this analogy one step further and make it as big as our Earth, it will give us an interesting perspective. Imagine that the flat plate 2D world of the Goombas is as big in diameter as our Earth. It would be kind of like a really giant "Ant Farm." Imagine that this Ant Farm is as big as the earth. In this 2D flat world are the Goombas. The Goombas have countries in their world.

Hyperspace in Scripture

Figure 15 shows an example of this and identifies three countries. Each country is a part of the 2D earth and are shown in the figure with lines. The line is the territory of that country. This represents a two dimensional flat world.

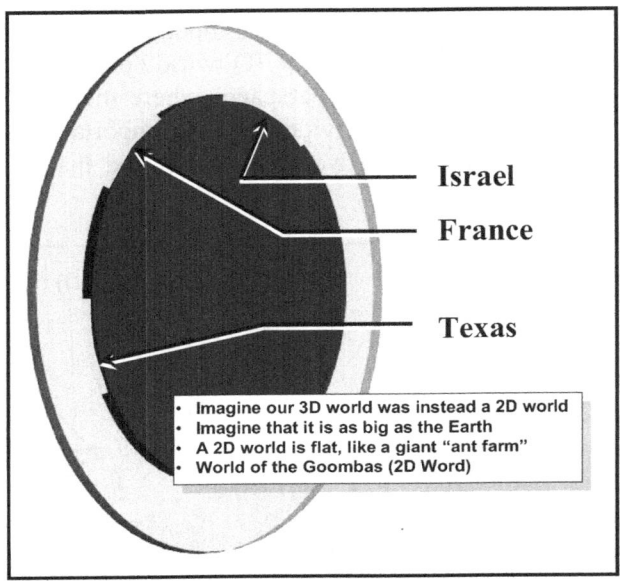

Figure 15 – Analogy of a 2D flat world of the Goombas (like an "Ant Farm") which is as big in diameter as our Earth

Now imagine that around or encompassing this 2D flat world is a 3D realm (as shown in Figure 16). The 3D realm would be spherical in shape like a ball. Because Goombas are flat, they are constrained to move only in the 2D Ant Farm like world. However, in an analogy with a 3D world, all around them is area, or perhaps better stated, more land. Notice now that the countries that were only lines in the 2D world are now areas or patches in the 3D world. What you can see in the figure is that the line which represented the country of Texas in the 2D world is now becomes an area or patch in the 3D world. That is the analogy.

Journey in Hyperspace

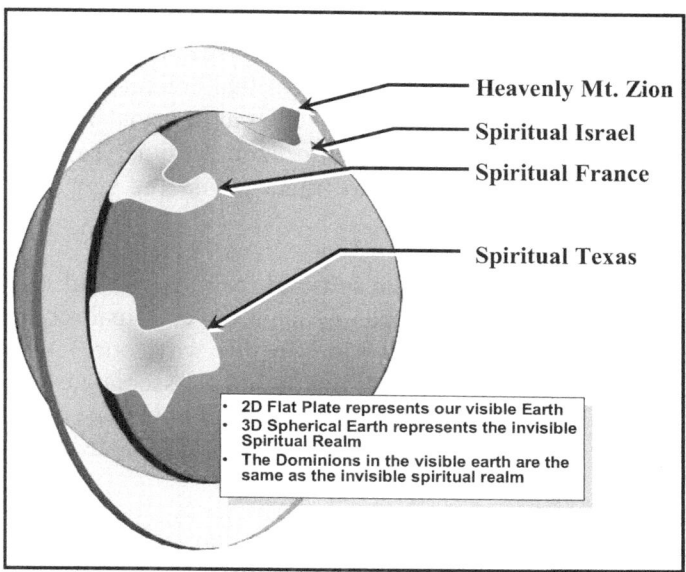

Figure 16 – Analogy of the 3D spiritual realm around the 2D world of the Goombas

So building the analogy; in a 2D world countries are lines and when they expand into a 3D world they become areas or patches. One thing that is interesting to note is that to the Goomba's, the lines seem big, like lots of area but when we see the spiritual side, the area really becomes very large indeed.

We can learn from this example of going from a 2D to higher 3D realm. In the same way, in our seen 3D world, we have countries that are areas. But when we expand to the higher dimensional 4D unseen realm, we find that what we see as our countries are actually embedded into a larger 4D reality. Don't try to imagine what this 4D reality looks like, we can't; but we know it is there. We can, however, see the 2D lines expanding to 3D areas and understand that. This is certainly very challenging to comprehend but my hope is that this 2D to 3D analogies helps you in that understanding.

Another insight from this 2D to 3D analogy is that of travel. If a Goomba goes from Goomba Texas to Goomba France, he travels in the 2D flat plate world until he gets there. If a spiritual creature was in Goomba

Hyperspace in Scripture

Texas, they could step back into the spiritual realm and be in Spiritual Texas (in 3D). What is worth noting is that not all places in the spiritual realm are at the same point. In other words, if a spiritual creature steps from Earthly Texas back into the spiritual realm, they enter at Spiritual Texas, they are not in Spiritual France. If a spiritual creature is in Spiritual Texas and wants to go to Spiritual France, they need to travel across the spiritual land to get there.

The point being is that the spiritual realm is big and very vast. The 2D ant farm world of the Goombas is actually very small compared to the spherical 3D Goomba spiritual world. In this way, our 3D Earth is very small compared to the vast spiritual realm that is associated with our Earth. The spiritual realm is a huge area and we would anticipate that the number of spiritual creatures far exceeds the number of people on Earth. And indeed, Scripture seems to indicate this. [45]

There is one additional example that might be helpful to understand. This approach isn't really a dimensional example but it does perhaps give some insight. Consider an example of a multi-story building. Imagine that we live on the first floor, which corresponds, to our earth. We travel around on the "floor" and can even move (to some degree) up and down. There are however, floors above us.

Imagine that the "Throne of God" is on the top floor (see Figure 17). If an angel was to come from there (the upper floor) down to the earth (the lower floor) he would have to pass through the other floors. In the case of Daniel's angel, there was an enemy who was on the floor above Daniel and he blocked or prevented the angel from passing through. To some degree, this illustrates the concept of traveling through territories to reach a specific destination.

---

[45] It is unclear as to exactly how many angels there are but some think that Scripture links angels and stars together (Job 38:7). If this is the case, it would imply that there are perhaps on the order of 10^{22} (which is 10 followed by 22 zeros) angels, a very large number. (also see Heb 12:22 and Rev 5:11)

Journey in Hyperspace

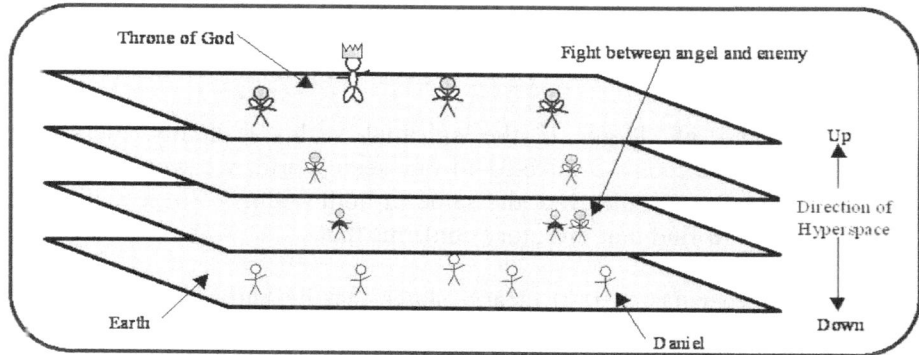

Figure 17 – Crude illustration of traveling through Hyperspace from the "Throne of God" to the Earth

Gold from Uphaz: There is an interesting side point of tangential interest because of its odd nature. Daniel gives us a fantastic description of the first majestic spiritual being that he sees. Daniel makes the point that the spiritual being is wearing a belt made of gold. Further, it is not just gold, but clearly identified as "fine gold from Uphaz" (Dan 10:5) The Holy Spirit chooses to highlight to us that this fine gold belt is fabricated from a very specific type of gold, from Uphaz. But, where is Uphaz? In Jeremiah 10:9, the prophet speaks of vain idols which are constructed of silver and gold. Jeremiah specifically speaks of gold from Uphaz. Clearly, the gold Jeremiah speaks of comes from the earth, from a place whose location seems to be a mystery, but none-the-less, made by human artisans.

But this raises an interesting question: "Is the golden belt of the mighty spiritual being made with gold from Earth or from the spiritual realm?" Either way you answer this question, it comes out somewhat shocking. If the being is wearing gold from Earth, that is surprising. Who made it and where did it come from? If the gold is from Uphaz in the spiritual realm, we would reasonably conclude that spiritual Uphaz is linked to earthly Uphaz, and therefore the gold of the land perhaps extends into the land of the spiritual realm.

Hyperspace in Scripture

Both conjectures are somewhat shocking, but plausible. Resolving between these two options seems beyond our current available information although it might be fun to ask when we get to Heaven.

Passage of Time: If the spiritual realm is really located in Hyperspace and directly connected to our seen world, we would naturally anticipate that time would flow the same in both realms. So, it really isn't very surprising to find that this story confirms that.

Daniel (in Dan. 10:2) clearly states that he had been fasting for a "full three weeks." This would be for a period of 21 days. He comments in verse 4 that this day of the event was now the 24th of Nissan (1st month of the religious calendar). This means that he must have started his fast on the 4th of the month and continued through Passover (14th of Nissan), Feast of First Fruits (a few days later) and the feast of unleavened bread (goes for a whole week after Passover ending on the 21st of Nissan).

So we have 21 days from Daniel's first prayer of understanding to the arrival of the angel. The angel in the description of why he was late specifically states in verse 12 that he was dispatched by God on the first day that Daniel prayed, unfortunately though he has been hindered from arriving, being in a fight, for the past 21 days (verse 13).

The 21 day fight between the angels perfectly corresponds with Daniel's wait of 3 full weeks or 21 days. A very reasonable conclusion from this is that time flows at the same rate in higher dimensions (the spiritual realm) as it does on this earth (3D world). This is a very critical insight and a very solid piece of data indicating that the invisible spiritual realm is contained within the time-space continuum that we know as our universe.

This is fully consistent and expected from a concept that locates the spiritual realm in the higher dimensions (hyperspace) of our universe. The insight that time flows in the spiritual realm along with time here on Earth is shocking in its discovery and comforting to realize that spiritual activity is synchronized with us.

Measurement of Length: Because the spiritual realm is in Hyperpsace and part of our space-time continuum, we would also anticipate that not only time would be the same as on earth, but length measurements would be the same as well.

This fact is confirmed from a look at Revelation 21:17 which describes the city walls of the future New Jerusalem: *"And he measured its wall, seventy-two yards, according to human measurements, which are also angelic measurements."* (NAS) Here the Holy Spirit informs us that the measure used on Earth is the same as the measure used by the angels in the spiritual realm. That is interesting. Tape measures that are used on Earth can be used in the spiritual realm and vice versa.

Again we see a connection, a link between dimensions in hyperspace and those of our 3D universe. From these two passages we understand that spatial (length dimensions) and the time dimension are the same for both realms. This further strengthens connectedness and unity between the unseen world of angels and the 3D world that we live in.

Hyperspace in Scripture

5.5 SUMMARY OF HYPERSPACE JOURNEY

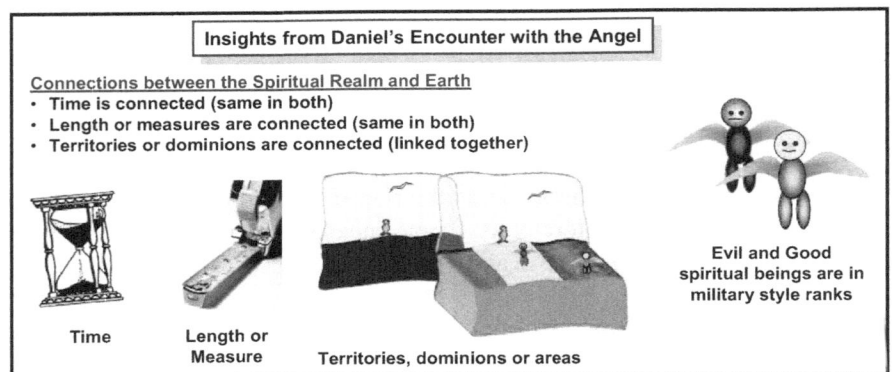

Figure 18. Connectedness or links between the spiritual world and Earth

Key take-aways from this section (see Figure 18):

✓ In the spiritual realm, there is distance to be traveled, presumably over land

✓ There is a physical connectedness between locations in the spiritual realm and our 3D world (see Figure 18) and dominions and territories in the seen world are directly linked with their corresponding territory in the unseen world.

✓ Because Hyperspace (the spiritual realm) is all around us, it can be entered at any point, but when you do, you are only in the corresponding spiritual location (example: if you enter the spiritual realm in California, you are in the California spiritual realm)

✓ If you are in the California spiritual realm and want to get to Florida spiritual realm, you will have to travel across Hyperspace to get there (or you can enter our visible realm in California, travel to earthly Florida here in the visible realm and then re-enter the spiritual realm once there in Florida)

Journey in Hyperspace

- ✓ There are evil angels who fight against God's angels, and are, in some cases, temporarily successful
- ✓ The angels (godly and evil) are organized and have ranks and assignments or territories (it is noted that the evil angel was a "Prince of Persia" and a second evil angel is mentioned who is "Prince of Greece" and Michael the Archangel is noted as one of the "chiefs" and is the "Prince" over Israel)
- ✓ There is a direct connectedness of activities between what is going on in our 3D world and activities in the spiritual realm
- ✓ Time in the spiritual realm flows at the same rate as it does on Earth (Angel was restrained 21 days which is the same as Daniel's 3 full weeks of waiting: Dan. 10:2 & Dan. 10:13)
- ✓ Measures of length are the same in the spiritual world as on Earth
- ✓ Prayer is a powerful activity and God directs angelic activity as a direct result of serious prayer

Hyperspace in Scripture

6 The Great City in Hyperspace (Map of Heaven)

"It may be said with confidence that it is not unreasonable to describe the Higher Space [higher dimensions] as the abode of our departed brethren, of the angels, and of our Lord Himself."[46] Theologian Arthur Willink, 1893

"The Bible is unique in that it presents a universe of more than three dimensions, and reveals a Creator that is transcendent over His creation. It is the only "holy book" that possesses such contemporary insights."[47] CEO and bible teacher Chuck Missler, 2002

6.1 INTRODUCTION TO HEAVEN AND IT'S LOCATION

If heaven is real, where is it? Scripture teaches that heaven is a real place. If that's the case, which is really good news by the way, then can't we identify from scripture where heaven is? And further, what exactly is heaven and who and what are there? Many of us refer to the place where believers go when they die as heaven. Is heaven the same as the spiritual

---

[46] Arthur Willink, *The World of the Unseen* (New York: Mcmillan and Co., 1893), 100.

[47] Dr. Chuck Missler, "Quantum Teleporting: Part 1"; Koinonia House; (Posted 2002) http://www.khouse.org/articles/2002/388/ (accessed May 10, 2010)

Hyperspace in Scripture

realm and therefore the same as Hyperspace? And what about the Throne of God; where is that? These are really good questions and several of them seem to come up frequently in discussions that many of us have. The approach taken here is that scripture does provide the answers to these very challenging questions, but we need to look carefully to discover it.

I love the big picture view. In many areas of my life I have trouble understanding details if at first I didn't get the big picture. So, let's describe in one paragraph the big picture. Then after that, in the subsections of this chapter, we will examine several key details to develop a deeper insight. Hopefully, we will be able to answer to a reasonable degree, the questions we just posed.

Big Picture: The time-space continuum that we live in consists of "seen" portions (3D plus time) and "unseen" portions (possibly as many as 7 higher dimensions). In physics, the un-seen portions of the time-space continuum (higher dimensions) are referred to as Hyperspace. From the Bible we have already discovered that the spiritual realm is in at least one of the higher dimensions of the time-space continuum (Hyperspace).

The spiritual realm is a vast region and has many different places. As example, Hades is located in the spiritual realm. Also, we have learned that there are regions in the spiritual realm that have their corresponding region (or country like Persia) in the earthly realm. Further, Scripture tells us of a marvelous place where believers go when they die. Jesus told us that He is there today preparing a place for us. We also know that Jesus is sitting at the right hand of the Father, in the Throne Room of God.

From this Biblical understanding, we can link together three places: (1) the place where the soul/spirits of believers go when we die; (2) the place that Jesus is preparing for us; and (3) the Throne of God are all in the same location. Scripture calls this place "Heavenly Jerusalem."

In Hebrews 12 it notes that Heavenly Jerusalem is full of angels, the souls of those who follow God (both from the Old Testament times and Christians from the New Testament times) and Jesus, the Christ, the Son of the Living God. This sounds like a great place to spend some time. This amazing place is located in the spiritual realm which is located in

Map of Heaven

Hyperspace.

But wait, there is even more good news. Scripture also gives us some pretty good insight into the location of Heavenly Jerusalem. Using this understanding, a "map" (if that word is appropriate) has been developed of the spiritual realm which notes the location of this important city. After having built the case from scripture that the spiritual realm is located in Hyperspace, we can now explore this unseen world further from scripture. I really hope you find this chapter absolutely fascinating.

6.2 BACKGROUND AND DEFINITIONS

John Philips comments on the Apostle Paul's journey to the 3rd heaven. "Yet it was other dimensional, spiritual, extraterrestrial too…What we gather from this is that heaven is localized. It is somewhere and it is substantial, because Jesus is living there now. There are many mansions, or 'abiding places,' there, Jesus said. That militates against smallness and narrowness." [48]

Different people use words like heaven to mean different things so it seemed wise at this point to create a little lexicon and define our terms before proceeding much further (see Figure 19).

Heavens: When most people speak of Heaven, they are thinking of the place where believers go when they die. That's good, but it is really only part of it. Genesis 1:1 notes that God created the Heavens. The word used is plural meaning more than one. Although some scholars view it differently, most agree that scripture speaks of three heavens. The first heaven is the air where birds fly; the second heaven is outer space containing the planets and galaxies and the third heaven is really the entire spiritual realm. The third heaven is the unseen world where the dominions of angels are. Therefore

---

[48] John Phillips, *Exploring the Gospel of John: An Expository Commentary* (Grand Rapids: Kregel Pub., 1989), 263-264.

Hyperspace in Scripture

the third heaven and the spiritual realm are really synonymous, the same thing.

Heavens (Plural)
- Genesis 1:1 "...God created the heavens and earth"
- 1st Heaven: Air (where the birds and airplanes fly: Gen 1:20, Jer 4:25)
- 2nd Heaven: Outer Space (also called the "Firmament"; where planets and galaxies are: Heb. 11:12; Gen 1:14-18
- 3rd Heaven: Spiritual Realm – Unseen World (where angels, souls of believers and the Throne of God are: 1 Kings 8:30; II Cor. 12:1-4)

Higher Dimensions of Space-Time Continuum (Hyperspace)
- Something in addition to our 3D plus time seen world
- Advance Physics suggest there might be a total of 10 dimensions (some say up to 26)

Spiritual Realm (or 3rd Heaven)
- Entire Unseen World
- It is proposed in this book that the Spiritual Realm is located in Hyperspace, in higher dimensions
- Contains the:
  - "Home of Believing Souls" (what many call heaven)
  - Throne of God
  - Places in the seen world are somehow linked to places in the spiritual realm (like spiritual Persia
  - Dominion of angels

Spiritual Jerusalem
- Specific part of the Spiritual Realm (Hyperspace): it has a specific location in Hyperspace
- Contains the:
  - "Home of Believing Souls" (what many call heaven)
  - Throne of God
  - Many but not all of the angels

Figure 19 - Definitions

Hyperspace from Physics: We are jumping ahead a little but in Chapter 9 we will show that modern physics, for the most part, believes that the space-time continuum contains much more than just the 3D spatial dimensions (our seen world) plus time. String Theory and M Theory, the dominating models in today's modern physics, view the space-time continuum as having at least 10 and possible up to 26 dimensions.

As example, they state that 4 of the 10 dimensions in the space-time continuum are our 3D seen world plus time. However, they also note that there are another 6 dimensions. These additional dimensions are un-seen. These un-seen dimensions are referred to as "higher dimensions" or Hyperspace.

So today, modern physics views the space-time continuum, the real universe, as containing the 3D seen world and higher dimensions (Hyperspace). Further, time is a property and is limited to only the space-time continuum. Amazingly, this is exactly what the Bible indicates.

Spiritual Realm: The spiritual realm is the term used to describe what scripture calls the "unseen world" (2 Cor 4:18). This realm is a very vast realm and contains many things. It is the dominion of angels, where they live and operate. As we have seen, the spiritual realm also contains territories or dominions that parallel what is on earth.

As example, we saw the Spiritual Persia of the spiritual realm that was adjacent to our Earthly Persia. Presumably, we would anticipate that Hades would be located in the spiritual realm. Also, what most people call heaven, where the souls of dead believers go when they die is also here in the spiritual realm.

Additionally, we find scripture describing the Throne of God which is also here in the spiritual realm. In this book we have built a case that the entire spiritual realm is located in the higher dimensions of the space-time continuum, or what is called Hyperspace.

Heaven (that most people think of): When most people think of Heaven, they think of the place where souls of believers go when they die. That Heaven for souls is specifically called in Scripture, Spiritual Jerusalem.

Spiritual Jerusalem: The book of Hebrews describes a most amazing place called Spiritual Jerusalem (also "Jerusalem Above" in Gal 4:26). Spiritual Jerusalem is in a very specific location in the spiritual realm there in Hyperspace. As we unpack the Scriptures here in Hebrews we will find that this is where the souls of dead believers are, where Jesus is making a place for us, where many of the angels are and very importantly, where the Throne of God is.

This is the place that Abraham longed for (Heb 11:10, 16), a place that we will call home. Oh, and here is some more good news; if you are a believer, you are already a citizen of Spiritual Jerusalem (Phil 3:20). It really is your home.

6.3 HEAVEN AND THE SPIRITUAL REALM

Philippians 3:20-21: *"For our citizenship is in heaven, from which also we eagerly wait for a Savior, the Lord Jesus Christ; who will transform the body of our humble state into conformity with the body of His glory, by the exertion of the power that He has even to subject all things to Himself."* (emphasis author – NAS) Our citizenship is in Heaven, Jesus is there now, and one day we will be joining Him there.

Don Piper who was declared legally dead at the scene of a traffic accident, possibly caught a glimpse of heaven: "With all the heightened awareness of my senses, I felt as if I had never seen, heard, or felt anything so real before…The best way I can explain it is to say that I felt as if I were in another dimension."[49]

Citizens of Heaven: When we become a Christian by asking Christ to become our personal savior a lot of good things happen. One of those good news items is that we become a citizen of heaven. We are given the status of dual citizenship. This means then that while we are citizens of some nation here on earth, we (believers) are also already citizens of heaven.

Heaven is our permanent and real home. We are now fulfilling our temporary role on this earth, and when that assignment is complete, we will

---

[49]Don Piper & Ceci Murphey, *90 Minutes in Heaven: Selections* (Grand Rapids: Revell, 2004, 2008), 41

be called to go to our real home. Our home in the spiritual realm is where our Savior dwells.

Personally I am really looking forward to the trip. I anticipate a new grand adventure as I transition from this world limited by 3D things to my real home, in higher dimensions. As Hebrews 11:9-10 notes, it is the place that Abraham sought: *"By faith he lived as an alien in the land of promise, as in a foreign land, dwelling in tents with Isaac and Jacob, fellow heirs of the same promise; <u>for he was looking for the city which has foundations, whose architect and builder is God</u>."* (emphasis author - NAS) Heaven is our home, our real home.

Place of More: As the spiritual realm comes into focus, our own 3D world seems to become dimmer. If we use the 2D to 3D analogy as we have previously, we can see heaven as being a place of more. With this analogy, our world would be like a 2D paper doll world, or like the 2D flat plate ant farm type world. In contrast, the spiritual realm in hyperspace becomes the 3D world, the one of true solids and substance.

This analogy highlights the difference between the seen world being one dimension less than the unseen world. By comparison, using this analogy, to the flat people (2D), everything they know is flat. In contrast, the unseen world would by a world of 3D or solid things. Noted physicists and believer Dr. Lambert Dolphin comments on this amazing insight:

> *The Bible depicts the spiritual realm as more solid, more substantial, more permanent than the present, observable, material world. When God created the universe he created it 'two-storied.' The spiritual realm is where the angels dwell. It is a so much more solid and substantial and permanent than our fading material world, that we can best describe ourselves as ghosts in a shadow-like world surrounded and embedded in the more substantial world of the spirit.* [50]

---

[50] Dr. Lambert Dolphin, "Is Empty Space Empty?", posted February 1997, http://ldolphin.org/update.html (accessed January 11, 2010)

Hyperspace in Scripture

Higher Dimensions: The spiritual realm is in higher dimensions with more solidness, more vibrancy, more dimension and just plain more of everything. Perhaps this is why Paul, who somehow got a glimpse of the magnificent place commented as follows in 2 Corinthians 12:2b-4: *"...whether in the body I do not know, or out of the body I do not know, God knows—such a man was caught up to the third heaven. And I know how such a man—whether in the body or apart from the body I do not know, God knows— was caught up into Paradise and heard inexpressible words, which a man is not permitted to speak."* (NAS)

"Inexpressible words" gives us the insight that it is nearly impossible to describe, and thus we would think so because how can a 2D creature describe the 3D world? How can 3D Paul visit the 4D heaven and describe it to us? Truly, it is difficult but through the scriptures, we anticipate that it is indeed, a very great place.

6.4 SPIRITUAL MT. ZION: CITY OF THE LIVING GOD

"But you have come to Mount Zion and to the city of the living God, the heavenly Jerusalem, and to myriads of angels, to the general assembly and church of the firstborn who are enrolled in heaven, and to God, the Judge of all, and to the spirits of the righteous made perfect, and to Jesus, the mediator of a new covenant, and to the sprinkled blood, which speaks better than the blood of Abel." Heb 12:22-24

"[Spiritual] Mount Zion is adjacent to the temple mount in old Jerusalem. To dwell in Zion is to have one's residence right next to the Lord's own holy dwelling."[51] Noted Bible Teacher John MacArthur

The City: Just the other side of the veil, in Hyperspace, in the unseen realm lays a city that is so marvelous that it is literally beyond description. Imagine a place that is completely devoid of all evil forces and the ugliness caused by fallen humans. Instead, what is there is an innumerable company of angels that are there serving a loving God and

---

[51] John F. MacArthur, *The Glory of Heaven* (Wheaton, Illinois: Crossway Books, 1996), 104.

carrying out His plans and purposes. Also there are the soul-spirits of everyone who have placed their faith in the God of Heaven for their salvation. Many of them have lived a life of toil and struggle in faithful service to God and now they have finally arrived at their true home and found rest. They are no longer strangers roaming the earth.

Hebrews, in the verse quoted above, gives three different names for this one city. It is called "Heavenly Jerusalem", "Mount Zion" (or more specifically we will use "Spiritual Mount Zion"), and the "City of the Living God". All of these are interesting and revealing names. Most importantly, God Himself, God the Father, is there as well. God is actually outside of time and space but we note that somehow, God the Father has in some way, a manifest presence there.

Also, Jesus, the Christ, the Son of God is there. They are in the Throne Room inside the Heavenly Temple. It is from that place that God reigns over the universe with great might, power, justice, mercy and love. It is therefore also appropriately described as the "Throne of Grace." How blessed and comforting it is to recognize that God rules the universe from such a place and in this way.

Scripture gives us some further fascinating insights into heavenly Jerusalem by noting who all is there, but we really aren't told much about the design and architecture of the city itself. Perhaps this is part of the *"inexpressible words"* that Paul, as an honored visitor to there, wasn't allowed to speak about (2 Cor 12:4). For this reason, we won't venture too far away from what scripture does tell us. Most folks do however, imagine a grand and glorious place and it sure seems like it would be all of that (see Figure 20).

Hyperspace in Scripture

Figure 20. City of the Living God, heavenly Jerusalem: *Left*, Jerusalem[52]; *middle*, Angels[53]; *right*, City[54]

Location of Spiritual Jerusalem: *"But you have come to Mount Zion and to the city of the living God, the heavenly Jerusalem..."* (Heb 12:22a)

But where is this very special place, this city that we all long for? Well, in some senses its sense its location may not come as a big surprise. We have seen in Daniel's experience with the angel that there are places in the spiritual realm that are directly adjacent to their corresponding place in the earthly realm. Earthly Persia, for example, was located next to Spiritual Persia (or really embedded into it). It turns out that the same is true for Spiritual Jerusalem. Spiritual Jerusalem is directly adjacent to Earthly Jerusalem. Even more specifically, Scripture links Earthly Mount Zion with Spiritual Mount Zion. It is here, on Spiritual Mount Zion that we find the Temple of God.

---

[52]"Heavenly City", Cosmic Conflict, http://www.cosmicconflict.com/Media/Gallery.aspx (accessed February 20, 2010).

[53]"Heaven", Divine Revelations, http://spiritlessons.com/Documents/7_Jovenes/English_7_Jovenes_Heaven.htm (accessed February 20, 2010).

[54]"New Jerusalem", Divine Revelations, http://spiritlessons.com/Documents/7_Jovenes/English_7_Jovenes_Heaven.htm (accessed February 20, 2010).

Map of Heaven

In the Book of Hebrews, after speaking of the great lives of faith the Old Testament saints had, it goes on to point out that their only real direct experience with approaching God was an earthly one. Back in Exodus 19, after passing through the Red Sea, the Israelites approached God on Mount Sinai.

Hebrews 12:18-24 makes the case that the experience they had in meeting with God was much different that what we experience. Theirs was a terrifying experience. We, on this side of the cross have a perfect sacrifice for our sin in Jesus. It is for this reason, by the blood sacrifice that Jesus made for us, that we can come forgiven to where God is now.

Figure 21. Earthly Mount Zion: *Left*,[55] ; *right*, [56]

And where God is located is the Heavenly Mount Zion. The implication behind Heb 12: 22 is that when you are on Mt. Zion on the earth, you are directly linked with the Heavenly Mount Zion. For these reasons, it then becomes clearer why God is so interested in the land of Israel and why when He had a temple built here on Earth to represent Himself here; it was

---

[55]Brenda Elliott, Jerusalem, http://therealbarackobama.wordpress.com/2009/09/24/klein-did-obama-call-on-israel-to-vacate-temple-mount-israeli-politicians-accuse-president-of-misrepresenting-history/ , posted September 24, 2009, (accessed January 8, 2010).

[56]Israeli Photos, Israel Ministry of Tourism, http://www.theodora.com/wfb/photos/israel/israel_photos_40.html , (accessed January 8, 2010).

on Mount Zion itself. Figure 21 Shows Earthly Mount Zion today with the Temple Mount location and the golden dome of the "Dome of the Rock" Islamic temple defining the skyline.

Earthly and Heavenly Temple: *"Now of the things which we have spoken this is the sum: We have such an high priest, who is set on the right hand of the throne of the Majesty <u>in the heavens</u>; A minister of the sanctuary, and of the <u>true tabernacle, which the Lord pitched, and not man</u>."* (Hebrews 8:1-2: emphasis author).

In reference to Jesus preaching at the Temple in John 8:20, Bible Scholar John Phillips notes: "They were standing on the portals of his [Jesus'] world. If there was one place where heaven came down to earth, it was there at the temple in Jerusalem."[57]

It comes as a surprise to many to discover that there is a real Temple in Heaven. This Temple isn't just floating is space somewhere with flying angels zipping in and out of the doors. This is a tangible, real building, which although located in Heaven, has its foundations sunk deeply into the solid rich ground of the spiritual realm. Scripture continually paints a picture depicting the spiritual realm as a real place with real dwellings. This is in stark contrast to Hollywood's portrayals of people and angels floating around on clouds. Let's dig in a little further.

As Dr. Chuck Missler likes to note, when Moses came down from the top of Mt. Sinai, he brought not only tablets with the 10 commandments (written by the finger of God), but he also brought a set of blueprint.[58] Blueprints? Yes, Moses received very detailed instructions on the design of the Tabernacle (Heb 8:5). The Tabernacle was to be the place where God would make His presence known among His people Israel.

---

[57] John Phillips, *Exploring the Gospel of John* (Grand Rapids: Kregel Pub., 1989), 163.

[58] I have heard this often in lectures but in print Missler notes a "very specific set of instructions." Dr. Chuck Missler, *Learn the Bible in 24 Hours* (Nashville; Thomas Nelson Pub., 2002), 54.

Map of Heaven

Referred to as the Shechinah Glory, for much of the Temple's history, there was a visible supernatural manifestation (smoke and light) indicating God's presence (1 Kings 8:10-11). Sadly, in Ezekiel's time, when Israel had slipped deeply into idolatry, the manifestation left (Ezek 9-11). But why would the design of the Tabernacle be so important? Why would it be placed on the level of importance with the 10 commandments?

This was also true of the great Temple that Solomon built. Solomon's Temple was one of the great wonders in the ancient world; an astounding feat of engineering, beauty and construction. Solomon's Temple was also built under very specific instructions from God as it replaced the Tabernacle, a temporary structure.[59] I'll suggest that the reason that God placed such a big emphasis on the design was that it was/is a representation of a very real Temple, the true Temple which is located in Hyperspace.

But wait, there is even more. Additionally, there appears to be a fascinating hyperspace reference related to the Temple. Let's look into that.

The Tabernacle and Temple were grand structures. The real glory of them was on the inside. There were two key rooms in the structures. First and larger was called the Holy Place and it contained the golden table of show bread, altar of incense and the light, the Menorah. An awesome massive veil or curtain separated the two rooms as a symbol barring access to God whose presence was behind the veil. That was until Christ's sacrifice was accomplished. At that time the veil was ripped in two by God Himself opening the way to the inner room (Matt 27:51; Mark 15:38; Luke 23:45).

The inner room is the Holiest of Holies and it contained the famous Ark of the Covenant with is solid gold "lid," which was really a separate

---

[59] As a point of bible trivia, it is interesting to note that the Temple where God dwells is a "type" of Christ. The Son of God first appears on earth in a body that is perishable, an earthly body like ours (which is represented by the Tabernacle, a temporary structure). The body of Jesus died but He was resurrected in an everlasting body (which is represented by the Temple, a permanent structure). The picture or "type" is that the dwelling of God on earth was initially temporary but intended to be replaced by a permanent dwelling.

Hyperspace in Scripture

piece of furniture, known as the Mercy Seat. It was here, on the Mercy Seat that God made His presence known. Materials used in the Temples construction included 3,334 pounds of gold (that's right; pounds), 11,467 pounds of silver and 8,071 pounds of bronze (Exodus 38:24-29). Without question, this is an impressive amount of precious metals.

It is also interesting that the Tabernacle (the earlier temporary structure) had a final covering over it of porpoise skin which is not very attractive (Ex 26:14). We recall that Isaiah 53:2 notes that the Messiah, Jesus, would physically not be attractive and people wouldn't take notice of Him.

Figure 22. Earthly Dwellings: *Left*: Tabernacle; *right*, Temple

However, in contrast, Solomon's Temple was a beautiful and marvelous wonder and when Jesus comes back in all His glory, in His everlasting resurrected body, He will be as well. Jesus' magnificent glory was premiered on the Mount of Transfiguration (Matt 17:2; Mark 9:2). Artist's depictions of these structures are shown in Figure 22.

Mt. Zion on Jerusalem has a fascinating history. The city of Jerusalem is on a hill or perhaps better stated, a mountain top and it is surrounded by valleys on three sides. In the Old Testament, it is referred to as Mt. Morriah and this is where Abraham was sent to sacrifice Isaac (Gen 22:2). David, in his conquest, captures this land from the Jebusites around 750 B.C. and established his capital, the capital of Israel there.

Map of Heaven

Mt. Morriah has 3 knolls or high spots on it. The south western knoll (1) is called Mount Zion but as time went on the entire hill top area became known as Mt. Zion. The Eastern knoll (2) becomes the location where Solomon constructs the Temple (2 Chr 3:1). Up to the time of David it had been a threshing floor, owned by a man named Ornan; David bought it from Ornan.[60] The last knoll (3) is the highest spot on the mountain and is on the northern side.

At the time of Christ, this high spot (knoll (3)) was just outside of the city wall. It was here that Jesus was crucified. The knoll is called Golgotha. Although rabbinical tradition suggests that Abraham's sacrifice was at the Temple knoll, some have suggested that it was more likely the high spot of the hill (Golgotha) where Isaac presented himself as the "type" of sacrifice, prophetically looking forward to Jesus. This is an awesome place with very deep supernatural history and roots.

About a third of a mile from the top of Mt. Zion lies the historic Temple Mount and the place where God once dwelt there in the Temple. Earthly Mt. Zion has an important place in scripture appearing 154 times.[61] It is first mentioned in the Bible in 2 Samuel 5:7 which notes that David conquered Zion and it became his capital, the City of David. Figure 23 shows the topography of Mt. Zion in Jerusalem and a satellite picture of the area today. The Temple Mount is North and a little East of Mt. Zion. Golgatha which is on the knoll of a hill and was the site of Jesus' crucifixion is only about one-third of a mile from the Temple. All of these things are in the heart of Jerusalem.

---

[60] This was after King David sinned by counting Israel's soldiers contrary to God's directive. Subsequently, this directly led to the breakout of a plague and 70,000 people dying as a punishment. The angel responsible for administering it temporarily stopped over the threshing floor of Ornan in front of Jerusalem. David saw the angel, pleaded for the city, buys the field, offered a sacrifice there and the plague was halted. (1 Chronicles 21:14-30)

[61] *Tsiyown*, Blueletterbible, http://www.blueletterbible.org/lang/lexicon/lexicon.cfm?Strongs=H6726&t=KJV (accessed February 27, 2010), Strong's #6726.

Hyperspace in Scripture

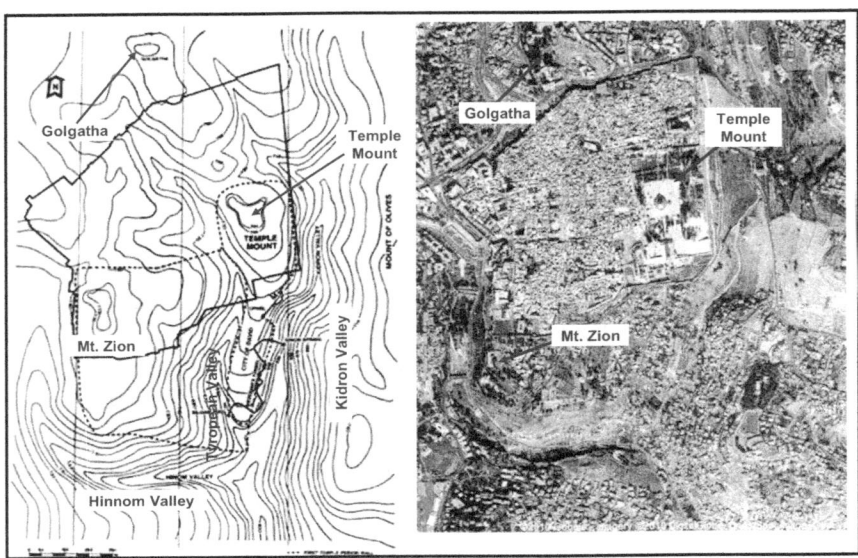

Figure 23. Mt. Zion: Left, Topography[62]; right, Satellite map today[63]

Higher Dimensional Heavenly Temple: *"Now if He [Jesus] were on earth, He would not be a priest at all, since there are those who offer the gifts according to the Law; who <u>serve a copy and shadow of the heavenly things</u>, just as Moses was warned by God when he was about to erect the tabernacle; for "See," he says, "that you make all thing according to the pattern which was shown you on the mountain."*(Hebrews 8:4-5 - emphasis author)

New Testament and Greek Scholar Kenneth Wuest commented; "…it [the shadow] merely is proof of the fact that there is a reality back of it. It [the shadow] is not itself solid or real. Just so, the earthly tabernacle is proof of the fact that there was a real one, the heavenly one where God

---

[62]Chuck Missler, "The Akedah", Koinonia House, http://www.khouse.org/articles/2008/758/ (accessed February 25, 2010).

[63]"Jerusalem; Satellite Map", Googlemaps, http://maps.google.com/maps?hl=en&tab=wl (accessed February 25, 2010).

Map of Heaven

Himself dwelt, where Messiah officiates as High Priest. The Aaronic priests performed their priestly rites in representation of the heavenly tabernacle."[64]

This verse gives us an unanticipated reference into Hyperspace. It speaks of the Earthly Tabernacle as a shadow and very specifically links it to the Heavenly Tabernacle. Further, the Holy Spirit makes the point of why it was so important that Moses built *"according to the pattern"* which was shown him. Why is all this so important? It is because the Earthy Tabernacle was a 3D model of the higher dimensional Hyperspace Tabernacle. Let me explain.

The word used here that is translated shadow is the Greek *skia* which simply means shadow.[65] [66] Also, the word copy is from the Greek *hupodeigma* which means "figure," "copy," or "example."[67] So, the earthy tabernacle was a shadow copy of the Heavenly Temple. The word "shadow" carries two meanings. One is like when we say someone is a shadow of their former self. This means that they (as a shadow) are perhaps somewhat less than what their real self once was. This certainly applies to the contrast of the Heavenly and Earthly Temples.

But of interest here, however, the word shadow also carries a more technical and insightful meaning. A shadow is actually a one dimension

---

[64] Kenneth Wuest, *Word Studies from the Greek New Testament* (1947, repr.: Grand Rapids, Eerdmans, 2002), II:141-142.

[65] *Skia*, Blueletterbible, http://www.blueletterbible.org/lang/lexicon/lexicon.cfm?Strongs=G4639&t=KJV (accessed March 2, 2010), Strong's #4639.

[66] Also, *"skia"* is further defined as "shadow thrown by an object"; Collin Brown gen. ed., *New International Dictionary of New Testament Theology* (Grand Rapids; Zondervan, 1967, 1986; VIII 554

[67] *Hupodeigma*, Blueletterbible, http://www.blueletterbible.org/lang/lexicon/lexicon.cfm?Strongs=G5262&t=KJV (accessed March 2, 2010), Strong's #5262.

Hyperspace in Scripture

lower form of an object which is very real. Example, a shadow of a tree on the ground is a flat 2D representation of a one dimension higher (3D) real tree. A shadow is just like a silhouette; a 2D representation of a 3D object. The word shadow specifically speaks of dimensions.

So, from this verse in Hebrews, we gain the insight that although real in itself, the Earthly Temple is a 3D, one dimension down from what is in Heaven. Therefore, the Heavenly Temple is not only very real, but must be a 4D structure. Can we draw a picture of this? No. As we have noted, it is impossible for us as 3D limited people to visualize what a 4D structure would actually look like. Fascinating isn't it? I've got one more.

Temple Veil: This is just a conjecture, and only a conjecture, but it is my opinion that the veil separating the two rooms in the Temple is perhaps also representative of the veil that separates the seen and unseen worlds today. Because of Christ's death, the veil was torn and spiritually, we now have direct access to God. Hebrews 4:16 notes we can now, with confidence or boldness[68] approach the God's Throne of Grace. The veil that spiritually separated man from God is now removed by the precious blood of Christ.

But there is more. When the 1,000 year reign of Christ (spoken of in Revelation 20) is complete, then we will move into the New Heaven and New Earth of Revelation 21. Perhaps the most striking key characteristic of this final age is the fact that God the Father comes to dwell with us, His people. The veil separating the seen 3D realm and the unseen 4D spiritual realm in Hyperspace will be removed. All will be united and another cool thing, God the Father's very presence is the light which illuminates the universe day and night. There will be no night, God's light continually shines (Rev 21:23-25). How glorious that will be. This is a great feature of our future that we can look forward to.

The fact that the two realms will unite in the New Heaven age is pretty clear from Revelation 21. My conjecture is that the splitting of the veil had an immediate message of access to God in the spiritual realm,

---

[68] The New American Standard and New International Versions translate this passage with the word "confidence" and the New King James uses the word "boldly".

spiritually; but additionally, I believe that the future uniting is also indicated by the splitting veil.

Throne of God: Here, in the City of the Living God, is where God makes His presence known. It is also where God's Throne, the *"Throne of Grace"* (a most elegant title: Heb 4:16) is. It is where our Savior resides. It is a most important place. This is the Throne of the Creator of the Universe. Revelation alone speaks of this place some 39 times. If we were talking about the United States, we would say 1600 Pennsylvania Avenue (the White House); if we were talking Great Britain we would say Number 10 Downing Street (the Prime Ministers Residence); if we were talking about my company, we would say Executive Row (where the CEO's office is). These are the places where the people in charge dwell; the person at the top.

Well, when we are talking the really big picture, everything seen and unseen, we are talking about God and He rules from His Throne which is in the Heavenly Temple, which is in the city of Heavenly Jerusalem, which is placed on the top of Spiritual Mount Zion, immediately adjacent to our Earthly Mount Zion.

In a sense, the Throne is the focal point of the Christian's life: *"fixing our eyes on Jesus, the author and perfecter of faith, who for the joy set before Him endured the cross, despising the shame, and <u>has sat down at the right hand of the throne of God</u>."* (emphasis author – Heb 12:2 NAS) We are to live our lives on a sight line that points directly at Jesus; who is sitting at the right hand of His Father's Throne.

It is customary, right and proper that everyone who comes into the presence of an earthly king will either stand or fall flat on their face. It is the same with God. When you come into His presence, you are either on your face or standing when instructed; everyone that is except our Savior. It is noteworthy that Jesus, the Son of God, now in a resurrected body, is sitting at the right hand of God the Father. Only an equal sits on the same level as the king.

We might be tempted to guess what the place looks like. Because we are only 3D creatures and the Temple and Throne are 4D spaces, we really can't grasp the majesty, beauty and wonder of the place; but there is

Hyperspace in Scripture

some good news. Two people have actually been there and returned to tell us about it.

Young Isaiah around 700 years before the time of Christ, went there, survived, and returned to give us a description. He recorded it in Isaiah 6. John the apostle, late in his life (perhaps some 80 years old at the time) also went there, survived and returned with the Book of Revelation. Revelation speaks many times of the Throne and provides a detailed description of it in Revelation 4-5. John actually describes activity in the temple on five different occasions (Rev 4-5; 7:9-17; 8:1; 15; and 16:17).

Isaiah's and John's accounts are extremely consistent. Although it is a real challenge to relate what they saw, their description seems to just ooze higher dimensional activity. Some of these features are noted in Figure 24.

Map of Heaven

Reference	What was witnessed (events)
Isaiah 6 (Old Testament Period)	Lord (King) on the Throne, lofty & exalted, train of His robe filled the temple
	Seraphim: six wings, two to cover face two to cover feet and two to fly
	Seraphim pronounce the Holiness of God
	The foundations and threshold of the temple shook
	Temple filled with smoke
	There is an altar there
Revelation 4-5 (Immediately after the Rapture)	One on the throne: like a jasper stone and a rainbow around the throne like emerald
	24 Elders on thrones around the throne (white garments, golden crowns)
	Out from the throne, flashes of lightning, sounds and peals of thunder \
	7 Lamps of fire which are the 7 spirits of God
	Sea of Glass
	4 Living Creatures; full of eyes in front and behind (lion, calf, man & eagle faces), 6 wings
	4 Living Creatures pronounce the holiness of God (joined by 24 Elders)
	Joined by myriads of myriads and thousand of thousands of angels
	Events just prior to 7 Seal Judgments
Revelation 7:9-17 (Middle of Tribulation)	Great multitude before the throne (all nations and peoples) in white robes and holding palms
	Tribulation martyrs
Revelation 8:1	There is silence in heaven for 1/2 hour
	Event just prior to the 7 Trumpet Judgments
Revelation 15	Tribulation martyrs on the glassy sea singing
	Temple was open
	One of the 4 creatures gives the last bowls of wrath to 7 angels
	Temple fills with smoke
	Just prior to the 7 vials (bowls) of wrath
	At this point, no one is allowed in the Temple with God
Rev 16:17	God cries "It is done" as the 7th Vial (bowl) of wrath is poured out
	The subsequent devastation to the planet earth is enormous (mountains leveled, islands sink, and an unprecedented unleashing of meteorites and bolides)

Figure 24 Biblical insights into the Heavenly Temple of God

What John and Isaiah see is Jesus in His glory and the Throne. These descriptions include: glory, radiance and light everywhere, foundation and threshold shaking; lightning, sounds and thunder, a mighty voice; dark smoke everywhere, and also mighty seraphim or living creatures.

Hyperspace in Scripture

I'll suggest that the reason that the colors, lights, sounds and motions are so difficult to describe is because all this is happening in 4D and our witnesses are simple 3D people. If the Throne of God is in a 4D higher dimensional space, this is the type of description that we would expect them to provide.

On a side note, a visit there must be an absolutely awesome (but certainly initially terrifying) experience. John description of a few minutes of activity in the Throne room is jaw dropping. *"Then I looked, and I heard the voice of many angels around the throne and the living creatures and the elders; and the number of them was myriads of myriads, and thousands of thousands, saying with a loud voice, "Worthy is the Lamb that was slain to receive power and riches and wisdom and might and honor and glory and blessing." And every created thing which is in heaven and on the earth and under the earth and on the sea, and all things in them, I heard saying, "To Him who sits on the throne, and to the Lamb, be blessing and honor and glory and dominion forever and ever." And the four living creatures kept saying, "Amen." And the elders fell down and worshiped."* (Rev 5:11-15) Man, that's a worship service!

One of the striking things to emerge from a look at the Biblical description of the Throne Room of God is the connectedness between clear and deliberate actions taken by God in the spiritual realm and its subsequent outpouring on the physical earth.

An example is Revelation 8:5: *"Then the angel took the censer and filled it with the fire of the altar, and threw it to the earth; and there followed peals of thunder and sounds and flashes of lightning and an earthquake."* Here we see and angel, operating in the spiritual realm by taking a censer filled with fire from the altar in the heavenly temple and then throwing it to earth. What follows is the 7 Trumpet Judgments which have a devastating effect on the earth. This is only one of many examples where we see a link in activity between the heavenly realm and that of the earth.

Residents: *"...to myriads of **angels**, to the general assembly and **church of the firstborn** who are enrolled in heaven, and to **God**, the Judge of all, and to the **spirits of the righteous made perfect**, 24 and to Jesus the mediator of a new covenant, and to the sprinkled blood, which speaks better*

Map of Heaven

than the blood of Abel." (emphasis author Heb 12:22c-24a)

Believer; do you want to know where you are going when you die? This is the time to read carefully. Several different groups are described here and most all Evangelical Scholars are in agreement as to who these folks are. They are itemized below:

- Angels: There is a seriously large group of angels there; it also seems that the phrase "general assembly" also refers to this huge gathering of these spiritual beings

- Church of the Firstborn enrolled in Heaven: This is the souls of believers who have been born again by the blood of Jesus. Jesus was the *"firstborn of many brethren"* referring to believers as the brethren who would follow (Rom 8:29). Believers are citizens of Heaven (Phil 3:20). Also, according to Luke 10:20 our names are recorded in heaven and also, according to Rev 21:27 our names are written in the "Lamb's book of life" so it is here that we are "enrolled"

- God: God the Father, the Judge of all, although omnipresent and outside of the space-time continuum, He chooses to manifest His presence here

- Spirits of Righteous Men Made Perfect: these are the souls of the Old Testament Saints, the people who followed God before Christ's death. The souls of Old Testament believers, upon death, went to upper Hades (or Abraham's bosom – Luke 16:22-23) to wait there until the death of Christ (their sacrifice) (Heb 11:40). After Christ's death, they now have a permanent covering for their sin, through Christ, so they were able to move on up to Heaven (Luke 4:18)

- Jesus, our Savior; and specific reference is made of His blood sacrifice. He is there, sitting at the right hand of the Father.

Hyperspace in Scripture

When a believer dies, he goes to Heaven. But much more specifically, when a believer dies, he goes to Heavenly Jerusalem, the City of the Living God.

The extremely large numbers of angels are alluded to both here in Hebrews as well as what John described in Revelation 5:11 as *"the number of them was ten thousand times ten thousand, and thousands of thousands."* It is unclear as to exactly how many angels there are but as scripture seems to links angels and stars together, it would imply that there are perhaps on the order of 10^{22} (which is 10 followed by 22 zeros), a very large number.

City of Contrast: Hebrews 4:16: *"Let us therefore come boldly unto the throne of grace, that we may obtain mercy, and find grace to help in time of need."* (KJV) In Hebrews 12 a great contrast is drawn between the Israelites who had an encounter with God on Mt. Sinai and our encounter with Heavenly Jerusalem.

Exodus 19-20 describes this supernatural encounter the Israelites had in directly meeting with God. Shortly after the Israelites had approached and met with God on Mt. Sinai they begged Moses not to ever let this happen again (Exodus 20:18-19). Hebrews notes that Moses himself, who had already spoken directly with God at the burning bush and other occasions, was so terrified that he was literally shaking uncontrollably in fear (Hebrews 12:21). Rumblings, thunder, blaring trumpets and a great earthquake must have really help make the harrowing experience.

The day the Israelites approached the base of Mt. Sinai and heard the voice of God goes down as perhaps one of the most dramatic encounters ever by a group of people to the presence of God. In the Book of Hebrews, that fearful encounter is contrasted with a believer who has been cleansed by the Blood of Christ coming to the City of God. The saved ones, the redeemed, can now approach the Heavenly Jerusalem, Heavenly Mt. Zion, with confidence and join the great assembly of angels and the souls of Old Testament and New Testament believers. Figure 25 notes some of these insightful contrasts.

Map of Heaven

Israelites Encounter on Mt. Sinai	Christians Arrive at the Heavenly City
• Temporary – God was only there once	• Permanent - City of the Living God
• Can't be touched – you will be struck dead	• Invited in – come fellowship
• 3D on this earth	• 4D – Heavenly Jerusalem
• Blazing Fire - Judgment	• All is forgiven – Church of the First born
• Darkness and Gloom	• Kingdom of Light (Col 1:12 (NIV)): General Assembly
• Even the beasts would be struck dead	• Myriads of Angels
• Trumpet blast and unbelievable sounds	• Jesus – the mediator of a new covenant
• Terrifying words	• Jesus, who speaks better than the blood of Abel
• Whirlwind – window to something better	• Come to God – who is the something better
• Those who heard, begged for it to stop	• The Spirits of the righteous made perfect

Figure 25. Contrasts between Mt. Sinai and Mt. Zion

Hyperspace Construction Project: John 14:1-3: *"Do not let your heart be troubled; believe in God, believe also in Me. In My Father's house are many dwelling places; if it were not so, I would have told you; for I go to prepare a place for you. If I go and prepare a place for you, I will come again and receive you to Myself, that where I am, there you may be also."* Jesus gives us a truly comforting promise that we, as believers, have a real home or place in Heaven waiting for us.

Jesus described an important activity, or more specifically, a massive construction project and He is the designer, architect and construction project manager.[69] So, in addition to ruling at the right hand of the Father, Jesus the Christ with the care of a truly loving leader is making sure that our real home will be ready for us.

As we have seen, the spirit/souls of dead believers are their in Heavenly Jerusalem today. But also, the Son of God is preparing a place for us and at the appointed time, Jesus will come to collect the remaining believers on Earth to join with the spirit/souls of those who have gone on before us (1 Thess 4:13-18 – this event is often referred to as the Rapture).

---

[69] As Warren Wiersbe points out, it is interesting that Jesus' job on earth was that of a carpenter: Warren Wiersbe, The Bible Exposition Commentary (Colorado Springs: Victor, Cook Communications, 2001)., N.T. Vol.I. 350.

Hyperspace in Scripture

The day is coming when we will go home, to our real home and Jesus Himself will draw us together.

6.5 ANALOGIES FOR HYPERSPACE

2D to 3D Analogy: Lets look again at the 2D flat plate world to help us understand the answer to this question: "Where is Heaven, the place for departed believing souls?" Using the 2D flat plate or ant farm type world of the Goombas, we find that they also have a 2D Mount Zion. When you are walking in Goomba land, if you come to Mount Zion, you will have to climb uphill to get to the top. If we were to create a 3D spiritual world around the 2D Goomba world, we would also find that there was a corresponding mountain that is adjacent to the mountain in the 2D Goomba land. This is illustrated in Figure 26.

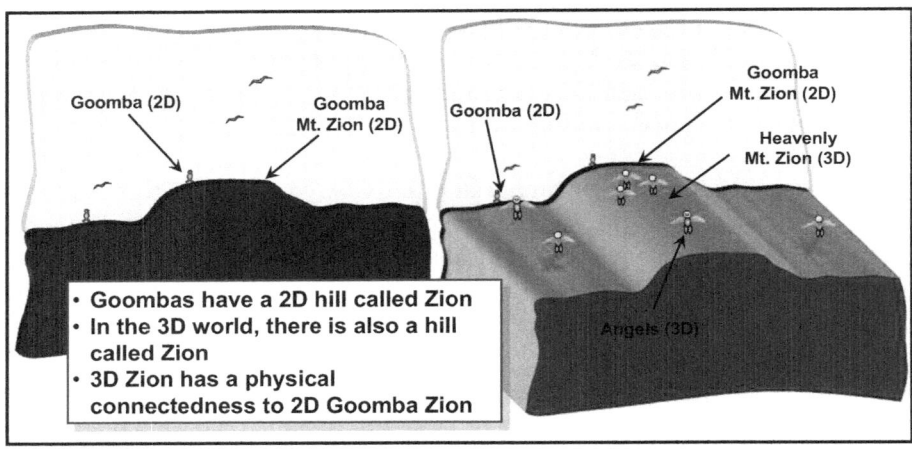

Figure 26. 2D to 3D analogy of Goomba Mount Zion and a connected 3D heavenly Mount Zion

In the drawing on the left, you can see the 2D Goomba mountain called Mt. Zion. On the right is the corresponding 3D Mount Zion complete with spiritual creatures. To the Goombas, the 2D Mt. Zion is very real, and it is. But by comparison, the 3D Mt. Zion is so much more. The 3D Mt. Zion is one dimension higher.

Also, it is important to recognize once again that there is a physical

Map of Heaven

and actual connectedness between the 2D Mt. Zion of the Goombas, and the 3D heavenly Mt. Zion. Heavenly Mt. Zion physically touches and builds from the 2D Goomba Zion. Even their shapes mirror each other at some point.

2D to 3D World Analogy and Location of Heaven: Carrying this analogy a little further to the world level, we can construct a 2D flat Goomba world which is like an ant farm. But this ant farm is as big as our earth. This is shown on the left in Figure 27.

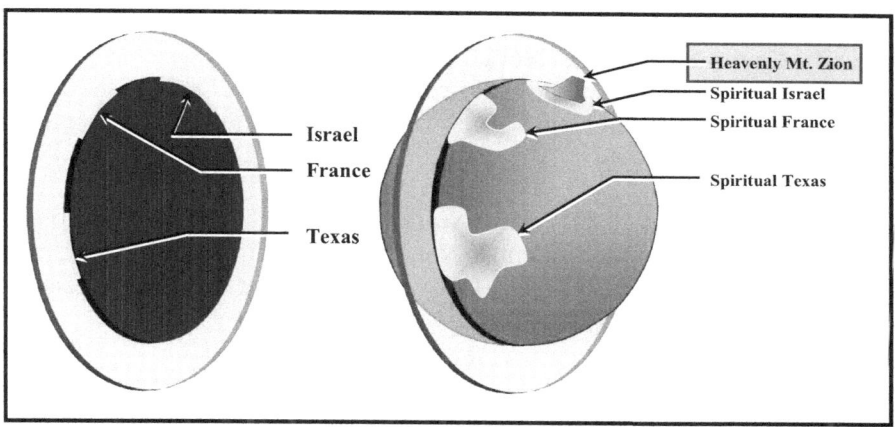

Figure 27 – 2D to 3D Analogy of the location of Heavenly Mt. Zion, the City of the Living God and home of the souls of departed believers

Territories such as Texas, France and Israel are noted as lines in the 2D flat world. When we view the full 3D spiritual world of the Goombas' we find that the territories that were simple lines in the 2D world are now areas in the 3D Goomba spiritual world. So, Texas, France and Israel are now areas in the full 3D world. We can also note that in the 2D Israel line, there is a mountain known as Mt. Zion.

In the 3D spiritual Goomba land, we note the corresponding 3D mountain associated with the 2D line mountain in the flat plate world. In this analogy, the Goombas, living in a 2D flat plate world have a mountain they call Mt. Zion. Adjacent to this, is an actual and real 3D mountain in the

Hyperspace in Scripture

Goomba 3D spiritual realm. The 3D mountain is also called Mount Zion. I refer to it as Spiritual or Heavenly Mt. Zion.

Let's come back to the big question again; "Where are the souls of believers who have died?" Answer: They are living on Spiritual Mount Zion. You might ask, "How do I get there?" Well, you need to get on an airplane, fly to Israel and then head up on to earthly Mount Zion. When you reach that spot, then all you will need to do is step through the veil separating the seen and unseen realms, and you will be there.

Everything is pretty easy except for that last part of stepping through the veil. Certainly stepping through the veil is the challenge, but none the less, if you could do that, you would end up there in the City of the Living God, Spiritual Jerusalem. Most folks who are there got there by another means.

Are you worried that when you die you might not be able to find your way to Heavenly Jerusalem? Not to worry. It appears from Jesus' description in Luke 16:19-31 (specifically verse 22) that there are angels that escort us to heaven.

This insight is gained from the fact that when poor Lazarus (poor man Lazarus – not the Lazarus raised from the dead) died, he was escorted by angels to Paradise. So some, and I am inclined to accept this also, feel that this is true for us when we die as well. We can take great comfort in the thought that when we die, Jesus will make sure we get to Heavenly Jerusalem to join up with Him there along with the other departed believers. It is then my opinion that Jesus uses angels to accomplish this: truly a comforting thought.

Spiritual Jerusalem a Land of Freedom: *"But the son by the bondwoman was born according to the flesh, and the son by the free woman through the promise. This is allegorically speaking, for these women are two covenants: one proceeding from Mount Sinai bearing children who are to be slaves ... and corresponds to the present Jerusalem ...**But the Jerusalem above is free**; she is our mother... And you brethren, like Isaac, are children of promise... So then, brethren, **we are not children of a bondwoman, but of the free woman**."* (Gal 4:21-31 – partial – emphasis author)

Map of Heaven

Jesus highlighted to Nicodemus, that in order to enter the "kingdom of Heaven" you had to be "born again" (John 3:3, 7). Further, Jesus noted that flesh gives birth to flesh (speaking of earthy birth – John 3:6) and the spirit gives birth to spirit, speaking of spiritual birth: being born again.

Scripture, in Galatians 4:21-31 gives us an analogy of these two births which solidifies our understanding of Heavenly Jerusalem. In the Galatians' analogy, those who are born in the flesh, all of us people are slaves to sin (Rom 6:6; 6:17). This corresponds to earthly Mt. Sinai. In contrast to this, those who have been born again, are now freed from the oppression and are now "free in Christ" (Galatians 5:1).

In the Galatians' analogy, those born again are born of promise (like Isaac from Sarah). Heavenly Jerusalem which is free is the analogy of those born free. The contrast between those born in slavery and those bore free are noted in Figure 28. Because of this contrast, we can deepen our understanding of Heavenly Jerusalem noting that it is characterized by freedom.

Hagar - Bondwoman	Sarah – Free woman
Son born of the flesh: son of the flesh	• Son born of promise (spiritual)
Covenant of Mt. Sinai: Born slaves	• New covenant of Christ: Born free
Mt. Sinai represents earthly Jerusalem	• Heavenly Jerusalem is free and our mother
• Slaves under the law	• Free men
• Like Ishmael, children of servants	• Like Isaac, we are "Children of Promise"
• Sons born of flesh persecute the free	• Sons of spirit will not share their inheritance with the sons of the flesh

Figure 28. Contrast between earthly-fleshly and heavenly-spiritual

This freedom goes beyond just the freedom of the people (spirits) and extends to the creation and land itself. Here on earth, our mountains and the terrain is in bondage (Rom 8:22-25). Under this bondage, our visible creation is groaning to be set free. But in the heavenly realm, things are already free.

6.6 GOD: CREATOR BEYOND TIME AND SPACE

"For thus saith the high and lofty One that inhabiteth eternity, whose name is Holy; I dwell in the high and holy place..." (Isa 57:15a)

"The Bible is unique in that it presents a universe of more than three dimensions, and reveals a Creator that is transcendent over His creation. It is the only "holy book" that possesses such contemporary insights." [70] Dr. Chuck Missler.

There are some today who suggest that "god is all and all is god." Further, a mother goddess is postulated as the focus of this god imbedded in all things. This position can not be held with sound logic. As example consider the problem of evil. The only way that believers in this system can account for evil is to declare it as illusionary. Intellectually, this is very unsatisfying and certainly to those who are victims of evil it doesn't begin to offer any real understanding.

In contrast, Scripture describes a Creator God who is beyond the space-time creation. From the very beginning God is declared not "as the creation" but the "Creator of the creation." Genesis 1:1; *"In the beginning God created the heavens and the earth."* God has created everything so by definition, He is beyond or distinct from that which He created.

The implications of this understanding are staggering. Because time is a property of the time-space continuum and God is outside of it, He has the ability to view or look across all time even before the continuum or universe began. He truly knows and *"declares the end from the beginning"* (Isa 46:10b).

So, God is bigger, more powerful and fully knowledgeable of all aspects of our universe, past, present and future. This is echoed in God's statement that He is the: *"Lord God Almighty, Who was and is and is to*

---

[70]Dr. Chuck Missler, "Quantum Teleporting: Part 1"; Koinonia House; (Posted 2002) http://www.khouse.org/articles/2002/388/ (accessed May 10, 2010)

come!" (Rev 4:8c). This means that God is beyond time and space and is the only being in such a position. None of the created beings, angels and other spiritual creatures, are outside of the space-time continuum or they would be able to see the past, present and future at the same time as God, but they can't. Only God has this unique "outside" of space and time position. Isaiah 57:15a (noted above) indicates that God inhabits *"eternity."* Eternity is not a location in either space or time, it is separate from that. Also, eternity is not a lot of time, it is a state devoid of time. Only God resides in eternity.

This is a very important point because the Bible is the only religious writing that identifies God as outside of or apart from the universe that He created. Hinduism, Buddhism and even Islam portray God as being ingrained or embedded into the universe.[71] Scripture, in contrast to this thought reveals that God is the Creator God, and is separate from His creation. We'll suggest an example for illustration.

Consider that all that God created is in a "box" as shown in Figure 29. This would include the 3D world plus time, what we perceive with our senses, the unseen spiritual realm and also higher dimensions (or hyperspace). Everything is in the box. As stated, because time is a property of the space-time continuum, time is also in the box. God is not in the box or even part of the box. He created the box with everything in it. God is the Creator beyond the box, beyond Time and Space.

---

[71]The Islamic god Allah is considered divorced from his creation, but also the universe and Allah have existed from eternity. See: Josh McDowell and Don Steward, *Handbook of Today's Religions* (Nashville: Thomas Nelson Pub., 1983), 393 and Walter Martin, *The Kingdom of the Cults* (Minneapolis: Bethany House Pub., 1965, revised – updated and expanded, 1997), 619.

Hyperspace in Scripture

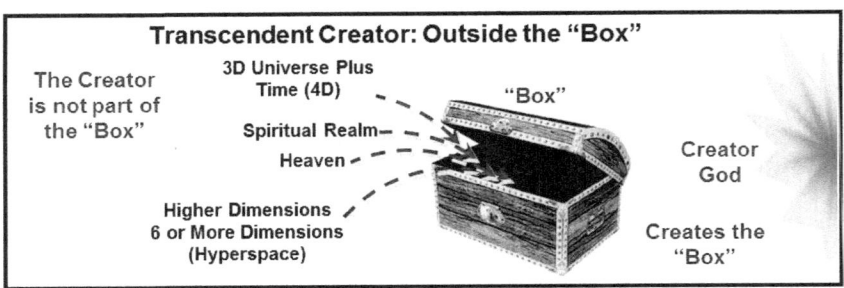

Figure 29. God's created "Box" contains all the things we know of

John Loeffler stated this very well:

> *If there is one concept that separates Judeo-Christianity from all other religions it is God's existence independently from the space-time universe, which we'll call the "box." God is outside the box. He existed before the box. He created the box and He continues to exist outside the box but maintains active communication with everything in the box. He is all-knowing, all-present, all-powerful but not a part of the box. In this He is transcendent. The books of the Bible were all written by men inside the box (inside space-time) but inspired by a Being outside space-time (outside the box). Having made the box, this Being understands everything there is to know about the box: its inhabitants, its past and its future. All other religions, monotheistic Islam included, have their God situated at some point inside the box, subject to space-time just as we are. Judeo-Christianity is the only faith that puts God outside the box.*[72]

Grasping the concept that God is outside time and space is very foundational and helpful but it does raise a question. "If God is outside of everything, how can He be sitting on a throne in Heaven?" It might seem confusing that the Throne of God and the Temple of God are located in the highest Heaven yet God is outside of everything created, including Heaven.

---

[72] John Loeffler, "The Unforgiving Watershed", Koinonia House, http://www.khouse.org/articles/2001/313/ (accessed April 8, 2010).

Map of Heaven

I'll suggest that we struggle to understand this because of our limited concept of God.

Scripture indicates that God is omni-present or present everywhere (1 Kings 8:27; Psalm 95:3-5; 139:7-10; Jeremiah 23:23-24), however, God the Father also seems to have the ability to have a local presence. Or perhaps better stated, God can manifest a local presence. Obviously, God is much bigger than just a local presence.

This thought was elucidated by Solomon at his dedication of the great Temple in Jerusalem. 1 Kings 8:27: *"But will God indeed dwell on the earth? behold, the heaven and heaven of heavens cannot contain thee; how much less this house that I have builded?"*. Solomon recognized that God was beyond the heaven of heavens or highest Heaven, appropriately seeing that God was beyond all time and space, outside our time-space continuum.

Theologian Wayne Grudem makes a similar point: "…how God is present everywhere but how He especially manifests His presence to bless in certain places. The greatest manifestation of God's presence to bless is seen in Heaven, where He makes his glory known, and where angels, or heavenly creatures, and redeemed saints all worship Him."[73] However, God did manifest Himself at the Temple Solomon built, with a presence that is referred to as the *shekinah* glory (2 Chronicles 5:13-14).

In the same way, God the Father is in some way present on the Throne in the highest Heaven as Stephen the martyr noted upon his death (Acts 7:56). Thus scripture identifies both that God is much bigger and cannot be limited to any one point of geography, however, at the same time, He does make His presence known upon His throne in the heavens. He is able to be both present near us locally, and be seated on His Throne at the same time.

---

[73] Wayne Grudem, *Systematic Theology* (Grand Rapids: Inter-Varsity Press, 1994), 1159.

Hyperspace in Scripture

6.7 SUMMARY OF HEAVENLY JERUSALEM

In this section the reality and dimensions of the spiritual realm have continued to come into focus. Key take-a-ways include:

- ✓ God is the Creator Beyond Time and Space; He is not part of or contained within the time-space continuum; He is outside dwelling in eternity
- ✓ There is a very real city called Heavenly Jerusalem in the spiritual realm (hyperspace) and residents include many angels, soul/spirits of people who have followed God but have died, Resurrected Jesus and a presence of God the Father
- ✓ Heavenly Jerusalem is also called Heavenly Mt. Zion and the City of the Living God
- ✓ There is a connectedness between earthly Mt. Zion and the Heavenly Mt. Zion
- ✓ The spiritual realm is in a sense, more real, more solid than our 3D world
- ✓ In many senses, Heavenly Jerusalem is indescribable to us (3D people can't visualize 4D) and God has put limits on available information about it
- ✓ The earthly temple is a 3D shadow of the 4D temple in Heavenly Jerusalem
- ✓ The earthly tabernacle and temple were a place on earth for God to manifest His presence among His people
- ✓ The earthly temple is on Mt. Zion in Jerusalem
- ✓ Although Solomon's Temple was an attractive structure, it pales in comparison with the real Temple in heaven
- ✓ There is an actual physical heavenly temple on Mt. Zion

in Heavenly Jerusalem and God sits there on the Throne of Grace in the Temple

- ✓ During the Millennium, Jesus will reign from Earthly Mt. Zion and sit on His Throne in the Earthly Temple (which is probably the Mercy Seat)
- ✓ Although we typically only think of buildings in Heavenly Jerusalem, there are certainly animals and it is very possible that it is complete with extensive vegetation

Hyperspace in Scripture

7 Hyperspace Underworld (Map of Hades)

7.1 INTRODUCTION TO THE UNDERWORLD

Jesus said: *"The Son of Man will send forth His angels, and they will gather out of His kingdom all stumbling blocks, and those who commit lawlessness, and will throw them into the furnace of fire; in that place there will be weeping and gnashing of teeth."* Matt 13:41-42

"Indeed, the mere fact that Christ utilized the rabbinic language connected with Gehenna [hell], such as 'unquenchable fire' and 'never-dying worms,' demonstrates beyond all doubt to any reasonable person that He deliberately used the word Gehenna to impress upon His hearers that eternal punishment awaits the wicked after the resurrection. No other conclusion is possible." [74] Theologian Dr. Robert A. Morey

The great news is that Heaven is a real place. As we have noted, it is an awesome place. With great longing, we look forward to the day when we get "called home" to forever be with the Lord. However, there is some difficult news. As strongly as the Scriptures proclaim Heaven, they also proclaim the reality of Hell. In fact, I'm going to suggest that there is a vast underworld in the spiritual realm and Scripture identifies several different places there. We are going to seek to identify and locate several of these underworld locations.

One group of inhabitants of the underworld are the fallen angels. It is a real mystery to many of us why a full one third of the angels, after being

---

[74] Dr. Robert A. Morey, *Death and the Afterlife* (Minneapolis: Bethany House Pub., 1984), 89.

with God in His Kingdom, chose to join Satan in his rebellion. It is difficult to imagine, after all the exposure they had. They directly saw God Himself, they witnessed the creation and after all of this, they would still chose to live separate from Him.

Another group of underworld residents are the soul/spirits of unbelievers. Sadly, many people have chosen to reject the God of the Bible and Jesus the Son of God. They have demanded an independent existence away from Him. For these people, tragically, what they chose in this life will come to pass in the next.

Jesus, the Son of God, humbled Himself, came to Earth and became obedient unto death, even the death on a cross. With unimaginable mercy and love deeper than the oceans, the blood of Christ was poured out in an incredible sacrifice. His life for ours. His blood is the only thing that will cleanse us from the sins that we all have which keep us separated from God. By grace, this sacrifice is extended to all.

To those who take this priceless free gift looking to Jesus as their savior have been saved, are citizens in Heaven and will escape the fires of Hell which we all truly deserve. It breaks our hearts that there are many who reject Jesus' sacrifice. He has already died for their sins; He has already paid the price for their wickedness and offers them freely eternal life. With great disappointment, we see many choosing to reject the blood sacrifice, obtained at the cost of the Son of God's life. To them, the Holy Spirit gives this most dire warning:

*"Anyone who has set aside the Law of Moses dies without mercy on the testimony of two or three witnesses. How much severer punishment do you think he will deserve who has **trampled under foot the Son of God**, and has regarded as unclean the blood of the covenant by which he was sanctified, and **has insulted the Spirit of grace**? For we know Him who said, "VENGEANCE IS MINE, I WILL REPAY." And again, "THE LORD WILL JUDGE HIS PEOPLE." **It is a terrifying thing to fall into the hands of the living God.**"* (Heb 10:28-31) (bold and underlining are authors)

It is indeed a terrifying thing to fall into the hands of the living God. On judgment day, those who have rejected Jesus' sacrifice; who have in essence, spit into the face of the Son of God will come to

Map of Hades

understand. While on Earth, they wanted nothing to do with God and yearned be separate from Him. In the afterlife, their desire will be fulfilled. Enough said.

The questions do however remain; "Where are the soul/spirits of those who have rejected God? Where are the fallen angels and where are these places located?" As we have mapped out the Heavenly realm we now attempt to map the underworld. In the same way the question was asked, "If heaven is real, where is it?" we now ask the question; "If hell is real, where is it?"

There are actually several different places in scripture that some refer to as hell. Our understanding of hell is artificially made difficult because of inconsistencies that the English Bible translators have made. For example, the Hebrew word *Sheol* is found 65 times in the Old Testament but is translated as grave 31 times, hell 31 times and pit 3 times.[75] The Hebrew *qeber* is used 67 times but is translated as grave 35 times, sepulcher 25 times and burying place 6 times.[76] Although some of the modern English Bible translations are now using the actual Hebrew or Greek (like Sheol and Hades), there still remains some inconsistencies in usage. And further, sadly, when Pastors refer to hell, it isn't clear whether they are talking about hades or the "lake of fire."

So here a careful examination of the Greek and Hebrew text is made. In summary form, each of the places referred to in scripture are identified below with a basic description. Subsequently, in this chapter, each one will be examined in detail to define it and highlight scriptural clues as to its location. Four different places will be examined:

---

[75] *Sheowl*, Blueletterbible, http://www.blueletterbible.org/lang/lexicon/lexicon.cfm?Strongs=H7585&t=KJV (accessed March 29, 2010), Strong's #7585.

[76] *Qeber*, Blueletterbible, http://www.blueletterbible.org/lang/lexicon/lexicon.cfm?Strongs=H6913&t=KJV (accessed March 29, 2010), Strong's #6913.

- **Grave**: the physical, earthly place where ones body is placed after death. Typically in the ground.
- **Hades** (Greek word and same as Hebrew: *Sheol*): place where the souls of those who have rejected God go. Identified as "down." Hades is described as having an "upper" and "lower" section. It is a temporary place or holding tank for those awaiting judgment
- **Bottomless Pit** (Greek: *abyssos*): place where some fallen angels are restrained in chains and also a place where some evil creatures (beasts) are released from during the tribulation. The fallen angels there are also awaiting judgment
- **Lake of Fire**: final destination of those who reject God; both men and angels. What most people think of when they think of hell. It is the final, eternal place of dwelling.

7.2 GRAVE:

"Now after the Sabbath, as it began to dawn toward the first day of the week, Mary Magdalene and the other Mary came to look at the grave." (Matt 28:1)

The Scriptural concept of grave is pretty straightforward. It is pretty much what we think of when we think of the grave. The grave is most often translated in the Old Testament from the Hebrew *qeber* or in the New Testament, the Greek *taphos*. Both words mean grave or sepulcher.[77] It is

---

[77] Taphos, Blueletterbible, http://www.blueletterbible.org/lang/lexicon/lexicon.cfm?Strongs=G5028&t=KJV (accessed March 29, 2010), Strong's #5028.

Map of Hades

the physical place on earth where a person's body is placed after death. A grave can be visited and is seen by people on earth. Graves are in our 3D earthly realm. Using the Goomba's 2D world analogy, the Goombas would burry their dead in the 2D flat plate, ant farm type world. This would be in their ground, below where they walk as shown in Figure 30.

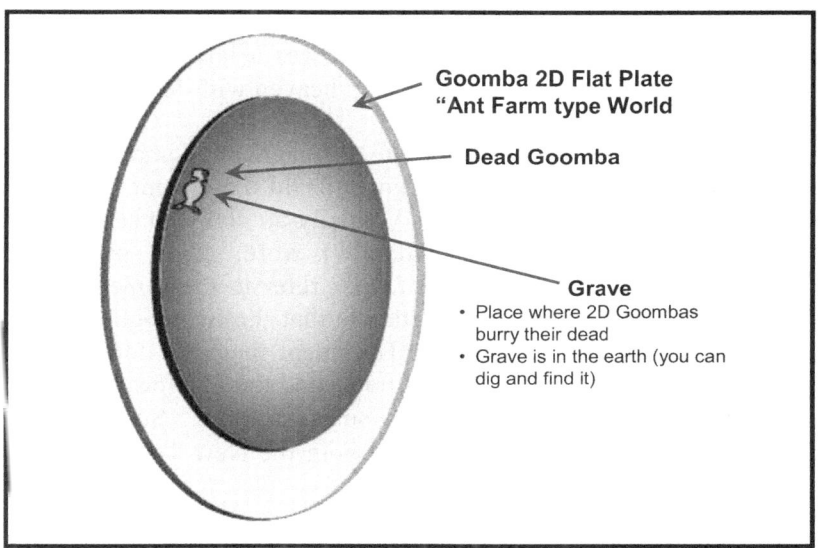

Figure 30. 2D analogy of a grave, in the ground below the Goombas

7.3 HADES OR SHEOL

"And you, Capernaum, will not be exalted to heaven, will you? You will descend to Hades [Greek hades]; *for if the miracles had occurred in Sodom which occurred in you, it would have remained to this day."* Matt 11:23

There are some subtleties to understanding Hades so a brief summary is given here first then it will be examined in detail in the following paragraphs. Basically Hades has two sections, "Lower Hades" and "Upper Hades." Lower Hades is where the soul/spirits of those who reject God go. It has always been this way and they still go there waiting for their final judgment. The soul/spirits of those who followed God used to go to Upper Hades. They couldn't go directly to "heaven" because a complete sacrifice for sin hadn't been given (Heb 10:11-12). Because of their sin, they would not have survived being in the presence of a Holy and Righteous God (Isa 6:5). When Jesus died, however, things changed. Jesus' death paid the full price for sins so the soul/spirits of those dead Old Testament saints went with Jesus directly to heaven (Eph 4:7-10). Now, when a follower of God dies, they don't need to go to Upper Hades, they go directly to heaven. That's why back in Chapter 6 it was stated that all believer go to heaven when they die. As example, my father who was a faithful follower of the Lord died several years ago. Today, he is in heaven with Jesus.

Hades and Sheol - what's the difference?: Simply, Hades and Sheol are the same place. Let's align the Old Testament and the New Testament teachings on this subject. Virtually all commentators agree that the Old Testament's (written in Hebrew) word, *Sheol* and the New Testament's word (written in Greek) *Hades* refer to the same thing or the same place. One primary reason for this is that the Septuagint, which is a Greek translation of the Hebrew Old Testament that was done nearly 300 years before the time of Christ always translated the Hebrew *Sheol* into the Greek *Hades*.[78] This is pretty solid substantiation. So, we can gain understanding about Hades by looking at both the New Testament (*Hades*) and the Old Testament (*Sheol*).

Hades – Old Testament Times: From the beginning of man up to the time of Jesus' death on the cross, the spirit/souls of all the dead went to Hades. Those who had rejected God went to the "lower" parts of Hades and those who followed God went to the "upper" part of Hades. Upper Hades is also referred to as Paradise (recall Jesus' comments to the thief on the cross: *"Today you will be with me in Paradise"* (Luke 23:43). Upper Hades was also referred to as *"Abraham's Bosom* (Luke 16:22).

The two parts of Hades are vividly illustrated in Jesus' story about the beggar Lazarus (not the same Lazarus who was raised from the dead) and the rich man found in Luke 16:19-31. The rich man who lived for himself and not God ends up in one part of Hades (lower Hades) and the beggar

---

[78] Dr. Robert A. Morey, *Death and the Afterlife* (Minneapolis: Bethany House Publishers, 1984), 76.

Map of Hades

Lazarus, upon his death, was escorted by angels to *"Abraham's Bosom."* Abraham's Bosom is also referred to as Paradise, and also Upper Hades. From the scriptures, it is clear that the rich man can see Abraham's Bosom but no one can travel between the two parts because of a great chasm (Luke 16:26) which separates them.

NIV and some commentaries state the opinion that Jesus' story here is a parable, but a closer inspection of the Scripture doesn't indicate this. Jesus refers to the individual by name (which doesn't happen in parables) and He describes the story in a literal or in a matter of fact way. Neither Jesus nor the author declares it as a parable as is done on many other occasions (Matt 13:13; 13:18; 13:24; 21:33; 24:32; Mark 4:13 and many others). Jesus doesn't define it as a metaphor or simile by stating: "The kingdom of heaven is like…" (Matt 13:31, 33, 34, 35 & others) as is done on other occasions. Jesus simply says: "Now there was a rich man…" (Luke 16:19a) which leaves a clear impression that he is relating real events. It seems clear then from the scriptures that Jesus is describing an actual and real place. Deuteronomy 32:22 confirms this and refers to one part of Hades as *"lowest hell* [Sheol].*"*

From Jesus' description we clearly note that there are two parts of Hades, "lower" and "upper." Lower Hades is for those who rejected God and upper Hades is for those who followed God. As explained by Jesus, Lower Hades is a place of torment for those who rejected God (Luke 16: 23, 28). Upper Hades, Paradise, is a place of comfort for those who followed God.

OK so far? Good, we'll keep going. Jesus changed everything. When Jesus was sacrificed on the cross for our sins, it had an impact that many people miss. Recalling that no one could go to Heaven because there was no permanent covering for our sins, when Christ died, this reason was blown out of the water. A way was now provided. When Christ died, those who had looked to God to save them now had a perfect sacrifice, one that could permanently remove sins. *"Every priest* [Old Testament priest in the temple] *stands daily ministering and offering time after time the same sacrifices, which can never take away sins; but He* [Jesus], **_having offered one sacrifice for sins for all time_**, SAT DOWN AT THE RIGHT HAND OF

Hyperspace in Scripture

GOD." (emphasis author - Heb 10:11-12) To those waiting in Upper Hades, this was incredibly blessed news.

Can you imagine the day that this news was proclaimed in Upper Hades? It must have been a marvelous and joyous celebration. The residents of Upper Hades needed to pack (but there really wasn't anything to pack) because they were going home. They were about to permanently relocate to their Heavenly home; to the City of the Living God.

Hades – New Testament Times: New Testament scriptures describe something very different for believers in Christ that what the Old Testament offered. What is happening now, what is going on today is quite different from the Old Testament times. Jesus did change everything. Now because of Christ's sacrifice and resurrection, when a person who has salvation through Christ dies, their spirit/souls go directly to heaven. This is noted by Paul in 2 Cor 5:8: *"We are of good courage, I say, and prefer rather to be absent from the body and to be at home with the Lord."*

This major change that occurred subsequent to Christ's resurrection is noted by Paul in Ephesians 4:8-10. It describes how Christ descended into the lower parts of the earth (this is in Hyperspace) and then ascended to Heaven leading a host of captives with Him (see also Acts 2:31). Jesus led those in upper Hades, in Paradise, up to Heaven, to Heavenly Jerusalem. The people of Paradise, the former residents, are now in Heaven. All of this happened because of Jesus. This is why back in Chapter 6 we observed that the Old Testament saints were there in Heavenly Jerusalem. This concept is elucidated by Dr. Robert A Morey (great Theologian who was mentored by the esteemed Dr. Walter Martin). Dr. Morey states:

> "In the New Testament, there is, therefore, a development of understanding which took place after Christ's resurrection. Before Jesus was raised from the dead, the apostles assumed that everyone went to Sheol or Hades. This Hades had two sections, one for the righteous and one fore the wicked. But Christ's resurrection changed this picture. Thus Paul uses the language of transition when he speaks of Christ taking the righteous out of Hades and bringing them into heaven (Eph. 4:8, 9)…by the time Paul wrote 2 Cor. 12:2-4, it was assumed that paradise had been taken out of

Hades and was now placed in the third heaven. According to the post-resurrection teaching in the New Testament, the believer now goes to heaven at death to await the coming resurrection and the eternal state. But, what of the wicked? The wicked at death descend into Hades which is a place of temporary torment while they await the coming resurrection and their eternal punishment."[79]

I hope I haven't confused you but perhaps a bottom line of what is going on during this present time is helpful. Simply put, all the spirit/souls of the wicked are in Lower Hades waiting for Judgment Day and the spirit/souls of the followers of God are in Heaven, specifically at the City of the Living God which is Heavenly Jerusalem.

OK, for the fun stuff: "Where is Hades?" Or perhaps more crudely; "Where in the Hell is Hades?"

Hades in Hyperspace: Now that we have established who is in Hades today (the souls of the wicked) we will examine some interesting technical aspects of Hades. In some sense, Hades is located "under the earth" and the direction to it noted by Scripture is "down." This is why some refer to it as the underworld. Jacob, upon hearing that his son Joseph had died noted that: *"Surely I will go down to Sheol in mourning for my son." So his father wept for him."* (emphasis author; Gen 37:35b) Isaiah refers to Hades as "Sheol from beneath" or "underworld" in Isa 14:9. These and many other passages (Gen 37:35, Psalm 63:9; Job 11:8; Isa 44:23; Ezek 26:20; 31:14, 16, 18; 32:18, 24) indicate that Hades (Greek) or Sheol (Hebrew) is "down."

Although Hades is "below the earth" it is still part of the spiritual realm. Hades is then, along with Heavenly Jerusalem in Hyperspace. As Dr. Morey has noted: "…Sheol is not a part of this world but has an existence of its own in another dimension."[80] For this reason, you can't dig your way

---

[79] Ibid., 86

[80] Ibid., 78.

down from the surface of our 3D Earth into Hades. It is not just a matter of digging down to get there because it is in the higher dimensions of the space-time continuum. It is in Hyperspace. But very importantly, in the same way that Heavenly Jerusalem and earthly Jerusalem are adjacent to and connected to each other, so Hades also has a connection to our Earth. So, in the same way, as Hades is down, that means that Hades is connected to or adjacent to what is below the surface of our earth. Fascinating isn't it. We'll get to the map in a moment but there is one more surprise.

Gates of Hades: A fascinating aspect of Hades is that it has gates. Hezekiah made mention of this when he thought he was going to die in the middle of his prime. He noted: *"I said, 'In the middle of my life I am to enter the gates of Sheol; I am to be deprived of the rest of my years.'"* (Isa 38:10, emphasis author) Wow; Hades has gates. Jesus also noted this point when talking to Peter: *"I also say to you that you are Peter, and upon this rock I will build My church; and the gates of Hades will not overpower it."* (Matt 16:18, emphasis author) This is a rather curious fact but we can conclude that is some way, you must pass through the "gates of Hades" in order to gain enterance.

Hades on the Hyperspace Map - 2D to 3D Analogy: In review, we have established that Hades is down and part of the underworld. Also, Hades is part of the spiritual realm and therefore in Hyperspace. Hades has gates from which it can be entered. Hades has two primary components, Lower Hades (inhabited by the soul/spirits of the wicked) and Upper Hades (now empty). There is a great chasm separating the two components. Now, lets put this information together and create a map.

To illustrate Hades we will create another 2D to 3D analogy using the Goombas. Imagine again a 2D flat plate ant farm world that is as big around as our Earth. We will pretend that this is where the Goombas live. Further, now imagine the Goomba's 3D spiritual realm which is connected to their 2D world. This is depicted in Figure 31 showing the 2D flat plate world on the left and the 3D spiritual realm associated with it on the 2nd left. To help see where Hades is located we need to look into the Goomba's 3D spiritual realm. We do this by the 3rd from the left graphic which shows a marked out section (like the slice out of an Orange). The last graphic (on the right) shows the slice that we have taken pulled out so we can see what is on

Map of Hades

the inside of the Goomba's 3D spiritual realm.

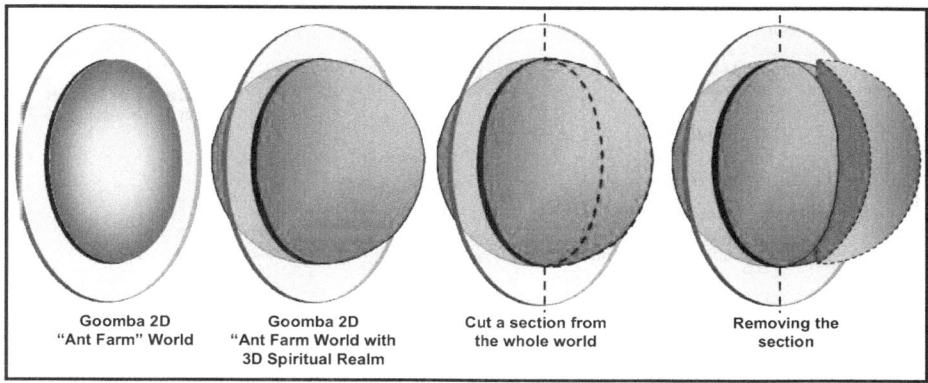

Figure 31. Example of 2D glassy plate world with a 3D spiritual realm associated with it

Now that we have pulled out this slice from the Goomba's spiritual realm we can now see what is going on inside. As we look at the slice, we are looking at the underworld of the Goomba's. Figure 32 shows a representation of what this would be like. We see Hades located there below the surface of the Goomba's spiritual realm. We see the two parts of Hades, the upper and lower sections with the chasm that is separating them. We can also note that there is a passage way to get into Hades and it does, as Scripture notes, have a gate at this entrance. Although Jesus noted "gates" plural, meaning there are more than one, only one is shown in our map here. We're not sure if the two gates are together in one place or if there are additional entrances. I'm inclined to guess that there is only one.

Hyperspace in Scripture

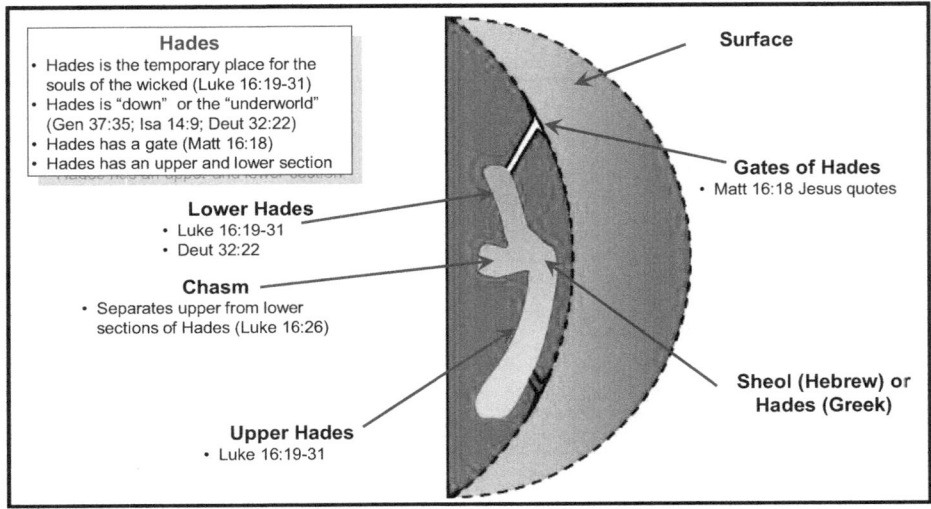

Figure 32. Section of spiritual realm showing Hades located inside

7.4 BOTTOMLESS PIT (ABYSS - *ABYSSOS*)

"And Jesus asked him, "What is your name?" And he said, "Legion"; for many demons had entered him. They were imploring Him not to command them to go away into the abyss [abyssos].*"* (Luke 8:30-31)

*"Then the fifth angel sounded, and I saw a star from heaven which had fallen to the earth; and the <u>**key of the bottomless pit**</u>* [abyssos phrear] *was given to him. He opened the bottomless pit, and smoke went up out of the pit, like the smoke of a great furnace; and the sun and the air were darkened by the smoke of the pit. Then <u>**out of the smoke came locusts upon the earth**</u>, and power was given them, as the scorpions of the earth have power. They were told not to hurt the grass of the earth, nor any green thing, nor any tree, but only the men who do not have the seal of God on their foreheads. And they were not permitted to kill anyone, but to torment for five months; and their torment was like the torment of a scorpion when it stings a man. And in those days men will seek death and will not find it; they will long to die, and death flees from them."* (Rev 9:1-6)

What is the Abyss and Who is There?: The Abyss is another place which is part of the underworld in Hyperspace. We see here from

Map of Hades

Scripture that this place holds some particularly evil spiritual creatures. Some commentaries suggest that the "Abyss" is the same as Hades. I'm inclined to think that Scriptures is telling a somewhat different story. The Biblical language and its descriptions, appear to indicate that the Abyss and Hades are indeed two distinct and separate places. Scripture also talks about the Bottomless Pit. It does appear that the Abyss and Bottomless Pit are the same place. Let's dig in.

The phrase "Bottomless Pit" is a translation of the Greek *abyssos phrear*. *Abyssos* literally means "without bottom" and *phrear* means pit or well.[81] [82] *Abyssos*, which is sometimes translated as the abyss, is found 9 times in the New Testament; Luke 8:31, Rom 10:7 and 7 times in Revelation.

Why do I think the bottomless pit and Hades are really two distinct and separate places? The key point is that there are two Greek words describing these places which leads to the natural conclusion that they are perhaps describing two separate places. A second point is that Scripture notes that Hades is the place for the departed souls of the wicked whereas the Bottomless Pit holds some very evil spiritual creatures. The inhabitants of the bottomless pit are:

1) Demonic beasts (Rev 11:7)
2) A demonic beast king named Abaddon (Rev 9:11)
3) Demonic locust creatures (Rev 9:2-3)
4) Satan when he is cast there in chains during the Millennium (Rev 20:3)

---

[81]Chad Brand et. all gen. ed. *Holman Illustrated Bible Dictionary* (Nashville: Holman Bible Pub., 2003),15.

[82]Phrear, Blueletterbible, http://www.blueletterbible.org/lang/lexicon/lexicon.cfm?Strongs=G5421&t=KJV (accessed March 29, 2010), Strong's #5421.

Hyperspace in Scripture

5) Demons themselves didn't want to go there when Jesus cast them from the demoniac at Gerasenes (Luke 8:31) indicating that demons are there

6) Possibly some of the fallen angels (Jude 6, 2 Peter 2:4) [83]

Scripture doesn't seem to indicate that human soul/spirits are in the bottomless pit. As Evangelical Theologian A. F. Johnson notes; "...while the abyss is the present abode of demonic spirits."[84] It is also possible that in a sense, the bottomless pit is part of or a subset of the more general description of Hades but this seems unlikely. Therefore, it seems reasonable to conclude that the Bottomless Pit is the same as the Abyss but it is not the same as Hades.

Location of the Abyss: From a Hyperspace perspective, Scriptures' use of the word bottomless is provocative. This possibly gives us an important clue as to the location of the Bottomless Pit. If we consider our earth for a moment, we would note that its gravitational field basically is pulling everything to the center of the earth. We are reminded of the important discovery of Newton noting that everything is pulled towards the center of the Earth.

Let's imagine for a minute a shaft or well that goes completely through the center of the earth. Also, let's imaging that at the center of this shaft, there in the middle of the Earth, is a big cavern. What do you think will happen if we throw something into the shaft? Well, gravity would pull it down and it would fall down the shaft until it reached the center of the Earth. There in the center, however, the forces of gravity are pulling everything towards the center. So when the object reached the center, it

---

[83] A parallel verse to Jude 6 is 2 Peter 2:4 which also speaks of the fallen angels being cast into "Tartarus." Tartarus is from the Greek *tartaroo* and is used only once in scripture which is here. As Chuck Missler has noted: "Tartarus is equal to the pit of darkness in the unseen world; [the] Greek term for dark abode of woe. Homer's Illiad: "as far below hades as the earth is below heaven..."" Chuck Missler, *The Book of Jude* (Coeur d'Alene, Idaho: Koinonia House Inc., 1996), 13.

[84] A.F. Johnson, "Abyss"; Walter A. Elwell, gen.ed., *"Evangelical Dictionary of Theology"* 2nd ed. (Grand Rapids: Baker Books, 2001), 21.

would basically float there in mid space; right in the middle of the earth. So there is in a sense, no bottom. Everything is pulled to the middle.

From this we could conjecture that somehow the bottomless pit is connected to the center of the earth. In the same way that Heavenly Jerusalem is adjacent to and connected to Earthly Jerusalem, and Hades is adjacent to and connected with the underground of Earth, it would appear that the Bottomless Pit is connected with the center of the Earth.

But remember, the Bottomless Pit is on the other side of the veil, in Hyperspace. So, we can't dig to the center of our Earth and see the creatures imprisoned there. Because Hyperspace is part of the space-time continuum, we would also expect gravity to be a force there.

Fallen Angels: Peter's link to the abode of some of the fallen angels in 2 Peter 2:4 refers to Tartarus which seems to be the same as the bottomless pit. Tartarus is from the Greek *tartaroo* and the word is used only once in scripture, and that is here.[85] Tartarus was a Greek term for the great pit that was located as far below Hades. Greeks thought that the distance between Tartarus and Hades was the same as the earth was below the sky. This was noted by Homer in his *Illiad*.[86]

Gate to the Abyss: Another curious fact about the bottomless pit is that it has a door or gate. The gate currently is locked imprisoning all these evil creatures. That's good news. The bad news however is that it won't always be that way. At some point in the future, during the 7 year time of distress that is to come upon the Earth, known as the Tribulation, it will be open. The opening of the pit brings some very disastrous results to the earth.

---

[85]*Tartaroo*, Blueletterbible,
http://www.blueletterbible.org/lang/lexicon/lexicon.cfm?Strongs=G5020&t=KJV (accessed April 1, 2010), Strong's #5020.

[85]Noted in Homer's Illiad 8.13 ff: as quoted on Aaron Atsma, "The Pit of Tartaros", Theoi Project, http://www.theoi.com/Kosmos/Tartaros.html (accessed April 1, 2010).

Hyperspace in Scripture

In Revelation 9, it is opened by a key and in Rev 9:2: *"He opened the bottomless pit, and smoke went up out of the pit, like the smoke of a great furnace; and the sun and the air were darkened by the smoke of the pit."* It is perhaps not surprising that great smoke is released from the bottomless pit when it is opened, but it is surprising that the smoke that is released effects the atmosphere here on earth. The sun and the air are effected because of the great extent of the smoke. The 5th trumpet judgment (which is part of the Tribulation period) is the opening of the bottomless pit. The smoke that rises from the pit brings a very dire warning to the inhabitants of the Earth. The smoke signals to all who are walking the earth that demonic plague of locust has just been released. These demonic locust will come from the very pit itself. Or perhaps more crudely stated, from the very pit of hell. This is the first of 3 great "woes" that are to come upon the earth. Without question, it will be a dreadful time for all the Earth dwellers and something so terrible that it has never been experienced in Earth's history.

2D to 3D Analogy of the Abyss: Returning to our 2D to 3D analogy of the world of the Goombas, it actually isn't too difficult to locate the Abyss. Being that the pit is bottomless and following our thought of the center of the earth, we can illustrate it in the Goomba analogy at the center of the slice. This is shown in Figure 33. Also drawn in the illustration is a shaft for entry and exit. Gates are shown located there on the surface of the spiritual realm.

Map of Hades

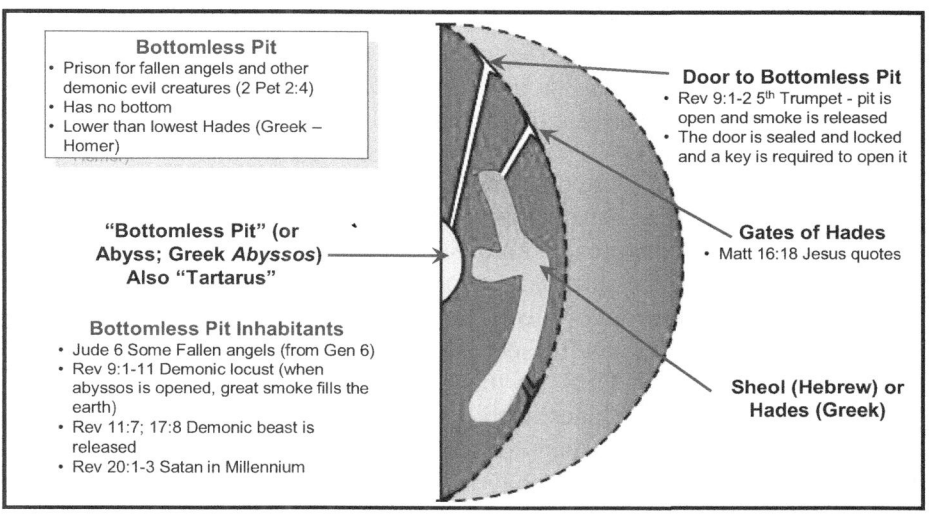

Figure 33. Section of spiritual realm showing the Bottomless pit

In summary, the Bottomless Pit (AKA: also known as the Abyss or Tartarus) is located in Hyperspace, in the spiritual realm. The Abyss is connected to the center of the earth. It serves as the prison for all sorts of demonic and evil creatures and includes the fallen angels. During the Tribulation, the door of the pit is unlocked and opened, releasing smoke that fills the earth. Hosts of demonic locust are released to bring a dreadful plague upon all those who have not chosen to follow God.

7.5 LAKE OF FIRE: GEHENNA

*"Woe to you, scribes and Pharisees, hypocrites! For you build the tombs of the prophets and adorn the monuments of the righteous, and say, 'If we had been living in the days of our fathers, we would not have been partners with them in shedding the blood of the prophets.' So you testify against yourselves, that you are sons of those who murdered the prophets. Fill up, then, the measure of the guilt of your fathers. You serpents, you brood of vipers, **how will you escape the sentence of hell** [geenna]?"* (emphasis author - Matt 23: 29-33)

"And the sea gave up the dead which were in it, and death and Hades gave up the dead which were in them; and they were judged, every

*one of them according to their deeds. Then death and Hades were thrown into the lake of fire. This is the second death, the **lake of fire**. And if anyone's name was not found written in the book of life, he was thrown into the **lake of fire**.*" (emphasis author - Rev 20:13-15)

Hell is not the same place as Hades. Both places are bad news and you don't want to spend time in either but they are two separate places. This is very clear from Scripture. In a nut shell, Hades, as we have noted, is part of the underworld in the spiritual realm. It is the temporary place where the soul/spirits of all those who reject Jesus as their savior are residing. On a future day, however, they will face judgment. After judgment, they will be thrown into the Lake of Fire. At this point in time, there will no longer be any need for Hades and Hades itself gets thrown into the Lake of Fire. The Lake of Fire becomes the final and eternal resting place for all those who have chosen the path of evil and have rejected God.

But "where is the Lake of Fire?" some may ask. Excellent question and we will look at that just after we see who all really ends up there.

Lake of Fire Inhabitants: The Lake of Fire plays a dominant role in the last few chapters of Revelation. It appears that Revelation's Lake of Fire and Jesus' descriptive term of Gehenna refer to the same thing primarily because of who will be there. Revelation 19 and 20 indicates very clearly who and what will be thrown into the Lake of Fire. This includes: (1) the beast of Revelation and (2) his false prophet (Rev 19:20), (3) Satan after the Millennium (Rev 20:10), (4) Death and Hades itself (after the Millennium and Great White Throne Judgment – Rev 20:14), and (5) everyone who was not found in the "Book of Life" (as they are being judged at the Great White Throne - Rev 20:15). Revelation 21:8 sums it up by basically saying it is everyone who did not follow God: *"But for the cowardly and unbelieving and abominable and murderers and immoral persons and sorcerers and idolaters and all liars, their part will be in the lake that burns with fire and brimstone, which is the second death."*

It is described as the second death because when the wicked die on earth, it is their first death; a physical death. The wicked are resurrected and judged at the Great White Throne (Rev 20:11-12). Subsequent to this, they are thrown bodily into the Lake of Fire; now their second death.

In the previous section, we have identified where all the evil creatures and the soul/spirits of the wicked are. Today, there are many evil spiritual creatures operating in the spiritual realm, on the surface so to speak. However, there are also many evil creatures who for one reason or another, are temporarily placed in the underworld of the spiritual realm. Scripture does not indicate that anyone today is in the Lake of Fire. So it would appear that the Beast of the Tribulation Period will be the first to end up there. That happens at the conclusion of the Tribulation. Subsequent to that, when the 1,000 reign of Christ is completed, all the wicked, evil spiritual creatures and soul/spirits of humans will be cast into the Lake of Fire. We will also find out that Hades itself will be thrown into the Lake of Fire.

Linking Gehenna and Lake of Fire: Jesus spoke several times of a place called Gehenna. In the New Testament the Greek word is *geenna*, and it is used 12 times, three times in combination with *pyr* which means fire.[87] Jesus, when he speaks out strongly to the Pharisees and scribes, he calls them "sons of Gehenna." Jesus highlighted that they can not escape the damnation of Gehenna (Matthew 23:15, 33). Jesus' use of the phrase *"sentence of hell* [Gehenna]" in Matt 23:33 implies that it is the final resting place of the wicked.

Because it is the final place, then that would occur when the wicked were in their resurrected form. Gehenna is therefore a place of final dwelling for the body, soul and spirit of the wicked. Another of Jesus' warnings about Gehenna included that the *"worm does not die"* and the *"fire is not quenched"* (Mark 9:47-48). This implies the eternal nature of the place and that the people there are in torment.

---

[87]*Geenna*, Blueletterbible,
http://www.blueletterbible.org/lang/lexicon/lexicon.cfm?Strongs=G1067&t=KJV (accessed March 30, 2010), Strong's # 1067; and *Pyr*,
http://www.blueletterbible.org/search/translationResults.cfm?Criteria=fire&t=KJV (accessed March 30, 2010), Strong's #4442.

Hyperspace in Scripture

The New Testament Gehenna is derived from the Old Testament Valley of Hinnom which was a real place just outside the city of Jerusalem (Josh 15:8; 18:16 and Neh 11:30). When the Jews fell into idolatry following the false beliefs of wicked nations before them, they did an abominable thing. In the Valley of Hinnom the Israelites set up a statue to the false god Molech. It was there that for a time, the Jews conducted the horrific practice of human sacrifice. Abandoning all that God had called them to, they burnt their children in the fire as noted in 2 Kings 23:10 and 2 Chron 28:3; 33:6). It was a deeply disturbing and evil place.

Later the Valley of Hinnom became the garbage dump of the city of Jerusalem. As Theologian Dr. Morrey notes: "Because garbage was constantly being thrown into the valley, the fires never stopped burning and the worms never stopped eating. This picture of an unclean garbage dump where the fires and the worms never died out became to the Jewish mind an appropriate description of the ultimate fate of all idol worshipers. Gehenna came to be understood as the final, eternal garbage dump where all idolators would be thrown after the resurrection."[88] This sentiment is echoed in Isaiah 66:24.

We can link Geheena and the Lake of Fire together because of who ends up there. As we have seen, Jesus clearly indicated that the Pharisees, because of their approach and rejection of Jesus end up in Geheena (Matt 23:33). The outcome of the Great White throne judgment noted in Revelation 20:15 for all the wicked (which clearly includes the Pharisees) is to be cast into the Lake of Fire. Primarily for this reason then we conclude that Geheena and the Lake of Fire are the same place.

Location of the Lake of Fire: But now let's ask the more interesting question involving Hyperspace: "Where exactly then is the Lake of Fire?" This turns out to be a very challenging question and one that is much more difficult to answer than locating Hades and the Bottomless Pit. First we will note that it isn't real clear from Scripture exactly where the

---

[88] Dr. Robert A. Morey, *Death and the Afterlife* (Minneapolis: Bethany House Publishers, 1984), 87.

Map of Hades

Lake of Fire is. What we offer then is some conjectures on the subject recognizing that the information we have is rather limited.

Jesus made a reference those who rejected Him as being cast into "outer darkness." This is a interesting phrase. Jesus stated in Matt 8:11-12: *"I say to you that many will come from east and west, and recline at the table with Abraham, Isaac and Jacob in the kingdom of heaven; but the sons of the kingdom will be **cast out into the outer darkness**; in that place there will be weeping and gnashing of teeth."* Outer is a translation of the Greek *exoteros*. [89] *Exoteros* is only used 3 times in scripture, all by Jesus and in all cases it is in conjunction with darkness, referring to this place (Matt 8:12; 22:13; 25:30).

Outer darkness seems to imply that it is an existence devoid of light. Perhaps this refers to both spiritual light, meaning God Himself choosing not to be present there, and also the absence of physical light itself. Outer would imply that it is outside of something. Outside of what? Perhaps the space-time continuum itself.

A speculation that the Lake of Fire is outside of the space-time continuum is in contrast with Hades of today. Today, Hades is part of the spiritual realm, in Hyperspace. Hyperspace is part of the space-time continuum. To be outside of that would be to be completely separated from the spiritual realm meaning to be separated from our space time continuum. To be outside of the space-time continuum brings up an interesting point that the Lake of Fire and its inhabitants are now apart from time itself.

Recalling that time is a property of the space-time continuum, if you are separated from it, you are in an existence that is possibly devoid of time. If the Lake of Fire is indeed outside of the space-time continuum, those inhabitants would not be experiencing time like we will be, they would just be perpetually in that state of existence. The thought that Lake of Fire inhabitants are really outside of time and in a some other perpetual state of

---

[89] *Exoteros*, Blueletter Bible; http://www.blueletterbible.org/lang/lexicon/lexicon.cfm?Strongs=G1857&t=KJV (accessed August 11, 2011), Strong's #1856.

Hyperspace in Scripture

existence is fascinating but I will quickly admit that the implications of this seems beyond my understanding.

7.6 SUMMARY OF THE UNDERWORLD

This chapter has covered the location of many unpleasant places; places that appear to be below the surface. We discussed the grave, which is in our world and then several places in the spiritual realm, in Hyperspace. These are challenging concepts to discuss because it brings to mind the harsh reality of these places of torment. Today, the souls of the wicked, everyone who did not follow God are in lower Hades. In the Abyss or Bottomless Pit are fallen angels and demonic creatures. Some if not all will be allowed out during part of the Tribulation to torment people on Earth. Both of these places are noted to have gates and are also noted as being "down" in some fashion, or in the underworld. Although difficult to determine, it also appears that the final abode of all the wicked, the Lake of Fire, is actually outside of our space-time continuum in a perpetual existence separated from us. Figure 34 illustrates these places in a 2D to 3D analogy.

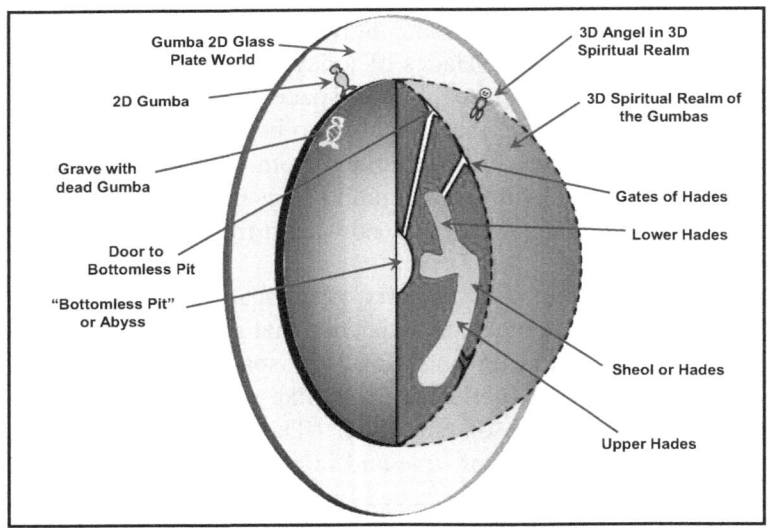

Figure 34. Summary analogy of the unseen underworld of the wicked

It does get confusing at times as to where everyone is so in Figure 35

Map of Hades

is a summary matrix identifying who is where. Hopefully this is helpful.

	Names		Reference	Inhabitants
Underworld	Bottomless Pit Abyss (Greek Abyssos) (and possible Tartarus)	Center of 4D Earth	Jude 6 Rev 9:1-11; 11:7; 17:8; 20:1-3 2 Pet 2:4 (tartarus)	Some Fallen Angels Demonic locusts Demonic beasts Future - Satan
Underworld	Hades (Greek) Sheol (Hebrews)	Upper Hades Place of Bliss Paradise Abraham's Bosom	1 Sam 28:13 Luke 16:19-31	Empty today: it used to contain the Soul/Spirits of those who followed God in Old Testament Times
Underworld		Chasm	Luke 16:26	
Underworld		Lower Hades (some refer to as Hell)	Deut 32:22 Luke 16:19-31	Soul/Spirits of those who reject God
"Outside"	Gehenna Lake of Fire	Some refer to as Hell	Rev 19:20; 20:10; 20:13-15; 21:8 Matt 5:22; 23:15-33	Future: all those who have rejected God Final resting place
"Outside"	Heaven	City of the Living God Heavenly Jerusalem Heavenly Mount Zion	Heb 12:22-24	Myriads of Angels Church (soul/spirits of believers) Spirits of Righteous men (Old Testament believers)

Figure 35. Summary matrix of who is in what place

Key Take-aways from this section include:

- ✓ The Biblical word grave refers to being buried in the physical earth
- ✓ Hades is located below the surface of the spiritual realm and is the current place where the soul/spirits of those who chose not to follow God go upon death. It is adjacent to or connected to the underground of our Earth
- ✓ Hades has both an upper and lower sections
- ✓ The bottomless pit appears to be different from Hades, located at the center core of the spiritual realm and is therefore linked with the center core of our earth.
- ✓ Inhabitants of the Bottomless Pit include fallen angels, demons and other evil spiritual creatures.
- ✓ Both the Bottomless Pit and Hades have a gate or door which can be locked

Hyperspace in Scripture

- ✓ Hades and all its inhabitants will eventually be thrown into the Lake of Fire
- ✓ Although speculation, it appears that the Lake of Fire is outside of our space-time continuum and lacks God's presence.

8 Hyperspace Universe

*"...And the heavens are the works of your hands, they will perish, but you remain, and they all will become old like a garment, and **like a mantle you will roll them up**; like a garment they will also be changed but you are the same, and your years will not come to an end."* (emphasis author - Hebrews 1:10b-12:)

"Some 500 years ago, the cabalists [group of Hebrew sages] theorized that at the instant of creation...God chose from the infinite realm of the Divine, ten dimensions or aspects and relegated them to be held within the universe..." Modern Physicist Dr. Gerald Schroeder [90]

8.1 INTRODUCTION:

Scripture consistently portrays a higher dimensional view of the space-time continuum. We have examined some powerful scripture events that really only can be explained or make sense when viewed from a Hyperspace or higher dimensional universe perspective. These in themselves represent a very strong case that the spiritual realm is located in Hyperspace.

In addition to this however, we also find that many other scriptures that speak of the properties of heaven, imply that higher dimensions do exist in the universe. In fact, scripture consistently portrays this view and never attempts to limit the universe to only the seen 3D universe. This fact alone separates the Bible from many other religious writings who state that what we see is all there is.

---

[90] Dr. Gerald Schroeder, Genesis and the Big Bang (New York: Bantam Books, 1990), 59. Dr. Schroeder references 13th century rabbi Ramban Nachmanides

Hyperspace in Scripture

In this chapter we will review 5 other key scriptural themes that support a Hyperspace or higher dimensional understanding to the space-time continuum. After that we will look at how Modern Physics sees these parameters of our time-space continuum. These scriptural themes are:

1) Our universe will be "rolled up" which implies that there is some dimension in which it is "thin" and is perhaps rather flat in that dimensions
2) The Fabric of Space can be "torn" implying thinness in some dimension
3) The Space-Time continuum was created by "stretching" it out from a small point: which is consistent with "Big Bang" creation type models (which are consistent with higher dimensions)
4) Time is actually a property of the space-time continuum and only began at the moment of creation: which is consistent with "Big Bang" creation type models (and consistent with higher dimensions).
5) Jesus gave an example of size using 4 spatial dimensions

8.2   ROLLED UP THIN UNIVERSE

A universe that can be "rolled up" implies that it is somewhat flat and also thin.

Rolled Up Universe: The Holy Spirit loudly declares who Jesus is, what He did and what He will do in the first chapter of the Book of Hebrews. Heb 1:9 directly announces Jesus as God with the phrase: *"...your throne O God..."* Then the Spirit in verses 10 & 11 states what Jesus the Lord had done: *"...you, Lord, in the beginning laid the foundation of the Earth and the Heavens are the works of Your hands, they will perish but You remain..."* Further the Spirit goes on to say what Jesus the Lord will do by speaking of the destruction of the universe. This includes a curious phrase in verse 12: *"...and they* [the universe] *all will become old like a garment, and like a mantle **you** **[the Lord]** **will roll them up**."* (emphasis author)   What a fascinating insight; the universe as we know it, will one day be "rolled up."

Thin Universe: Curiously, if the universe can be "rolled up" and

Hyperspace Universe

"torn" (as we will see in the next section) as scripture indicates, this implies that in some dimension, the universe must be thin. So, although not directly stated, Scripture would seem to imply this thinness. Theologian Arthur Willink speculated on higher dimensional space more that 100 years ago and suggested this very same thing. Willink commented on spiritual beings in higher dimensions seeing this as he noted: "Or in other words, a dweller in Higher Space [meaning like angels in 4D or Hyperspace] will look upon our Space [our visible 3D world] as having only the thickness of one atom."[91]

This is a stunning scientific insight from scripture revealed 100 years ago. It has only been in recent times, perhaps less that 25 years ago that secular scientists began speculating on our universe must be thin in the higher dimensions.

This appears to be another amazing scientific insight that the Bible has stated, long before science has even been able to conceive or establish these thoughts. Modern quantum physics, although not yet definitive, seems to indicate the thinness of the universe as well. The 10 dimensional universe, defined by string theory (which will be explained in the next chapter), indicates that 6 of the higher dimensions are very small and curled in on themselves. It is suggested by modern physics that these higher dimensions are perhaps less than an atom in thickness.[92] It is always a pleasant surprise to see an almost incomprehensible statement of scripture being validated by modern science.

The predominant views in secular science is that all of the higher dimensions of Hyperspace are small and then. Although scripture notes that one dimension is thin, it would seem that at least one dimension, the one containing the Spiritual Realm, would be rather large. It is further interesting that as secular science further grows its theories, it now seems to suggest that there some of the higher dimensions could be large.

As example, the most modern emerging theory known as "M-theory" suggests that the universe could be much thicker than an atom. Physicist

---

[91] Arthur Willink, *The World of the Unseen* (New York: MacMillian and Co.,1893), 91

[92] Michio Kaku, *Parallel Worlds* (New York: Doubleday, 2005), 200.

Hyperspace in Scripture

Kaku comments as follows: "However, M-theory also features membranes; it is possible to view our entire universe as a membrane floating in a much larger universe. As a result, not all of these higher dimensions have to be wrapped up in a ball [or curled up]. Some of them, in fact, can be huge, infinite in extent."[93] A floating membrane concept is very consistent with scripture, indicating thinness in at least one of the many dimensions and thereby enabling the possibility of the universe being rolled up, torn or broken up.

A Flat Universe:

Recognizing that the space-time continuum is thin in at least one of the higher dimensions of hyperspace, it raises the question of: "What is the shape of the universe?" Scriptural statements of being "rolled up like a scroll" and reference to a garment would suggest that the universe is basically flat.

Among the physical constants that define the universe include two that describe the shape of the space-time continuum. Together, these constants known as Omega and Lambda could be either great that one, equal to one or less that one. If greater than one, the universe would have positive curvature like a ball. If less that one, it would have negative curvature like a horse's saddle. If Omega and Lambda are equal to one, then the space-time continuum would be flat. As it turns out, after extensive study and some interesting experiments, science has come to embrace an Omega – Lambda value of one, therefore recognizing that the universe is basically flat.

As an example, renowned modern day Physicist Dr. Michio Kaku notes: "For any reasonable value of Omega at the beginning of time, Einstein's equations show that it should almost be zero today. For Omega to be so close to 1 so many billions of years after the big bang would require a miracle. This is what is called in cosmology the fine-tuning problem. God, or some creator, had to 'choose' the value of Omega to within fantastic accuracy …In other words, at the beginning of time the value of Omega had to be 'chosen' to equal the number 1 within one part in a hundred trillion,

---

[93]Michio Kaku, *Parallel Worlds* (New York: Doubleday, 2005), 217.

Hyperspace Universe

which is difficult to comprehend." [94] Dr Kaku has also noted that: "WMAP satellite data shows that Omega plus Lambda is equal to 1, meaning that the universe is flat." [95] Michio Kaku

Once again, modern physics is confirming what the scriptures have pointed out more than 2,500 years ago. A research satellite exploration of the early 1990's provided initial data to indicate a flat universe. This NASA program known as the Cosmic Background Explorer (COBE) provided some amazing initial insights into the shape of the universe. However NASA's Wilkinson Microwave Anisotropy Probe (WMAP) satellite which became operational in 2001 provided a much more accurate and comprehensive database clearly defining the shape of the universe.

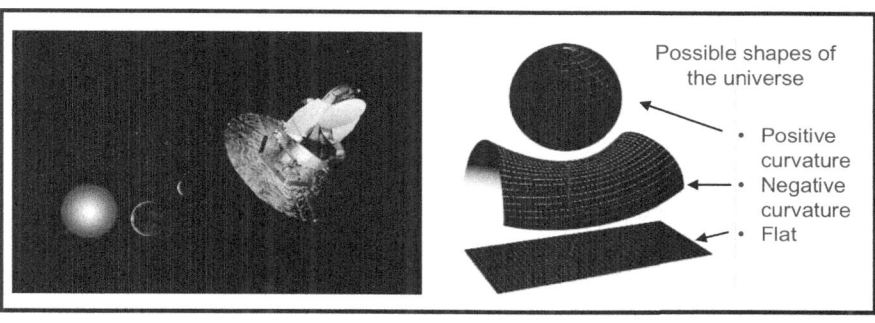

Figure 36 Fabric of Space: *Left*, WMAP Satellite, NASA[96]; *right*, Curvature of the Universe, NASA[97]

Three possible shapes to the universe were envisioned and are shown in Figure 36. Using a variety of extremely accurate instruments and careful planning of experiments, measurements of the distribution of mass

---

[94]Michio Kaku, *Parallel Worlds* (New York: Doubleday, 2005), 87

[95]Michio Kaku, *Parallel Worlds* (New York: Doubleday, 2005), 42

[96]"WMAP Spacecraft", NASA, http://map.gsfc.nasa.gov/media/990387/index.html (accessed December 28, 2009).

[97]"Is the Universe Infinite?", NASA, Universe 101, http://map.gsfc.nasa.gov/media/ContentMedia/990006b.jpg (accessed December 28, 2009).

Hyperspace in Scripture

and that of dark energy and mass around the universe were made. WMAP was able to make an accurate assessment declaring the universe to be truly "flat." WMAP defined the curvature of space to be flat to within 1% confirming what was declared by scripture.[98]

8.3 TEARING THE FABRIC OF SPACE

The fact that space-time can be torn implies that it must be somehow thin in at least one dimension.

Isaiah 64:1a: *"Oh that thou wouldest rend the heavens..."*

"By late 1991, then, at least a few string theorists had a strong feeling that the fabric of space *can* tear. But no one had the technical facility to definitively establish or refute this striking possibility" [99] Rhodes Scholar Physicist Dr. Brian Greene

The whole concept of being able to "tear the fabric of space" seems very challenging. It is further surprising to see Scriptures making this statement. Isaiah's statement of *rending*, which means tearing speaks of bringing what is in the unseen world into our world. Modern physics also refers to "tearing of the fabric of space" implying what appears to be very similar to what Isaiah speaks to.

If the space-time continuum can be torn, this also would imply that at least one of the dimensions is thin. The rending of heavens is therefore also consistent with it being rolled up. Modern physics appears also to echo the thought of being able to rend the heavens.

8.4 CREATION COSMOLOGY & BIG BANG

---

[98]"Wilkinson Microwave Anisotropy Probe," NASA, http://map.gsfc.nasa.gov/ (accessed December 27, 2009).

[99] Dr. Brian Greene, *The Elegant Universe* (New York: W.W. Norton & Co., 1999), 269

Hyperspace Universe

In the context of creation, God declares that it was "stretched out": Jeremiah 10:12 (See also Jeremiah 51:15): *"It is He who made the earth by His power, who established the world by His wisdom; and by His understanding He has stretched out the heavens."* (emphasis author - NAS)

Psalm 104:2: *"Who coverest [thyself] with light as [with] a garment: who stretchest out the heavens like a curtain"* (emphasis author)

Hebrews 11:3: *"By faith we understand that the worlds were prepared by the word of God, so that what is seen was not made out of things which are visible."* (emphasis author - NAS)

Or perhaps more simply: "First there was nothing, then it exploded!"[100] CEO, Engineer and Bible Teacher Dr. Chuck Missler

Scripture, Creation and Stretching the Heavens: Scripture, in some 16 places, describes creation as a stretching out process. Stretching is the Hebrew *natah* which means "to stretch out," "spread out," "extend," "incline," and "bend."[101] The book of Hebrews (Heb 11:13) gives us the further insight that the universe that we see and live in was made from something that is "not seen." This is also consistent with Genesis 1:1: *"In the beginning God created the heavens and universe."*

Together, the Bible tells us that from a point so small it cannot be seen, the entire universe was stretched out. Centuries ago, Nachmanides, a famous Hebrew sage, using Scripture described the creation in this way. Lets take a close look.

There are three Hebrew words used to denote building or creating something. One is *Yatsar* meaning "to form" or "fashion," like in Genesis

---

[100] Dr. Chuck Missler, *Book of Genesis: Comprehensive Workbook* (Coeur d'Alene ID: Koinonia House Pub., 2004), 30.

[101] *Natah*, Blueletterbible.com, http://www.blueletterbible.org/lang/lexicon/lexicon.cfm?Strongs=H5186&t=KJV (accessed December 28, 2009), Strong's 5186.

Hyperspace in Scripture

2:7 where God "formed" man from the dust of the ground.[102] A second is *Asah* which means "to make" like in Genesis 1:16 where God "made" two great lights (Sun and Moon).[103] The third is *Bara* which means "to create" out of nothing.[104] Genesis 1:1: uses *bara* with the declaration that it wasn't that something existed and from that, God made the universe. With unfathomable wisdom and unsearchable understanding that only God possesses, He created, out of nothing, the universe, the time-space continuum that we now live in.

There is another interesting facet to this. As difficult as this is to grasp, it is important to note that particles of matter didn't "explode" into a space that was there. There was no space. There were no dimensions of space. What seems to be implied from Scripture is that God created out of nothing a tiny spot. A spot so small it can be seen. Think of it as a seed, that contained all the particles of the universe (not atoms and molecules yet). All the particles of the universe are packed together in a micro space.

Then the process of creation continues as God then "stretches" this seed out creating space in the process. There was no space and then, as the seed is stretch, it forms the space. Creationists (those who believe that God created the universe) refer to this as "Creation Ex Nihilo" or "from nothing." They recognize that God created the seed from nothing. Scripturally, this is our understanding.

Nachmanides: Check out this quote: "Now with this creation, which was like a very small point having no substance, everything in the heavens and on the earth was created."[105] That's a pretty good assessment of how,

---

[102]*Zondervan NASB Exhaustive Concordance* (Grand Rapids: Zondervan, 2000), *Yatsar*, Strong's #3335, 1405.

[103]Ibid., *Asah*, Strong's #6213a, 1452.

[104]Ibid., *Bara*, Strong's #1254, 1373.

[105]Ramban Nacmanides, *Commentary on the Torah: Genesis*, trans. Dr. Charles Chavel (New York: Shilo Publishing House, Inc., 1999), 25.

now in the 21st century, quantum physics views the beginning of the universe. Shockingly however, this statement was made by Ramban Nachmanides in 1265 AD. You read that right, about 800 years ago, Nachmanides, one of three of the most venerated Hebrew rabbis' viewed the creation as starting from a single point and expanding outward.

For hundreds of years, this was viewed as a "quaint" thought. With the advent of quantum physics and its subsequent development in the 20th century of various "Big Bang" theories, Nachmanides' nearly millennial old thought becomes very descriptive of what is taught in advanced physics classes of today. "Big Bang" is the phrase given to most modern theories that are being developed that describe the origin of the universe. Modern physicists and cosmologists typically ascribe to one of the "Big Bang" type concepts which, simply stated, describe the formation of the universe as starting from an extremely small point and bursting forth, expanding outward creating space and inaugurating the beginning of time.

Modern Physics and the Big Bang: Modern physics describes very much the same thing. Physicist Tom Flandern defines the Big Band Theory as follows: "Big Bang Theory....all matter and energy in the entire universe was contained in an infinitesimal point at the 'beginning'; then for some unknown reason it all exploded...."[106] Most physicists today believe in some form of a big bang start to the universe.

The basic premise is that the entire universe started at one point, at one instance in time. The best Big Bang theory that we have today (suggested by Alan Guth), is referred to as the Inflation Model. Although still speculative, it states that the entire universe started from a single point of incredibly large mass, but no space. It doesn't contain atoms-they haven't been formed yet- but particles. From this speck, an explosion started (growth).

Very early on, when the time-space continuum was very small and still in the early states of growth (10^{-25} seconds and 10^{-24} centimeters in size – much less that a second and much smaller than an atom) something happened. Physicists today state that an outside force that is not in action

---

[106] Tom Van Flandern, *Dark Matter, Missing Planets and New Comet,* revised ed. (Berkeley, Calif.: North Atlantic Books, 1993), xv.

Hyperspace in Scripture

today must have been exerted on the space-time continuum when it was very small. Some type of anti-gravity force is postulated. The scientific implication the secular world struggles with, is that a Creator is implied in this model. Isn't that interesting?

As we have stated and although very difficult to grasp, it is important to recognize that matter and the material that we can see did not explode into space. There was no space and there was no time. From this invisible "seed" of the universe, space and time itself came forth. Space was created as the seed burst forth and time began as the seed burst forth. Secular physicist Tom Van Flandern makes the point: "This is because the Big Bang is an explosion *of* space and time, not an explosion *into* space and time."[107]

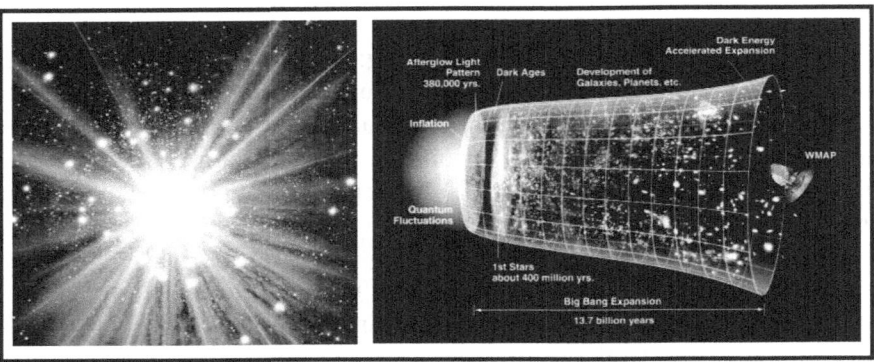

Figure 37 Big Bang: *Left*, Image, Nathan Siegel[108]; *right*, History, NASA[109]

---

[107]Tom Van Flandern, *Dark Matter, Missing Planets and New Comet,* revised ed. (Berkeley, Calif.: North Atlantic Books, 1993), 391.

[108]Ethan Siegel, "Starts with a Bang", http://scienceblogs.com/startswithabang/2009/11/when_i_make_an_assumption.php (accessed December 30, 2009).

[109]"Big Bang", WMAP, NASA, http://map.gsfc.nasa.gov/news/index.html#timeline (accessed December 30, 2009).

Hyperspace Universe

Figure 37 shows an illustration of how secular scientists view the beginning of the universe according to the Big Bang. It shows the continual expansion or stretching of space-time which is believed to be ongoing today. Notice that the illustration notes the creation of space itself as the "stretching" process continues. The space-time-continuum is stretched out from something smaller than an atom to now be some billions of light years across.

"Big Bang" models have stemmed from the theories of relativity which provides the analytical basis for this thought. Specifically:

- ✓ Special Relativity – Einstein 1905; defines as $E=mc^2$
- ✓ General Relativity - Einstein 1915: No distinction between time and space: four-dimensional continuum

The theory of General Relativity has been confirmed 12 ways to 5 decimal places and is therefore becoming pretty solid. Einstein's only real mistake, which as later self-admitted, was a cosmological constant, a "fudge factor" he included to formulate a static model. Einstein's static model meant that it was not changing and stable. The basic theory implied a creative act for the beginning, a point he was not willing to make at the time, so the "fudge factor" allowed for an always existing, static universe. He later regretted making this step as the biggest blunder of his career.[110]

Secular physicist Tom Van Flandern comments on the continually expanding universe and the cosmological constant: "So the Big Bang postulates that the cosmological expansion occurs not because galaxies move apart through space, but because more space is being continually added between them. This continual creation of space *ex nihilo* (from nothing) is an integral part of the theory. Without it, the cosmological principle would be violated."[111] This is a very revealing statement that if correct, implies the stretching is still going on and God is still involved in the process.

---

[110] Michio Kaku, *Hyperspace* (New York: Anchor Books, 1995), 267.

[111] Tom Van Flandern, *Dark Matter, Missing Planets and New Comet,* revised ed. (Berkeley, Calif.: North Atlantic Books, 1993), 391.

Hyperspace in Scripture

Bottom Line: Let's clarify something here which is important. Please don't think we are trying to force-fit a Big Bang creation model back into Scripture. What we are noting here is that the Scriptures have been declaring for some 3,500 years the process that God used to create our time-space continuum. From nothing, God created a "seed" that was so small it couldn't be seen. Then, this seed which contained all the material in the universe was stretched out and in the process, created space itself.

As noted, Nachmanides clearly published this insight from Scripture some 800 years ago. What is fascinating is that just in the past 100 years, modern science is coming to embrace this very concept and further, many modern physicists recognize (although not widely published) that involvement from a creator from the outside is actually necessary to produce the time-space continuum that we see today. But wait, there is one more fascinating scientific tidbit associated with the Bible's description of how the time-space continuum was formed; this is the beginning of time itself.

8.5 BEGINNING OF TIME

Genesis 1:1: *"In the beginning God created the heavens and the earth."* (NAS) (See also John 9:32)

2 Timothy 1:8-9: *"...God, who has saved us and called us with a holy calling, not according to our works, but according to His own purpose and grace which was given to us in Christ Jesus before time began."* (emphasis author - NKJV)

Titus 1:2: *"...in hope of eternal life which God, who cannot lie, promised before time began."* (emphasis author)

Eph 2:10: *"For we are His workmanship, created in Christ Jesus for good works, which God prepared beforehand, that we should walk in them."* (emphasis author - NAS)

Jude 25: *"...to the only God our Savior, through Jesus Christ our Lord, be glory, majesty, dominion and authority, before all time and now and forever. Amen."* (NAS)

John 1:1-3: *"In the beginning was the Word, and the Word was with*

Hyperspace Universe

God, and the Word was God. He was in the beginning with God. All things came into being through Him, and apart from Him nothing came into being that has come into being. ..." (NAS)

"Put your hand on a hot stove for a minute, and it seems like an hour. Sit with a pretty girl for an hour, and it seems like a minute. THAT'S relativity." Albert Einstein[112]

"In the beginning was the Word, and the Word was with God, and the Word was God. He was in the beginning with God." John 1:1-2 Renowned Bible Commentator John Phillips speaking on John 1. "In each case it sets before the reader not something past, or present, or future, but something ongoing. It refers to a mode of existence that transcends time. Time is a device to help finite beings relate to their mode of existence. The verb John uses takes us into the sphere of the timeless. In other words, the one John calls "the Word" belongs to a realm where time does not matter. The Word did not have a beginning." [113]

It generally comes as quite a surprise to most people to realize that time is really just a property of this time-space continuum. Not only that, but this property of time displays some rather fascinating features. A proper understanding of time is very helpful in comprehending God and His grasp and relationship with the future.

Scripture instructs us on several major points concerning time, none of which are intuitive or obvious. These points are: (1) time began at the beginning of creation and (2) God is eternal and existed before time began (3) God lives outside of time and space. (4) Jesus, as God, was pre-existent before time. For centuries, much of the scientific secular world viewed our universe as eternal in existence and infinite in size. With the understanding provided by Einstein's theories, science is now in agreement that time did indeed begin with the creation of the universe. Also, as we previously noted, the universe is also finite in size. Science has demonstrated that time is

---

[112] Albert Einstein, Quote DB, http://www.quotedb.com/quotes/14 (accessed December 31, 2009).

[113] John Phillips, *Exploring the Gospel of John* (Grand Rapids: Kregel Pub., 1989), 17.

Hyperspace in Scripture

mutable, flexible and varies with mass, speed and acceleration. These facts are some of the most shocking to come from the study of advanced physics. For this reason, initially the scientific community had great difficulty accepting this.

This section will (1) develop a scriptural understanding of time and then relate it to our understanding of God and (2) show how modern science, after millennia of controversy, is finally in agreement with Scripture.

Scriptures Declare when Time Began: In several verses as noted above, scripture declares to us that time did indeed have a beginning and that prior to that, some things had occurred. Titus 1:2 as an example clearly noting that the believer's promise of eternal life was *"promised before time began."* This is hugely challenging because we would be naturally inclined to think that (1) time has always been; (2) is the same for everyone and (3) is continuing forward.

Recognizing that time did begin at some point raises the question: "When did time begin?" Scripture answers this question although it takes some close looking to see. The answer is found in Genesis 1:1, the first verse of the Bible. A closer examination of this verse reveals an answer in the subtly of letters as shown in Figure 38. Genesis 1:1 is made up of 7 words and a total of 28 letters, the product of 7 times 4.[114] Seven, being the number of spiritual perfection and 4 the number of creation, reflects from the beginning the perfect order that was established in the initial creation.[115]

---

[114] Arthur Pink, *Gleanings in Genesis – Vol I & II* (Chicago: Moody Press, 1922), 13.

[115] E.W. Bullinger, *Number in Scripture* (1910, repr., Grand Rapids: Kregel Pub, 1967), 158 & 123.

Hyperspace Universe

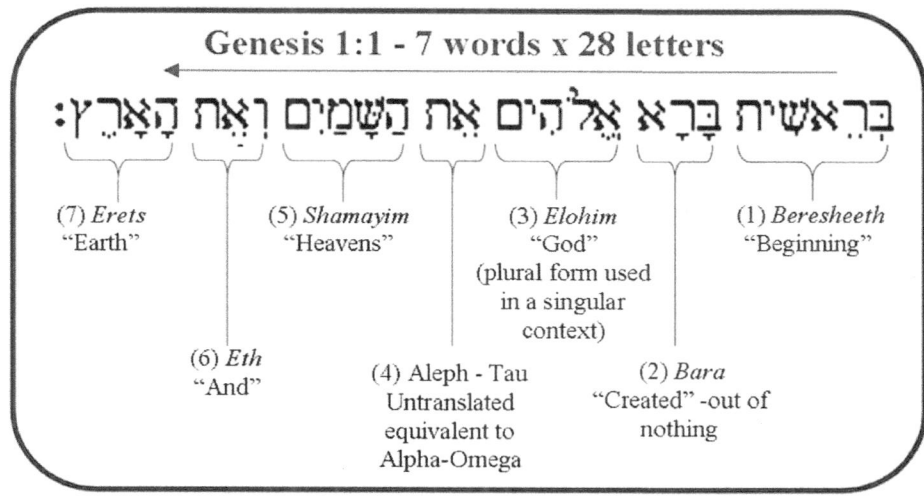

Figure 38. Genesis 1:1 analysis

The first word in scripture is *"Bershetes"* (sometimes written *"reshith"*) meaning "in beginning."[116] As Dr. Gerald Schroeder notes, the first letter is shaped so as to indicate that what precedes this event is unknowable. "The first letter of the first word...is the Hebrew letter *beth* ב. [Hebrew reads from right to left (not left to right as English) so the *beth* is at the right of the page and indicating a close to the right of it (or before) and an open to the left (or after)]. It is on this seemingly irrelevant fact that the sages based their understanding that any knowledge of what preceded the beginning is unattainable by investigation...because of the shape of *beth*."[117]

For those who may feel that this is a bit contrived, I have some bad news. Remember one of the three great Hebrew sages we mentioned a little while back? He lived about 800 years ago in the 13th Century so he did not have the benefit of understanding Einstein's theories. In spite of this however, Nachmanides noted in 1265 AD that time came into being in the

---

[116]Re'shiyth, BlueLetterBible, http://www.blueletterbible.org/lang/lexicon/lexicon.cfm?Strongs=H7225&t=KJV (accessed December 31, 2009).

[117]Gerald Schroeder, Ph.D., *Genesis and the Big Bang* (New York: Bantam Books, 1990), 56.

Hyperspace in Scripture

first verse of Genesis 1. Nachmanides further observed this from Genesis 1:5 noting that it was not "the first day"(which would have implied an already existing series) but it is more literally stated as "Day One" (implying the beginning of time).[118] (see also John 9:32).

Maimonides, another Hebrew sage of the 11th century AD also wrote of time beginning in Genesis 1:1: "We consider time a thing created..."[119] These ancient Hebrew sages confirm the point that scriptures indicate that time began with the beginning of creation.

Science Comes to Understand the Beginning of Time: Secular scientists of the late 1800's and early 1900's insisted that the universe had existed "forever". We find today that this thought was in error. Modern cosmologists mostly follow one of the many "Big Bang" theories. All the Big Bang theories recognize that time began at the beginning of the "Big Bang". Time is a property of this time-space continuum and prior to the existence of the universe, there was no time. We find that the biblical text is in agreement with this concept, or perhaps better stated, the fact that time began at the beginning of creation was revealed in scriptures 3,500 years ago. The fact that time Began at Creation is a difficult concept to grasp. However, this realization became very apparent to Einstein from his theories of relativity.

In his book, "About Time", popular author and secular physicist Paul Davies remarks on the incredible discovery that time began at the beginning of the universe. "Modern scientific cosmology is the most ambitious enterprise of all to emerge from Einstein's work. When scientists began to explore the implications of Einstein's time for the universe as a whole, they made one of the most important discoveries in the history of

---

[118]Ramban Nachmanides, *Commentary on the Torah – Genesis*, Trans. Rabbi Dr. Charles B. Chavel (New York: Shilo Publishing House, 1999, 32.

[119]Maimonides, one of three venerated Hebrew sages, wrote in the 11th century AD.. Maimonides, *Guide of the Perplexed*, trans., M Friedlander (New York: Hebrew Publishing Co.,1901), Part II Chapter XIII Page 63; Maimonides, one of three great venerated Hebrew sages, wrote in the 11th century AD.

human thought: that time, and hence all of physical reality, must have had a definite origin in the past. If time is flexible and mutable, as Einstein demonstrated, then it is possible for time to come into existence-and also to pass away again; there can be a beginning and an end to time."[120]

Physicist Tom Van Flandern on the subject of time; "The Big Bang theory is the accepted model for the origin of the universe. This theory requires us to accept the following: Time and Space have not always existed; both began a finite time ago; and both the age and size of the present universe are finite."[121]

1978 NASA astronomer Robert Jastrow, a self described agnostic stated: "I am fascinated by some strange developments going on in astronomy-partly because of their religious implications and partly because of the peculiar reactions of my colleagues. The essence of the strange developments is that the universe had, in some sense, a beginning-that it began at a certain moment in time, and under circumstances that seem to make it impossible - not just now, but ever…"[122]

Bottom Line: Scripture declares a God who is transcendent from His Creation, the space-time continuum. God is outside of space and time. Scripture has also declared from the very beginning, standing for over 3,500 years, that time actually is a property of the universe and actually began, started ticking so to speak, when the universe began. From a world view perspective, we find that the Bible is unique among religious writings in it's declaration of the universe that has a beginning. Other religious writings declare that the universe always was. Surprisingly, we find that in the past 100 years that modern science is now embracing a view that time started at the beginning of the universe (the Big Bang).

---

[120] Paul Davies, *It's About Time* (New York: Simon and Schuster, 1995), 17.

[121] Tom Van Flandern, *Dark Matter Missing Planets and New Comets*. Rev Ed. (Berkley, Calif.: North Atlantic Books, 1993), XV.

[122] Robert Jastrow, *God and the Astronomers* (New York: W.W. Norton & Company, Inc., 1978), 11.

Hyperspace in Scripture

Additionally, it is worthy of note that because God is transcendent and outside the space-time continuum, He can see across all of time all at once. He in essence can observe all of history at the same time. For this reason, God truly is: *"Declaring the end from the beginning, And from ancient times things which have not been done, Saying, 'My purpose will be established, And I will accomplish all My good pleasure.'"* (Isa 46:10).

For this reason, God alone knows the future and confirms this fact to us through Scripture. God has validated that the Bible is His words by including extensive prophetic information into the very pages of Scripture themselves.[123] It is marvelous how God speaks with scientific accuracy and prophetic accuracy. Only a real God could. Only a God outside of time can know the future.

8.6 CHRIST'S LOVE IS HYPERDIMENSIONAL

*"So that Christ may dwell in your hearts through faith; and that you, being rooted and grounded in love, may be able to comprehend with all the saints what is the **breadth** and **length** and **height** and **depth**, and to know the love of Christ **which surpasses knowledge**, that you may be filled up to all the fullness of God."* (emphasis author - Eph 3:17-19)

Unveiled here in Ephesians is perhaps one of the most masterfully crafted and exciting passage in all of Scripture. It begins with the revealing of a mystery hidden not only from people, but also hidden from angels up to this time. The mystery is glorious news for each of us personally and the center piece of this is Christ and His love for us. As the gifts of grace are described the Holy Spirit goes on building the excitement. Then, to cap off the understanding, the Spirit includes an analogy of higher dimensions. This higher dimensional analogy is used to cement the marvelous impact of the understanding of Christ's love for us.

While reading the passage, our own excitement builds and then when we get to the higher dimensional analogy, it forces us to stop. We

---

[123] Scripture contains some 1,817 different prophecies and is some 27% prophetic: J. Barton Payne, *Encyclopedia of Prophecy* (Grand Rapids: Baker Books, 1973), 675.

Hyperspace Universe

question ourselves and are driven back to consider what we have just read. As the reality of Jesus' huge gift to us comes into focus, our understanding begins to grow and we see His efforts done on our behalf. Not just for man in general, but for reader in a very personal way. A tear begins to form in our eye as we see how much Jesus loves each of us personally and the fact that He has chosen this very moment in time to let us know. Then, a smile of great joy forms across our face as we recognize through the Holy Spirit's use of higher dimensions to help us see that we will never really be able to fully comprehend how much God really loves us in such a very personal way.

Ephesians 3 is just a marvelous passage that describes the mystery, hidden from the beginning of the world that not only is salvation available to Gentiles, but surprisingly, because of Jesus, God actually dwells in the hearts of believers. This is fantastic news, well worth celebrating. It is all available to us because of Christ's love for us. The Holy Spirit then chooses an elegant analogy to describe Christ's love for us. He uses a higher dimensional analogy relating that Christ's love has 4 dimensions. We typically describe the size of something with 3 dimensions (length, depth and height). The Holy Spirit in this instance uses 4 (length, depth, height and breadth). As we have noted, comprehending Hyperspace (4 dimensions) is challenging for us. Certainly then it is not by coincidence that the Holy Spirit then notes that Christ's 4 dimensional love *"surpasses knowledge"* (Eph 3:19).

The 4 dimensions from Ephesians 3:18:

- Breadth (Greek - *platos*)

- Length (Greek - *mēkos*)

- Depth (Greek - *bathos*)

- Height (Greek - *hypsos*) – link with the spiritual realm

It actually appears that one of these dimensions (height) is used predominately in Scripture as a link to the spiritual realm. The Greek word used here for height is *"hypsos."* *Hypsos* is only used 5 times in scripture. It is translated to height (2 times); high (3 times) and high position (1 time). Here in (Eph 3:18) it is one of dimensions of a 4D Hyperspace example.

Hyperspace in Scripture

Another use is Eph 4:8 where it states that our Resurrected Lord *"ascended on **high** [hypsos]"* speaking of going to Heaven in the spiritual realm. Provocative! Another use is in Revelation 21 where it describes the size of the city of New Jerusalem.

Although controversial, I'll suggest that the use of *hypsos* is another reference to the spiritual dimension, the 4th dimension (this will be covered in detail in my second book on Hyperspace). In fact, in context, the passage very specifically links distance measurements in our 3D earthly realm with the same dimensions in the spiritual realm. Rev 21:16b-17: *"...its length and width and **height** [hypsos] are equal. And he measured its wall, seventy-two yards, according to **human measurements, which are also angelic measurements**."* (emphasis author) It is pointed out in the "Dictionary of New Testament Theology" that; "Used absolutely, *hypsos* often denotes the heavenly realm." [124] In the Greek translation of the Old Testament, the Septuagint, in Psalm 68:18 is the phrase: "...ascended on high..." It is the prophetic reference to Jesus, leading captives to heaven in Eph 4:8. The word "high" is translated to the same Greek word *hypsos*. [125] These examples build a strong case linking the dimension high (*hypsos*) with the spiritual realm and Hyperspace.

8.7 SUMMARY OF BIBLICAL COSMOLOGY:

The description that Scriptures gives of the time-space continuum is not only consistent with a higher dimensional universe, but they actually proclaim this. Scripture tells us that the heavens can be "rolled up," "rend" meaning "torn", they will "wear out," be "shaken," "burnt up," and "split apart." These properties in themselves (summarized in Figure 39) clearly imply a higher dimensional universe. Scripture's description of the universe is surprising and to consider that something the size of the universe could

---

[124] Colin Brown gen.ed., *New International Dictionary of New Testament Theology* (Grand Rapids: Zondervan Pub., 1986), II 199.

[125] Psalm 68:18, Septuagint, Blueletterbible, http://www.blueletterbible.org/Bible.cfm?b=Psa&c=68&v=1&t=LXX#conc/18 (accessed August 11, 2011).

Hyperspace Universe

exhibit these properties or experience these things is indeed challenging. From a hyperspace perspective, these properties give further insight including: (1) there must be more than 3 physical dimensions, (2) at least one dimension of the universe must be thin, and (3) the fact that its life is limited.

Property	Biblical Reference	Revelations, Implications and Confirmations
Stretching the Heavens	2Sam 22:10; Job 9:8; 26:7; 37:18; Ps 18:9; 104:2; 144:5; Isa 40:22; 42:5: 45:12; 48:13; 51:13; Jer 10:12; 51:15; Eze 1:22; Zech 12:1	Declared before the time of Christ: A creative process by which the universe is created in a process of being stretched out. This creative process described by Scripture is descriptive of a Big Bang type creation event, and advanced inflationary models not defined until the 1900's
Torn	Isa 64:1; Heb 1:11-12	Some 2,800 years ago Isaiah describes a property that implies (1) the universe has more than 3 physical dimensions and (2) the universe is thin in one dimension: both of which are consistent with advanced String theories of today
Worn out like a garment	Psalm 102:25; Isa 34:4	Confirms the 2nd Law of thermodynamics (Law of Entropy) which wasn't defined until the 1850's
Shaken	Hag 2:21; Hag 2:6; Isa 13:13	Must be a dimension for it to move
Burnt up	2 Pet 3:12	Speaks of eventual "heat death" which is a primary consideration of the eventual destruction of the universe (possible atomic fission)
Split apart like a scroll	Rev 6:14 (Sky)	Universe must be "thin" in some dimension
Rolled up like a mantel or scroll	Heb 1:12; Isa 34:4 (Sky)	Universe must be "thin" in some dimension and basically flat which has been confirmed by the WMAP satellite program in the early 2000's

Figure 39 - Properties of Hyperspace

For over 2,500 years, and against 150 years of ridicule of many in the scientific community, the Bible has made some staggering claims concerning the properties of our space-time continuum. In the face of strong opposition, we discover that Scriptures have clearly declared an astounding insightful and detailed grasp of our time-space continuum. This meaningful insight includes describing the creation process, laws that govern its existence, and its higher dimensional nature. In this area alone, at least 5 different and rather surprising scientific revelations are made in scripture. It is fascinating that only in the past 50 years has modern science come to embrace these concepts and now finds itself in amazing agreement with the Bible.

Hyperspace in Scripture

Over the past 100 years, God has allowed mankind to discover several of the secrets of the universe which include the properties of Hyperspace. These revelations include: (1) there are more than 3 physical dimensions to the universe, 10 are estimated today by string theories emerging in late 1980's; (2) the universe is thin and is in one of these dimensions, generally thought to be less than one atom; (3) the universe is basically flat, measured in 2001-2009 to be flat within 1%; (4) the universe will wear out, which is consistent with the 2nd and 3rd laws of thermodynamics defined in 1850; and (5) God created the universe by stretching it out from a small point, consistent with all Big Bang type creation models since the 1900's. A summary of these revelations that the Holy Spirit declared millennia ago are noted in Figure 40.

	Scientific Understanding	Reference from Scripture	Secular Science Comes to Understanding
1	The universe is more than 3 Dimensions	From Genesis 1: documented in 13th Century	Proposed by science in 1850's
2	In one dimension, the universe must be "thin"	From the recognition that it can be "rolled up": Heb 1:12 & Isaiah 34:4	Consistent with the emerging String and M-Theories since the 1980's
3	The universe is basically flat	From the recognition that it can be "rolled up": Heb 1:12 & Isaiah 34:4	Verified by satellite experiments of the 1990's
4	The universe is wearing out (entropy)	From Psalm 102:25 & Isaiah 34:4	Consistent with the 2nd Law of Thermodynamics developed in the 1800's
5	The universe began as a "seed" and was stretched out to form the universe; the space-time continuum	From Genesis 1 and many references to the heavens being "stretched out" (2 Sam 22:10; Job 9:8; Ps. 18:9...)	Consistent with the various "Big Bang" theories from 1927

Figure 40 - Scientific revelations from scripture recently accepted by science

Personally we are fascinated by what Scriptures tell us of hyperspace and we watch with joy as modern physics unfolds concepts that are in alignment with the Bible. Key takeaways from this chapter include:

- ✓ Scriptures imply a higher dimensional nature of the universe by stating that it can be rolled up and torn
- ✓ From these descriptions, Scriptures also imply that one of the higher dimensions is flat and thin
- ✓ Commensurately and recently, modern science has

Hyperspace Universe

    determined by analysis and experiment that the universe has higher dimensions and at least one is very thin and also very flat

- ✓ An ancient Hebrew sage of the 13th Century noted from Scripture that the universe started as something like a "seed" and was stretched out to the universe we know today as the space-time continuum

- ✓ Modern "Big Bang" theories all are based on a concept that the entire universe started from an extremely small point in space and then space itself was expanded to the universe we see today; similar to the Scriptures

- ✓ Ancient 11th and 13th Century Hebrew sages noted from Scripture that time began at the moment of creation

- ✓ Modern physics notes that time is a property of the time-space continuum and therefore began at the instant of creation; just like the Scriptures

- ✓ Jesus, in describing His love, did so using an analogy of 4 spatial dimensions, just like Hyperspace

Hyperspace in Scripture

History

9 History of Hyperspace Thought

> 2005 A.D.: Michio Kaku (PhD physicists): Henry Semat Professor of Theoretical Physics at the Graduate Center of City University of New York:
>
> Historically, the concept of hyperspace has been resisted strenuously by physicists; they scoffed that higher dimensions ...Scientists who seriously proposed the existence of unseen worlds were subject to ridicule. With the coming of M-theory, all that has changed. **Higher dimensions are now in the center of a profound revolution in physics** ...Only in ten- or eleven-dimensional hyperspace do we have 'enough room' to unify all the forces of nature in a single elegant theory .
>
>
>
>
>
> 1265 A.D.: Ramban Nachmanides (venerated Jewish Rabbi): Stated that **Scripture informs us that there are 10 dimensions to the universe**; 4 are knowable and 6 unknowable. This was developed from a study of Genesis 1.

126 127

2 Corinthians 4:18: *"while we look not at the things which are seen, but at the things which are not seen; for the things which are seen are temporal, but the things which are not seen are eternal."* (NAS)

In 1995 renowned modern day physicist Michio Kaku comments on heaven and Hyperspace: "For uncounted centuries, clergymen had skillfully dodged such perennial questions as where are heaven and hell? and where do

---

[126] Michio Kaku *Parallel Worlds* (New York: Doubleday, 2005), 185

[127] Ramban Nachmanides, *Commentary on the Torah – Genesis*, trans. Rabbi Charles Chavel (13th Century, reprt.; NewYork: Shilo Pub House Inc., 1999), 21. This interesting insight was pointed out by Dr. Gerald Schroeder, *Genesis and the Big Bang* (New York: Bantam Books, 1990), 59.

angels live? Now, they found a convenient resting place for these heavenly bodies: the fourth [spatial] dimension."[128]

Kaku further comments on the birth of higher dimensional understanding: "...Georg Bernhard Riemann, [wrote down] the fundamental mathematics of higher dimensions (which were then imported wholesale decades later into Einstein's theory of general relativity). In one powerful sweep, in a celebrated lecture Riemann delivered in 1854, he overthrew two thousand years of Greek geometry and established the basic mathematics of the higher, curved dimensions that we use even today. After Riemann's remarkable discovery was popularized in Europe in the late 1800's, the 'fourth dimension' [4th spatial dimension] became quite a sensation among artists, musicians, writers, philosophers, and painters."[129]

The history of the development of Hyperspace (higher dimensional) thought and its interplay and impact on spiritual understanding is absolutely fascinating. Christians accept by faith through the scriptures that a spiritual realm exists although its location remained a mystery until recently. It is by definition, the world of the unseen (2 Cor 4:18).

When higher dimensional concepts began to be explored in the scientific community, in the believing community it was like a light went on. All of a sudden, there was a plausible explanation for where the spiritual realm was located and why it was indeed, "un-seen." Hyperspace provided a natural physical context that enabled, for the first time in the history of man, a way by which people could understand how the spiritual realm could be literally directly adjacent to our earthly realm yet remain "un-seen"

Overview: For most all of history, secular scientific thought was dominated by Euclidian thinking which clearly limited the universe to 3 dimensions. A huge shock occurred in 1854 when a mathematician, the son of a Lutheran pastor suggested to the scientific world that higher dimensions existed. His claim rocked man's understanding so deeply that it is still being

---

[128]Michio Kaku, Hyperspace (New York: Anchor Books, 1995, 55.

[129]Michio Kaku, *Physics of the Impossible* (New York: Doubleday 2008), 232.

History

felt today. All of a sudden, higher dimensional thinking replaced limited 3D thought.

In the late 1800's, the believing community embraced this higher dimensional understanding and began to postulate that many of the Scriptural events that seemed rather bizarre could all of a sudden be explained, or perhaps better stated, understood, when viewed from a Hyperspace perspective. This began to shake up the secular scientific world because it seemed that they had in essence, virtually proved, or certainly created the possibility, of the existence of other life beyond what we could see. Science realized that they had identified a place where angels could operate.

Recognizing this and with the advent of quantum mechanics in the early 1900's, secular science retreated and began to deny the existence of higher dimensions. In this process, they could continue to deny a place where angels could roam. Unfortunately for critics of the Bible, that was a position that wouldn't last. Beginning in the late 1950's and coming on strong in the 1980's were new, more complete, leading edge physics concepts.

These new theories provided a better and more complete understanding of how things behaved. What was surprising is that all of these newer theories were based on the existence of higher dimensions. These higher dimensional theories such as String Theory and M-Theory are nearly universally being pursued with only a rather small group of physicists who are holding on to a belief against higher dimension.

The exciting news is that in the later 1980's, a brave few within the believing community who possessed a good understanding of scriptures, began to note and teach that the Bible proclaims a higher dimensional universe. As example, Dr. Chuck Missler, who is perhaps the leader in Scriptural higher dimensional thinking clearly proclaimed, using extensive Biblical references, that God's created universe was obviously higher dimensional.

It is incredibly exciting for us to note that Scripture which has declared the existence of a higher dimensional heaven and the spiritual realm for 3,500 years is now in an odd way, being validated by modern physics.

Hyperspace in Scripture

9.1 BIRTH OF HIGHER DIMENSIONAL THOUGHT

"In this sense, the introduction of higher dimensions has been one of the pivotal scientific discoveries of all human history." [130] Modern day Physicist Michio Kaku commenting on Einstein's theory of special relativity

Birth: It is clear from Scripture that many ancients believed in God and a heaven. It is unclear where they thought heaven was located. It is reasonable to speculate that they would naturally have thought it must be somewhere beyond what was known as our universe. We are unaware if any really connected Heaven with higher dimensional space. Historically, back in fourth century B.C. the great Greek mathematician Euclid, who founded Euclidian geometry, believed that there could be no more than three dimensions to the universe. This thought was also echoed later by Aristotle and Ptolemy. It could probably be stated universally that throughout the majority of history, nether people of faith or skeptics believed in the possibility of higher dimensions.

We will also note that those in the believing community couldn't really elucidate in any meaningful way where Heaven actually was. The simple answer given was that it was in the spiritual realm. But where is the spiritual realm? That question went unanswered for most of the history of man.

However, that was about to change. Major shifts in human understanding often come from what might initially be seen as a common event. In 1854 a lecture was given at the University of Gottingen in Germany by a simple, sickly and young mathematician. He was a very unassuming son of a Lutheran Pastor. However, this nearly transparent individual shattered a system of mathematics that had stood for over 2,000 years. That ancient system had been the backbone of all science and engineering for millennia. This man's lecture changed all of that and our

---

[130]Michio KaKu, *Hyperspace* (New York: Anchor Books – Random House, 1995), 13.

History

understanding of the universe was forever altered because of the introduction of Hyperspace.

His name was Georg Bernhard Riemann and the lecture he gave received an enthusiastic reception. As modern physicists Michio Kaku notes: "In retrospect, this was, without question, one of the most important public lectures in the history of mathematics. Word spread quickly throughout Europe that Riemann had decisively broken out of the confines of Euclidean geometry that had ruled mathematics for 2 millennia."[131] Riemann proposed that the universe could be better understood if viewed with higher dimensions. He postulated a 4th spatial dimension thereby adding one to the 3 that we can see.

Riemann's concepts laid the foundation and paved the way for subsequent greats like Clerk Maxwell, Albert Einstein and all the great physicists of the 20th and 21st Centuries. This is extremely significant. It was Riemann's higher dimensional thought that led to the Maxwell's foundations of electromagnetics which paved the way for Einstein." [132] It was also Riemann's concepts that broke from Newton's gravity force and more accurately described gravity as a warping of space; a concept that Einstein more fully developed. Kaku further noted the importance of Riemann's discovery stating that Riemann was: "the first to state that nature finds its natural home in the geometry of higher-dimensional space."[133]

Impact: With Riemann's breakthrough lecture, the scientific world began accepting and embracing a universe of higher dimensions. Riemann's thought was that the forces like gravity, magnetism and electricity didn't operate by magic through space from one object to another, but through bending of a fourth and higher dimension. Hyperspace thought birthed a

---

[131] Michio Kaku, *Hyperspace* (New York: Anchor Books, 1995), 37.

[132] Some examples of the links between Reimann and modern physics can be seen with: Ibid: page 36 and Roberto B. Salgado, "Einstein-Riemann Spacetime: Introducing Curvature", Department of Physics - Syracuse University, http://physics.syr.edu/courses/modules/LIGHTCONE/einstein-gr.html (accessed May 14, 2010).

[133] Michio KaKu, *Hyperspace* (New York: Anchor Books, 1995), 29 & 30.

fervor of interest by the arts, sciences and religious world. However, things began to change as the 20th Century started. Critics began claiming there was no supporting evidence for a 4th or higher spatial dimension.

Subsequently then the study of higher dimensions started becoming very controversial. However, also at the beginning of the 20th century, the science world was rocked once again by another young person, this time by Albert Einstein. Einstein made the shocking and amazing discovery that time was linked with mass, velocity and energy and was therefore relative. If time was relative, it was a property of the time-space continuum and therefore a dimension in itself.

Time relativity means that the measure of time can be experienced differently by people doing different things. A classic example is one of twin astronauts. One of the twins goes on a trip to the closest star at a very high speed (relative to the speed of light) and then returns to Earth. We then discover that he is years younger than his brother who stayed on Earth. This is because for the astronaut traveling at a very high rate of speed experiences time at a much slower rate than his twin living on earth. Einstein published this shocking discovery which became known as the theory of special relativity in 1905. Einstein showed that time is a dimension, and it is popularly referred to as the 4th dimension.

Physics Higher Dimensional Theory: Another significant leap towards hyperspace was made in 1919 when Theodr Kaluza proposed to Einstein that the universe had another special dimension (like Riemann). Kaluza proposed that when Maxwell's electromagnetic theories were combined with Einstein's theory by using another spatial dimension, the 5th dimension, a single solution resulted. Kaluza combined two complex theories into one single theory. This new theory, which became the Kaluza-Klein theory dominated the world of physics up into the 1930's, but, things were about to change in a very dramatic way. The theories of quantum mechanics which describe the world of the atomic structure, was about to be unleashed.

A summary of the historic development of high dimensional thought is shown in Figure 41.

History

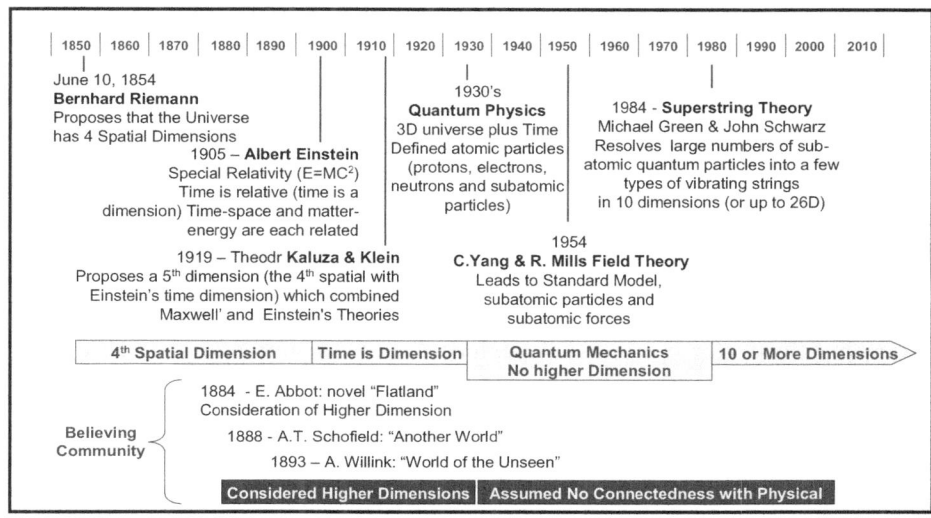

Figure 41. History and development of higher dimensional thought

9.2 QUANTUM MECHANICS, STRING THEORY AND M-THEORY

"In fact, it is often stated that of all the theories proposed in this century, the silliest is quantum theory. Some say that the only thing that quantum theory has going for it, in fact, is that it is unquestionably correct." [134] Modern day Physicist Michio Kaku

Quantum Mechanics: Quantum Mechanics (the study of materials at the atomic level) has made an impact on the world that is perhaps beyond estimation. Over 60% of the Gross National Product of the United States of America is dependent on the theories of Quantum Mechanics. Theories of Quantum Mechanics led to an explosion of understanding and opened many doors to new frontiers. As this happened, it quickly overshadowed any high dimensional thinking. Historically, this would last for quite a while. As the

---

[134] Michio KaKu, Hyperspace (New York: Anchor Books – Random House, 1995), 262

Hyperspace in Scripture

theories of quantum mechanics continued to expand, new developing knowledge led to many amazing discoveries. His new knowledge, however, also uncovered many perplexing insights.

These insights were so perplexing that they seemed to begin to actually destroy our understanding of reality. Recognizing the situation, Niels Bohr, who is known as the Father of Quantum Mechanics noted: "Anyone who is not shocked by quantum mechanics has not understood it."[135] This illustrates the unusual perspective of our universe that was being developed from Quantum Mechanics.

Some of the amazing results that grew out of an understanding of quantum mechanics included the atomic bomb, transistors, lasers and eventually computers. The electronic industry we know today with all its associated products like radios, phones, television and computers was completely created with knowledge derived from quantum physics. The scientific world was focused on a 3D plus time universe. That is until further emerging new and more complete theoretical solutions began to appear.

These new solutions were very complex and other more difficult problem began to arise. The quest to find a more complete physics theory that included gravity and other things not all that well understood began. This quest quickly found itself very limited because of the complexities associated with quantum theory. Then another huge breakthrough occurred that once again rocked the world of scientific understanding. Once again, higher dimensions were to come to the rescue.

Issue: The problem was that in Quantum Mechanics, the number of sub-atomic particles was getting out of control. Sub-atomic particles are particles that are smaller than just the proton, electrons and neutrons. The number of these particles that had been identified had grown into the hundreds. With so many different sub-atomic particles to consider, it was

---

[135]Dr. Neil Shenvi ,"Quantum mechanics and materialism," Postdoc at Yale Chemistry Department, http://www.chem.yale.edu/~tully/nashenvi/quantum.html, (accessed January 14, 2010).

becoming very difficult to make sense of it all. Sub-atomic particles include quarks which turned out to have many varieties. They come in what is called 3 "colors" and 6 "flavors". There are also anti-quarks, mesons, leptons and many others sub-atomic particles. Physicists dealing with all these hundreds of sub-atomic particles were struggling to keep up with the very complex math they demanded. So, a fresh approach was required.

Higher Dimensional Solution: In 1984, Michael Green and John Schwarz made history by introducing Superstring Theory which said that all these particles were really just a few particles with different vibration patterns. The kicker is that they vibrate in 10 dimensions. All of a sudden, Hyperspace was back on the scene and it appears that it is here to stay. Since then, Superstring theories have advanced and there are a few different models around.

One of the differences in these models is the number of dimensions in the universe. They range from 10D up to 26D. It is not known for sure how many dimensions there are in the universe, however, every modern physicist is working with some form of higher dimensional physics (Hyperspace) as an assumption. Modern science and the world of physics has now accepted hyperspace as a given.

Lets back up for a minute and explain how this has come together and where Modern Physics is currently heading. For the past century, physics has fully embraces the concepts of Quantum Mechanics in describing the world of sub-atomic particles. Physicists have also fully embraced the theory of General Relativity which provides an excellent understanding of things at a large, macro, level.

However there is a large gap in our understanding. It would seem that a more complete theory should be able to combine the understanding from everything, Quantum Mechanics and General Relativity. Up to recently there has been no successful way to bring these theories together into a single common model that accurately represents the entirety of understanding. String theory, and more importantly the new emerging M-theory purports to be able to accomplish this. M-theory is an outgrowth of string theory that is specifically developed to unify the two critical theories of physics, that of relativity and quantum mechanics.

Hyperspace in Scripture

Science is in a continued pursuit of a single model, or theory that will explain everything. Referred to as the "theory of everything", some believe that M-theory may be a major if not complete step towards achieving this much anticipated scientific milestone.

As popular physicists Michio Kaku states:

> Today, the mystery and lore surrounding the fourth dimension are being resurrected for an entirely different reason: the development of string theory and its latest incarnation, M-theory. Historically, the concept of hyperspace has been resisted strenuously by physicists; they scoffed that higher dimensions were the province of mystics and charlatans. Scientists who seriously proposed the existence of unseen worlds were subject to ridicule.
>
> With the coming of M-theory, all that has changed. Higher dimensions are now in the center of a profound revolution in physics because physicists are forced to confront the greatest problem facing physics today: the chasm between general relativity and the quantum theory. Remarkably, these two theories comprise the sum total of all physical knowledge about the universe at the fundamental level. At present, only M-theory has the ability to unify these two great, seemingly contradictory theories of the universe into a coherent whole, to create a "theory of everything"...Only in ten- or eleven-dimensional hyperspace do we have 'enough room' to unify all the forces of nature in a single elegant theory.[136]

9.3   CONNECTING HYPERSPACE AND THE SPIRITUAL REALM

Believing Community of the late 1800's: With the suggestion of possible higher dimensions to the universe being made in the middle of the

---

[136] Michio Kaku, *Parallel Worlds* (New York: Doubleday, 2005), 185.

History

19th century, a door was opened wide for the religious and spiritists of many kinds to exploit the concept.

Several prominent charlatans rose during this time that leveraged higher dimensions and linked it with the occultist spirit world. These were discredited for the most part by the early 20th century. More serious thought took place within organized religion to link the spiritual realm with higher dimensions. Some of these were believers in the scientific accuracy of Scripture and they noticed that several of the Biblical stories had a hyperspace connection.

One very notable work was that of Christian headmaster of the City of London School, E. Abbot. He wrote the broadly known novel "Flatland: A Romance in Many Dimensions." [137] Abbot's work was a very clever use of people in a lower dimension denying or trying to understand a higher dimension. He started with 1D people who are invaded by 2D people. Then the 2D people have an experience with 3D people and so on. The work is an enjoyable satire that pokes fun at all of us. Of interest to us is Abbots 3D people who continually deny that anything more exists beyond their little 3D world. Abbot's work shows how impossible it is to visualize something in higher dimensions but makes it clear that just because we can't see them doesn't mean that they aren't there.

Two other key works of the turn of the century connected the spiritual world with higher dimensions making the case from Scripture. These were medical doctor A.T. Schofield's "Another World" [138] and church pastor A. Willink's "World of the Unseen".[139]

These are ground breaking works and the earliest works that extensive research could identify that related the spiritual realm to higher dimensions or Hyperspace. As example, both works noted the relationships between Biblical events like Jesus appearing in a closed room, Daniel and

---

[137] Edwin A. Abbott, *Flatland: A Romance of Many Dimensions* (1884; repr., United Kingdom. Dodo Press)

[138] A.T. Schofield, *Another World* (London: Swan Sonnenschein & Co., Lim., 1888)

[139] Arthur Willink, *The World of the Unseen* (New York: Macmillan & Co., 1893)

the handwriting on the wall and several other insights with an understanding of higher dimensions. With these they built a strong case for the spiritual realm being located in Hyperspace.

These works are however somewhat limited in scope, only making that basic assertion. They were limited because of the limited understanding of higher dimensions that was available in the 1800's. For this reason no real analysis, scriptural or otherwise, was done. That aside, these works are an important step that goes beyond just guessing that the spiritual world may be in hyperspace to making initial scriptural correlation.

Loss of Hyperspace Understanding: Sadly, several things happened and our understanding of heaven being located in higher dimension slipped away. As previously noted, in the physics community, higher dimensions fell into disfavor early in the 20th century. Also at this time "Higher Criticism" became popular. Higher Criticism began to challenge from both inside and outside of the believing community any scientific veracity that the Scriptures may have. With the rise of evolutionary thought and the complete denial of the supernatural world, many pastors and Bible teachers retreated from a position that recognized the scientific value of what the Holy Spirit had communicated through the pages of Scripture.

In general, most of the world's focus became heavy on the "seen" versus the "unseen" realms. For these reasons, the believing or religious world faded in their interest of the concept as well. From the 1930's to the 1990's almost no one in the believing community spoke of higher dimensions as a potential location of the spiritual realm.

Believing Community of Today: Toward the end of the 20th century, a few science and engineering professionals who took the scriptures seriously, and were aware of the major transformations taking place in the world of physics, began to re-think the possibility of the spiritual realm being located in hyperspace. One of these is physicist Dr. Lambert Dolphin. Very appropriately, Dolphin sees the spiritual realm as part of the created universe and of a higher order. He is careful about not specifying exactly what or which dimension the spiritual realm is in. He does however, recognize that spiritual realm is higher dimensional and he makes the

History

following very important point: "Actually the physical, material world is EMBEDDED in the spiritual. The physical universe is a small district within the heavenlies. So in our bodies we interact with the physical world (which is perishing) and in our spirits we tune into to the heavenlies which are eternal."[140]

Another person who speaks of the potential connection between the spiritual realm and hyperspace is Dr. Chuck Missler. Missler uses an analogy of 2D paper doll flat people he calls "Mr. and Mrs. Flat" to help communicate the concept of higher dimensions.[141] These recent pioneers have opened the door to considerations of higher dimensional thought as it relates to the spiritual realm in recent times.

9.4 SUMMARY OF HIGHER DIMENSIONAL HISTORY

Followers of God have consistently believed in the supernatural realm or the spiritual realm from early on. Its actual location has however been a mystery until the rather recent development of higher dimensional understanding. Key points are noted as follows:

- ✓ Although throughout history, followers of God believed in a spiritual Heaven without understanding its location
- ✓ Throughout history, up to the 1850's, science never considered higher dimensions (Hyperspace)
- ✓ In 1854 Reimann's suggested a 4th spatial dimension. He was taken seriously and interest in higher dimensions grew over the next several decades impacting major scientific developments including Maxwell and Einstein.

---

[140]Dr. Lambert Dolphin, "Is heaven a fifth dimension?", The Paraclete Forum Archive, http://paracleteforum.org/archive/email/apologetics/fifthdimension/dialogue.html (accessed January 15, 2010)

[141]Dr. Chuck Missler, *The Book of Genesis: Comprehensive Workbook* (Coeur d'Alene, Idaho: Koinonia House, 2004), 29.

Hyperspace in Scripture

- ✓ A few Christian thinkers as far back as the 1880's began postulating that the spiritual realm could be located in higher dimensional space

- ✓ In the 1930's with the advent of quantum mechanics, science focused on atomic structure (the micro level), which did not require higher dimensions in their models. This caused higher dimensional thought to fall out of favor

- ✓ In 1984 Super String theory was introduced which resolved many of the issues associated with current quantum physics models by postulating 10 higher dimensions (possibly even 26)

- ✓ Today, most all of physics embraces higher dimensional approaches including the latest M-Theory. All of these emerging theories continue to envision 10 or more dimensions to the universe

- ✓ A few brave thinkers in the Christian community began to suggest that Scriptures speak of the universe as consisting of Higher Dimensions

- ✓ With this recent research, the case for the spiritual realm being located in the higher dimensions of the space-time continuum is becoming solidly established

10 Visualizing Hyperspace

"The only ones who can picture hyperspace are mathematicians and little children"[142] Engineer, CEO and Bible Scholar, Dr. Chuck Missler.

"This means that the beauty and symmetry found in nature can ultimately be traced back to higher-dimensional space" Modern Physicist Dr. Michio Kaku[143].

"The universe is not only queerer than we suppose, but queerer than we can suppose." Pioneer geneticist J. B. S. Haldane[144].

The Bible really does tell us about higher dimension but what exactly are they? Is there anyway to visualize higher dimensions or perhaps understand them a little better physically? Yes… well, probably more no. Suggested here are some exercises that are designed to help us grasp the concepts of Hyperspace a little better. But, we also need to note our limitations as 3D human beings.

Because we are only 3D creatures we really don't have the capacity to fully visualize or understand directly what higher dimensions would look like. There are, however, analogies and some mathematics which certainly can facilitate our ability to comprehend. In prior chapters 2D flat Goomba friends were introduced and they served as analogies going from 2D to 3D which hopefully illustrate what it would be like to go from 3D to 4D. In this

---

[142]Quoted from memory by author from Genesis study by Chuck Missler. I have heard it several times in his lectures but couldn't find it located in print. I love the quote.

[143]Michio Kaku, Hyperspace (New York: Anchor Books, 1995), 159.

[144]J. B. S. Haldane, National Review, posted December 17, 2007, http://www.encyclopedia.com/doc/1G1-172050909.html (accessed January 5, 2010).

chapter we will cover some models and do a little mathematics. But don't worry, our math is pretty straightforward (Junior High School level).

Encouragement: By the way; in my personal life I constantly encounter new things that I have great difficulty in understanding. As I enter into conversations and discussions with some high level scientists and people who are leaders in their field, I can quickly get lost and have trouble keeping up in the conversation. Often in these and other situations I have come to rely on the Holy Spirit. God has given us the promise that when we lack wisdom and understanding He will help us.

He has given us the Holy Spirit in part to do just that. Although when I ask, understanding doesn't come to me like a light bulb was turned on, but through questions, reading and study, God does answer my prayer and He faithfully leads me to understand things that perhaps were complete mysteries to me only a short while ago. For sure, there are so many things I don't understand, and I will most certainly always be in a learning mode. Hopefully I will continue to encounter people who know so much more than me whom I can learn from.

But often, when do I pray for wisdom and understanding My God is so gracious and faithful to deliver. Even though my grasp on the concept of Hyperspace is still fresh and limited, what I do understand has come from repeated prayers of: "God, I don't understand this? What does this mean? You know all God, in fact you created all. Please help me understand what You have done so I can praise your mighty name even more." James 1:5: *"But if any of you lacks wisdom, let him ask of God, who gives to all generously and without reproach, and it will be given to him."*

10.1 THE HYPERSPACE YOU HAVE ALWAYS KNOWN

Here is something you can surprise your Christian friends with. Have you every considered that there are angels around us? Do you ever think about the fact that even though we can't see them, there are angles that join us in our worship times at church? If you have, if you believe that there are angels operating around us, only we just can't see them because they are in the spiritual realm, that is super. Because, what you have pictured all along, a spiritual realm that is next to us but just invisible, is exactly what

Visualizing Hyperspace

Hyperspace is. You have all along had an understanding of Hyperspace.

Really, all that has been done here is the establishment of the physics behind the concept. If you can comprehend an unseen spiritual realm that is adjacent to our seen world, a realm where angels are active, you already have a good perspective of what higher dimensions are, what Hyperspace is. All we are really seeking to do is to identify the ordnance of God, or otherwise stated, the law of physics, that God has put in place which governs the actions of spiritual creatures and how that impacts our 3D physical realm. If you have some mental picture of angels operating around us, accomplishing God's directives, you have a great start towards understanding Hyperspace.

10.2 SPATIAL DIMENSIONS

Dimension: A term that we have used frequently is the word "dimension". A dimension is a measurement in a particular direction. Classically the word dimension is defined as: "measure in one direction; specifically: one of three coordinates determining a position in space or four coordinates determining a position in space and time ."[145] A dimension is basically a particular direction.

An example is a box. A box can be described in three dimensions (3D) using length, width and height. In a larger picture, any position anywhere in space can be marked by its latitude (lat.), longitude (long.) and altitude (alt.). If the latitude, longitude and altitude of something is known, we know exactly where it is. By using three dimensions, we can describe a specific and unique point in space. Every point in space can be described with 3 coordinate dimensions and 3 coordinate dimensions only describe one unique point.

Movement in Space: People can move in the three dimensions of our universe. We can go forward or backward, side to side and up and down. Each of these is a movement in one of our three dimensions. This concept is illustrated in Figure 42. Time is also considered as a dimension, sometimes referred to as the fourth dimension (although in this book when

---

[145]Dimension, Meridian-Webster Online Dictionary: http://www.merriam-webster.com/dictionary/dimension (accessed May 14, 2010).

Hyperspace in Scripture

we use the term 4th dimension, we have primarily been speaking of a 4th spatial dimension recognizing that there is a time dimension as well). As humans we are limited and can only move forward through time, we can't really go back.

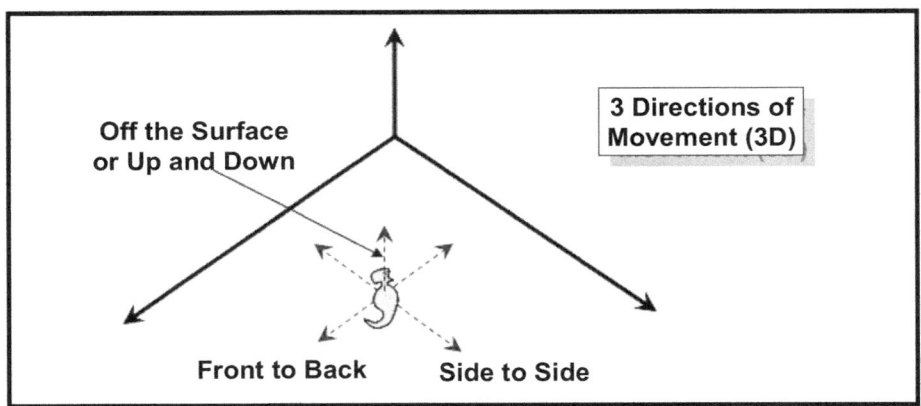

Figure 42 – Moving in 3 spatial dimensions

The first 3 dimensions are referred to as "spatial" dimensions, spatial meaning where a physical measurement is possible. The subject of this work is the study of what is referred to as "higher dimension". Higher dimensions are additional spatial dimensions beyond the 3D that we experience and live in. These higher dimensions are every bit as real as our 3 spatial dimensions that we know.

Higher dimensions are not theoretical. The fact that they are unseen doesn't mean that they are not real and physical, they are just unseen. Further, from Revelation's description of Heavenly Jerusalem (Rev 21:17), we know that the spiritual realm is a physical, measurable dimension. Hyperspace is a term for these higher dimensions and the two terms are used interchangeably. Movement in hyperspace is just the same as going sideways or up and down, it is just not in one of the 3 dimensions that we know, but moving in a different direction, one of a higher dimension.

Math of Higher Dimensions: A math example can be helpful for our understanding. This example will build up the math of progressive dimensions (you can do this). A single dimension is described as a line.

Visualizing Hyperspace

Movement along a line is to go in one direction, in one dimension (1D). We can illustrate this by simply drawing a line on a piece of paper. We want to build a progressive understanding of dimensions as an example so we will start with a line drawn on a paper and we will call its length "L". So, our line is one dimensional and has the length of "L."

Now, if we progressively grow our example from a 1 dimensional line to a next level up dimension, we accomplish that by drawing a square. The square is a 2D (two dimensional) object. Our square lives in a 2D framework which can be described as a flat plate. Technically, a two dimensional (2D) surface is referred to as a plane. It can be thought of as like the surface of a table top. For our 2D example, we have defined a square with the length of "L" on each side. The area of a 2D square is the length of one side times the length of the other or L times L which can be written as L^2.

We live in a three dimensional (3D) space. As stated, we can move in any of three different directions. An example of a 3D object with three equal sides is a cube. A cube which has each side of length L has a volume of L times L times L or L^3.

Now, let's go one more. Here's the Challenge, even though we don't have a reference to visualize what a four dimensional (4D) object would look like, we can see from the progression that has just been developed, that mathematically, its "size" would be L^4. So, simply put, we can't visualize a 4D object but we can do the math. Our example has grown from a 1D "L", to a 2D "L^2" to a 3D "L^3" and now to a Hyperspace 4D of "L^4." Fascinating.

Figure 43 illustrates this concept an object. Please note that the 4D hypercube depicted in the illustration is not really what a 4D object looks like. It is virtually impossible to draw or visualize a 4D object.

Hyperspace in Scripture

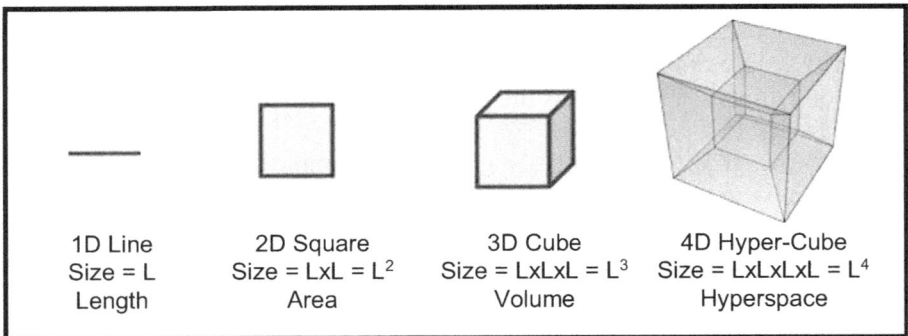

Figure 43. Example of object of length "L" in higher dimensions

10.3 ATTEMPTS AT VISUALIZATION

Hypercube: Even though we really can't visualize 4D objects or draw them, it is often a topic of discussion so we have included some objects that are commonly shown when people discuss 4D objects. So, we can't really draw a 4D object but perhaps they are somewhat useful as we consider the subject. So please recognize that when people attempt to illustrate 4D objects, at best, it seems to stretch our imaginations, but I'll suggest none of us really can picture the object in our minds. In spite of that, let's give it a try.

What does a 4D object of unit sides L look like? Shown in Figure 44 are two standard representations of a hypercube that you see in many books. On the far left is an attempt to show the pulling out of the corners of a 3D cube into a higher dimension. The picture on the right is simply a 3D cube with sides of equal length "L" that is extended in one direction with a length "L" extension. Also depicted in the middle of the figure is what I will call a 3D shadow of a 4D hypercube.

A 3D shadow of a 4D hypercube can perhaps be understood with the following process. Imagine being out in the sunlight and holding a wire frame of a cube over the ground. On the ground you would see the shadow of the cube you held up. The shadow would change shapes as you rotated the cube. If you got the cube just right, its shadow would be a simple square. Now, if we can imagine someone taking a 4D wire frame and holding it into the light so that it would cast a 3D shadow, the 3D shadow would look like

Visualizing Hyperspace

the middle picture of the figure. In a sense, we are truly creating a "shadow" of a hypercube.

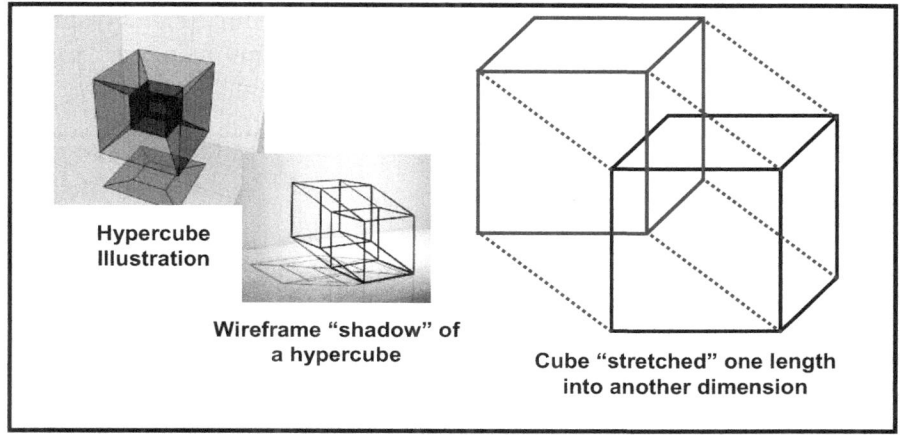

Figure 44. Illustrations of 4D hypercube, *Left*, wireframe[146]; *middle*, Wireframe extended cube[147]; *right*, wireframe 3D cube with extension

Flat Patterns: Another technique that might be helpful in understanding Hyperspace is an unwrapping or flat pattern. If you were to take a paper cube, cut it along some of its sides and then unfold it flat, it becomes a cross shape flat pattern. Because it is flat, it is now a 2D object. In this process, a 3D paper cube has been turned into a 2D flat pattern.

Similarly, if a 4D hypercube was cut and unfolded into 3D space, it would look like the middle picture in Figure 45. The 3D cube had 6 sides and unfolded into a 2D flat pattern, there are 6 squares in the pattern. A 4D hypercube has 8 sides so when it is unfolded into a 3D "pattern" it ends up as 8 cubes.

---

[146] Anthony Beckwith, "Hypercube", Topology, http://mail.colonial.net/~abeckwith/topo.html (accessed January 5, 2010)

[147] Peter Forakis, "Hyper-cube", http://www.austinchronicle.com/gyrobase/Issue/review?oid=oid%3A721403 (accessed January 5, 2010)

Hyperspace in Scripture

Just for fun, on the right of Figure 45 is shown a picture painted by artist Salvado Dali. He worked to capture the higher dimensional nature of the crucifixion through the use of a hypercube in his painting, "Corpus Hypercubicus".

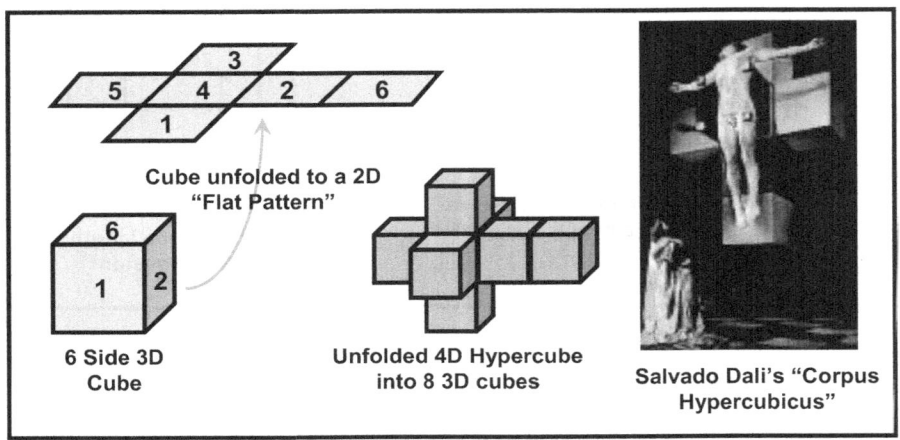

Figure 45. Unfolding, *Left*, 3D cube unfolded into a 2D flat pattern; *middle*, 4D hypercube unfolded into a 3D pattern; *right*, Salvador Dali's painting[148]

3D to 2D Interaction Example: A final area of visualization is also helpful for an encounter of what Belshazzar experienced in the Book of Daniel (covered in Chapter 3). This technique considers what something may look like as it passes through lower dimensions. Let's imagine a 2D flat plane world that is inhabited by our 2D Goomba friends. Now consider what it would look like to them as we pass a cone through their little 2D world. As it first touches, it would be a point and as it penetrates into the 2D world, it makes a circle in their world. As the cone penetrates further and further, the circle continues to grow until it passes completely through and then disappears from visibility in the 2D world. This is illustrated in Figure 46.

---

[148] Salvador Dali, "Corpus Hypercubicus ", http://gallery.cabri.com/en/hyperCube.html (accessed January 5, 2010).

Visualizing Hyperspace

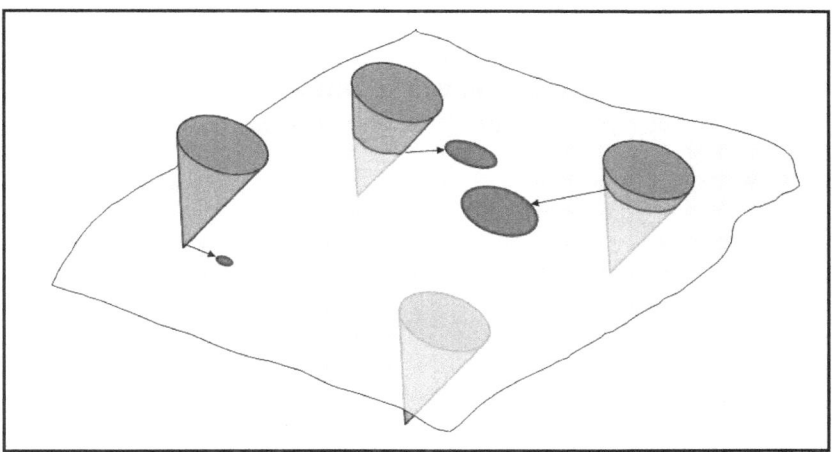

Figure 46. 3D cone passing through a 2D world

If you have made it this far, congratulations are in order. I'm proud of you. Trying to comprehend Hyperspace is not easy. We have just covered what we will call the mathematical insight into multiple dimensions. I didn't want to say that upfront because I thought it would scare everyone. Also, don't worry if some of this was confusing, because we really can't visualize the fourth dimension. In spite of these things, it is my hope that these examples help you grow a little in your understanding of Hyperspace.

10.4 SUMMARY OF VISUALIZING HIGHER DIMENSIONS

- ✓ It is virtually impossible to visualize higher dimensions
- ✓ The mathematics of higher dimensions are very workable
- ✓ A spatial dimension is a dimension into which we can move or travel a distance
- ✓ Christians who recognize that there is a spiritual realm around us where angels move about are really, in a sense, visualizing Hyperspace.
- ✓ A being from a higher dimension (like an angel in 4D Hyperspace) can insert himself into a lower dimension

Hyperspace in Scripture

(like our 3D seen world) but we can't go the other way (not yet anyway)

11 Big Picture & Summary

11.1　　GENERAL SUMMARY

For some of us, this has been a very thrilling study. Attempting to identify from Scripture where Heaven really is has been a challenging endeavor. But the good news is that Scripture has provided many good passages that inform us that Heaven and the spiritual realm is really located in Hyperspace. The Holy Spirit Himself has given us these nuggets of spiritual knowledge and we have thoughtfully arrayed them together like pieces of a jigsaw puzzle and the picture that has emerged is truly majestic. We have not had to build our case from only a few verses out of context, but instead, we have pulled from a wealth of Biblical references.

All of this information points only to and clearly to one viable solution for the location of the spiritual realm. Only the solution of Hyperspace, the higher dimensions of our space-time continuum, as the location for the spiritual realm is a consistent with all these Biblical passages. This is very encouraging because as the Holy Spirit has given us the ability to understand this so that we can dramatically grow in our appreciation and comprehension of Heaven.

It has been fun to learn that in the spiritual realm horses and chariots of fire are roaming around with all the angels. The fact that the Heavenly City of the Living God is directly connected to Mount Zion in Israel is eye opening. Recognizing that God is outside of our space-time continuum facilitates our understanding of His unique knowledge and control of the future.

It also has been challenging to come to grips with the reality of the underworld in the spiritual realm. Coming to and understanding of Hyperspace has given us a more comprehensive understanding of God's created universe. This results in a bigger view of God. We have a greater

Hyperspace in Scripture

appreciation leading us to praise Jesus our Lord for what He has created rules and sustains. Truly our God is an awesome God.

11.2 SUMMARY OF THE CASE FOR HYPERSPACE AND HEAVEN

The Case for Heaven and the spiritual realm being located in higher dimensions of our space-time continuum has been made on four key points. Each of these points are substantiated by several Biblical stories or events. The total weight of this Scriptural evidence makes for a very solid case. No other even remotely viable explanation has been brought forward. The key points are noted below and in Figure 47:

1) Biblical Events indicating hyperspace activity
    a) Jesus appears in a closed room (John 20:19; 20:26; Luke 24:31)
    b) Handwriting on the wall of Daniel (Daniel 5:5-6)
    c) Our earthly 3D Temple is referred to as a model and "shadow" (one dimension less) of the 4D Heavenly Temple (Hebrew 8:5)
2) Scripture links the realms of the seen and unseen together (implies connectedness or higher dimensions) (Ephesians 6:12)
    a) Elisha's servant sees into the spiritual realm (2 Kings 6:16-17)
    b) Gabriel traverses across the spiritual realm to get to a place on Earth where Daniel is (Daniel 10:1-13)
    c) Jacob sees angels leaving and coming to Earth (Genesis 28:12)
    d) Stephen sees into hyperspace (Acts 7)
    e) Hebrews links earthly Zion to the spiritual realm Zion (Hebrews 12:18-24)
    f) Both length (physical) and time measurements are the same in the spiritual realm as on Earth which implies linking of the earthly (3D

Big Picture

+ Time) and spiritual realm (higher) dimensions (Daniel 10:2, 13; Revelation 21:17)

3) Biblical model of the universe is consistent with a time-space continuum with higher dimensions
   a) Universe can be rolled up and torn (implies that it must be "thin" in at least one dimension (Heb. 1:10-12; Isa. 64:1; Isa. 34:4)
   b) Time had a beginning (Gen. 1:1; 2 Tim. 1:8-9; Titus 1:2; Jude 25; John 1:1-3)
   c) The universe will "wear out" and be destroyed (Psalm 102:25; Isa. 34:4; 2 Peter 3:10-12)

4) Other scriptural information is placed in a more understandable context
   a) Gates of hades (Job 38:17); Door to the "Bottomless Pit" (Rev. 9:1-3); Door to Heaven (Rev. 4:1)
   b) Location of Hades (down: Gen. 37:35; Isa. 14:9; Gen. 37:35; Psalm 63:9; Job 11:8) and Heaven (up) are linked in reference as direction from our world
   c) Creatures (angels, horses and chariots of fire) and activity in the spiritual realm
   d) God is outside of the space-time continuum and therefore knows the "beginning from the end."

Hyperspace in Scripture

① Biblical Events Indicate Hyperspace Activity
- Jesus appears in a closed room (Jn 20:19)
- Handwriting on the wall described in Daniel (Dan 5:5)
- Earthly Temple is 3D (a shadow) and the Heavenly Temple is 4D (Heb 8:5)

② Scripture Links the Realm of the Seen and Unseen Together
- Elisha's servant views the spiritual realm (2Kings 6:16)
- Gabriel travels across spiritual realm to reach a point on Earth (Dan 10)
- Jacob view's angels leaving and coming to Earth (Gen 28:12)
- Stephen sees into the spiritual realm (Acts 7)
- Hebrews links earthly Zion with Heavenly Zion (Heb 12:18)
- Length (physical) and time measures are the same in the spiritual realm and on earth (Dan 10:2, 13; Rev 21:17)

③ The Biblical Model of the Universe is Consistent with a Time-Space Continuum of Higher Dimensions
- Universe can be rolled up and torn (Heb 1:10-12; Isa 64:1)
- Time had a beginning (2 Tim 1:8-9)
- Universe will wear out and be destroyed (Psalm 102:25)

④ Places Other Scriptural Insights into Context
- Gates of Hades (Job 38:17); Door to Bottomless Pit (Rev 9:1-3); Door to Heaven (Rev 4:1)
- Hades is down (Gen 37:35) and Heaven is up
- Spiritual Creatures and activity in the spiritual realm
- God is outside of space-time and therefore knows the future as well as the past

Figure 47. Four Key points of the case for hyperspace and Heaven

Alternative views of Heaven being out beyond some distant planet or some ethereal type existence have some significant conflicts with scriptural insight. Envisioning Heaven in higher dimensions or hyperspace is not only consistent with scripture, but also assists us in understanding such odd things resurrected Jesus appearing and disappearing out of nowhere and realities such as a door to the bottomless pit. A few of these are also noted in the figure.

The conjecture that the spiritual realm is located in higher dimensions of our space-time continuum has provided a straight forward framework of understanding of how the spiritual realm relates to our 3D world. All Biblical events describing interactions between these two can be understood from a Hyperspace perspective.

Further, the concept of higher dimensions has clarified several difficult passages. Our proposed solution (Heaven in Hyperspace) creates no other difficulties with other scriptural passages that need to be dealt with. It is very consistent with scripture.

Big Picture

11.3 SUMMARY OF SCIENTIFIC AND SPIRITUAL FINDINGS AND DISCOVERIES

Spiritual Findings: The study of hyperspace and the spiritual realm has proven to be a fertile field for findings and discoveries. As a professional in the engineering Research and Development (R&D) field, I find that most of what our group accomplishes is building on foundations that others have laid. That has proven to be the case here as well.

We have built an extensive structure of understanding on the key foundation that was laid over 100 years ago by insightful people who believed in the scientific accuracy of Scripture and took the Bible seriously. That foundation was the thought that the spiritual realm was located in higher dimensions.

This assertion and 7 others related to hyperspace and the spiritual realm are noted in Table 1. 5 Are noted as findings which are defined as truths that others have asserted previously. 3 Are labeled as discoveries which are defined as something that has not been previously advocated by anyone else; they are new thoughts. The likelihood that these discoveries will one day prove to be true are noted. In our planned Volume II on Hyperspace, an additional 4 discoveries and findings will be claimed. This indeed has been a fruitful study.

Hyperspace in Scripture

Table 1 Spiritual findings and discoveries resulting from the Biblical study of Hyperspace and the Spiritual Realm

	Findings and Discoveries	Asserted	Supported
1	Heaven is located in higher dimensions of our space-time continuum	• Asserted as early as 1890	Finding: with this work, we have extensively further developed our understanding and have built a conclusive case from scripture
2	God is outside of the fully created universe	• Asserted by implication for 1,000's of years (see Solomon) • Asserted recently via physicists who understand creation: "*Creator Beyond Time and Space*"	Finding: Concept has been previously developed but here it is placed in a broader context (Isa 57:15)
3	Mapped Heaven's location	• New Discovery by author (very likely correct)	Discovery: Developed 2D to 3D analogy map indicating location
4	There is an actual physical connectedness between the seen and unseen worlds	• New Discovery by author (very likely correct)	Discovery: Example - Mt. Zion is adjacent to Earthly Mt. Zion (Heb 12)
5	Angels and Resurrected Jesus can travel directly in and out of hyperspace	• Asserted as early as 1890	Finding: Further developed in the context of hyperspace (John 20:19, 26)
6	Mapped part of the underworld of the spiritual realm locating Hades and the Bottomless Pit	• New Discovery by author (likely corrrect)	Discovery: based on the "down" direction identified in scripture mapped with 2D to 3D analogy the underworld
7	Nature of the Space	• Asserted by several over the past 50 years	Finding: further developed and aligns with modern physics
8	Identified creatures in the Spiritual Realm (horses)	• Asserted for 1,000's of years but not widely declared	Finding: collaborated with scripture

Scientific Understandings: Also of high interest is how science has really caught up in recent years to what Scripture has proclaimed for several thousand years. Science now finds itself very much in agreement with the properties of the universe or what the Bible refers to as the "ordnances of heaven."

Twelve of these key understandings (see Table 2) which are derived from the pages of Scripture and are related to higher dimensions and the

Big Picture

time-space continuum are noted (2 more will be noted in Volume II of Hyperspace). Over the period of the last 100 years, without knowing it, secular science has come to embrace an understanding of the universe that has been declared by the pages of scripture for some 3,000 years. These concepts are beyond our ability to even imagine and visualize, yet they have been clearly communicated to us from the Holy Spirit from the very beginning.

Table 2 Biblical scientific insights related to the Time-Space Continuum confirmed by science

	Scientific Understanding	Reference from Scripture	Secular Science Comes to Understanding
1	The universe is more than 3 Dimensions	From Genesis 1: documented in 13th Century	Proposed by science in 1850's
2	The universe began as a "seed" and was stretched out to form the universe; the space-time continuum	From Genesis 1 and many references to the heavens being "stretched out" (2 Sam 22:10; Job 9:8; Ps. 18:9…)	Consistent with the various "Big Bang" theories from 1927
3	The "seed" from which the universe was made was too small to see	Indicated by Hebrews 11:3	Consistent with the various "Big Bang" theories from 1927
4	Time Began at the creation of the universe	From Genesis 1 & 2 Tim 1:8-9, Titus 1:2, Eph 2:10, Jude 25, Jn 1:1-3	Consistent with the various "Big Bang" theories from 1927
5	The universe is finite	From Genesis 1 and Isaiah 40:12b	Consistent with the various "Big Bang" theories from 1927
6	The universe is basically flat	From the recognition that it can be "rolled up": Heb 1:12 & Isaiah 34:4	Verified by satellite experiments of the 1990's
7	In one dimension, the universe must be "thin"	From the recognition that it can be "rolled up": Heb 1:12 & Isaiah 34:4	Consistent with the emerging String and M-Theories since the 1980's
8	There is more to the universe beyond out 3D perception, the spiritual realm exists	All of scripture speaks of an unseen Spiritual Realm (Colo 1:16; 2 Cor 4:18)	Concepts of parallel universes and hyperspace were proposed in the late 1800's
9	The universe is wearing out (entropy)	From Psalm 102:25 & Isaiah 34:4	Consistent with the 2nd Law of Thermodynamics developed in the 1800's
10	Dark Matter exists	God created darkness (Isaiah 45:6-7; Job 38:19-20)	Recognition only in the past 30 years and it remains a scientific mystery
12	Travel through hyperspace is possible (Jesus)	Consistent theme throughout scripture: example is Jesus (Jn 20:19-26)	Conjectured from science since the 1850's

The alignment of the most current models in physics, that of Super-String theory and M-Theory, to the Biblical model of the time-space continuum from its beginning to today is absolutely staggering. This reality should give the student of the Bible great confidence that what he is reading is nothing less that very Words of God, something we really have always known.

11.4 VALUE OF HYPERSPACE RESEARCH

Jesus could have walked from the road from Emmaus, opened the door to the disciples' room and walked in, but He didn't. Instead, He disappeared from the dining room in Emmaus then amazingly reappeared in the locked room in Jerusalem; seemingly out of nowhere by just stepping in from hyperspace. God could have directed an angel to walk into Beltachazzar's room to deliver a message, but He didn't. Instead He directed an angel to poke his hand through the fabric of space and write a scathing indictment on the palace wall. Scripture tells us these things in this way for the purpose of opening our eyes to the higher dimensions of the universe.

Gabriel didn't have to give Daniel an excuse for his 21 day delay. But he did and he described in detail his travel across the land of Spiritual Persia to reach Daniel in Earthly Persia. Elisha could have comforted his servant and encouraged him in his faith to just simply trust but he didn't. Instead he asked God to open the servant's eyes so he could peer into the spiritual realm that was right adjacent to them. As God enables him, the servant sees mighty angelic forces and chariots of fire ready for battle. Scripture informs us of these things so we can recognize the close connectedness and links between the spiritual realm and our Earth.

The Holy Spirit didn't need to include the details in the scriptures of our universe letting us know that it could be rolled up, torn and would one day wear out, but He did. The Holy Spirit didn't need to tell us that time had a beginning, but He did. In this way, believers, for thousands of years have had the insight that modern physics has only just begun to realize.

Far from being an academic intellectual exercise, the study of the spiritual realm becomes very personal. Far from being just text book drama, the study of higher dimensions opens our eyes to the reality of Heaven and its richness. Not to imply that our 3D world is not real, but in perspective, the beauty, fullness and richness of Heaven and the spiritual realm far exceeds that of our ordinary of our world. As a 2D paper doll pales next to a

Big Picture

3D person, so does our world compare to that of higher dimensions.

The value of a study of hyperspace and the spiritual realm lies in the expanded view of God that is gained. Heaven has become more real. Comfort has been gained through the knowledge that God is directing angelic activity on our behalf. Trust has been strengthened as we see how physics seems to be paralleling scriptural insights. Encouragement has been found in the reality of our fantastic future lives in the Heavenly City of God. And just for fun, joy has been achieved as we consider what we might be doing in the hyperspace-capable resurrected bodies that we have been promised.

11.5   THANK YOU

If you have taken the time to read this, God bless you my brother or sister. I take it as a very sacred duty to diligently seek out and present truth as derived from the scriptures. It has been my goal and prayer that your time invested here is rewarded with growth in both the knowledge of Jesus our savior and most importantly, in your relationship with Him.

The older I have gotten, the more it seems that I look forward to Heaven, to home. Like Abraham, I feel more and more like I am a wanderer on this earth. Heaven is my home, it is where my eternal citizenship lies; it is a deep longing in my heart. The day will come, and perhaps it is not all that far off when Jesus will return to take us home, to our real home that He has prepared for us (John 14:3). And on that day, that great and glorious day, in a moment, in the twinkling of an eye we will be forever changed (1 Cor. 15:52). We will shed our earthly bodies and be transformed into our everlasting bodies; bodies that won't wear out or won't decay (1 Cor. 15:54). On that day, our Lord and Savior will escort us into the spiritual realm, into higher dimensions. And on that day, we will go home, to the place we have longed for all our lives. On that day our grand adventure will really begin. And on that day, I will turn to you and say: "Congratulations! You have just entered hyperspace."

Hyperspace in Scripture

12 Appendix I
Eternal Life

The Heavenly City of God is a fabulous place. It is filled with people and angels that are engaged in a lot of activity, but perhaps is well described as a place of great joy and love. What is missing is injustice, pain, sorrow and evil, and those aren't really being "missed". Instead it is a place of comforting justice, ease, excitement and goodness.

Everything has purpose and great meaning. Far from sitting around on clouds and strumming on harps, the Bible relates that people are active and busy. Even better, whatever we will be doing, we will discover that it was what we were made to do. Our personalities, interests and desires will find fulfillment as we engage in what God has prepared specifically for us. Unlike never before, as we do something, a satisfaction and joy will well up in our souls and we will find wholeness and completeness that is well beyond anything we have experienced or imagined. God has prepared them exclusively and individually for us and as we do them, God becomes glorified and we become satisfied.

And when we rest and relax, it will be like never before. Many have trouble today relaxing and just being quiet because the constant troubles, trials and concerns of life crowd into our thoughts and rob us of real peace. In Heaven, when we stop to rest and breathe, every breath will be one of soothing peace. We will take great joy and pleasure just in the way things are. A moment of reflection will bring a smile to the face and comfort to the soul. Gratefulness, thankfulness and praise will be constantly flowing from our hearts because of how blessed, how well rewarded and how much good we will have. If you ever have had a brief moment and thought as you reflected on something really good brought into your life and it gave you a feeling of great thankfulness, perhaps you have had a very small taste of what it will be like constantly.

Hyperspace in Scripture

Life in the Heavenly City is good, rich and full because it is the dwelling of God and all the goodness that God plans for us, that He created us for, that will satisfy our deepest longings, will be fully realized. Heaven is fantastic because its creator, owner and leader is God Himself. Like a very wealthy and deep pocketed king whose major desire is to share in love all he has with his family and will richly lavish them with all that is good, we find that God lacks no resources and will provide for us in such great abundance we will constantly be overwhelmed by His generosity and goodness. True love will be the order of the day and joy and contentment will overflow from us.

However, there is a problem; a big one. All of us have sinned and fallen short of the glory of God (Rom. 3:23). We are born with a fallen nature that rebels and turns from God. Even if we wanted to, we cannot do enough good to cover our sins and earn our way to Heaven. Instead, we are going to get what we deserve. True justice will demand punishment for all the offenses, wrongs and hurts we have brought to others and to God. We are headed for eternal punishment for all the sins we have committed. We cannot even stand up to our own vision of what people should be. We will be condemned by our own words of what we thought and say people should do (Revelation 20:11-15). We are in serious peril. We will all be judged and found wanting; found to have come well short of the mark that even we have established. Our only hope is a savior. We desperately need a savior. Because God is perfect in love and justice, He won't be able to just ignore and be blind to our sins. Punishment for them is demanded and real justice will be served. We're toast unless we can find a savior.

But wait, there is some really good news. I've found the savior and His name is Jesus. God's Son, God Himself, emptied Himself and took on the flesh of man (John 1:1). In fulfillment of Scripture, He was born of a virgin. He lived a perfect and sinless life to qualify Himself as a sacrifice. He became our savior; He took upon Himself the sins of each of us and paid the ultimate price. He died in my place, paying all my debt. Yet as Scripture predicted, He rose victorious from the grave conquering sin and death and He has extended salvation to all who choose Him; choose to place their faith, trust and life in His hands. There is no way we can earn salvation on our own, but it is extended to us free of cost if we accept it in simple faith (Eph. 2:8-9). With a simple act of faith, in prayer, we open our heart, recognize

Eternal Life

our sin, turn from it (repent) and ask Jesus to save us and place our lives in His hands. Jesus referred to the process as being "born again." (John 3:3) It is a great phrase because when we ask Jesus Christ to be our savior, the impact is much more that just simply cleansing us from sin, we are born spiritually, a new creature (2 Cor. 15:17). Everyone who comes to Jesus, everyone who calls on His name will be saved, it is His desire. And more good news, when we are born again, God sends the Holy Spirit to live in us as a seal and guarantee of eternal life with Him in Heaven (2 Co.r 1:22).

I'm getting old so most everyone is becoming a precious daughter or a highly valued son to me. To you who are reading these words, if you have not yourself been given new life in Christ; I plead with you to do so. I have prayed for you, even though I don't know you, I have prayed for you, the one who reads these words. I have prayed that you will see your need of a savior and open your heart to Jesus, the only one who can save you from destruction and give you eternal life. He is not looking for you to clean up your act and then come to Him, He wants you now, just as you are. He will give you new life and lead you on a new path. If you do turn to Him, He will save you from eternal destruction; that's mercy. And if you do turn to Him, He will give you amazing eternal life in Heaven filled with abundance; that's grace (Eph. 2:7). If you don't know Him, turn to Him today.

If you have chosen to embrace Jesus Christ as your savior, let me express my congratulations and joy at your decision. Even the angels of Heaven rejoice with you (Luke 15:10). I would encourage you to seek out a church that teaches the Bible, the Word of God every week. Look for a church that has you open your Bible and then helps you understand what it is saying. If a church just quotes a few bible verses to bolster what they are saying, beware. If they tell everyone to bring their bibles each week, and they open them, read them and talk about what it says, the whole passage and in context, you are in a good place. I have prayed that God will go before you and lead you to a good place. Trust Him to lead you and let the Holy Spirit guide you. Bless you my child, I will see you in Heaven and I personally guarantee that we will have some real fun.

If you would like to talk with someone more about this or have any questions, please call my friends at Mission Community Church. They would be happy to talk and help you find a church in your area as well. Just

Hyperspace in Scripture

ask for the Pastor on Call. You can contact them at: http://www.mission68.org or call them at 480-545-4024.

13 Appendix II
Study Group Discussion Questions

Chapter 1 - Introduction

1) What do you think most people think that heaven is like? What do you think it will be like?
2) Do you think the Bible is scientifically accurate? Does it even speak about science? Can you cite some examples?
3) Do you think the spiritual realm is real and who lives there?

Chapter 2 - Stepping Through the Veil

1) Do you think there is a difference between Lazarus's body and that of resurrected Jesus? What are those differences?
2) There are several options as to how Jesus just appeared in a room with a closed door (see pages 13-15). What do you think is a reasonable understanding and why?
3) Does the analogy of the Goomba entering a house make sense to you? (page 17)
4) When it is said that there is a "connectedness" between the spiritual realm and earthly realm, what does this mean?
5) When you consider the "Road to Emmaus" story, does it seem reasonable that Jesus had to travel in the spiritual realm from the place where they ate back to Jerusalem?

Chapter 3 - Poking Thorough the Veil

1) If you were in Belshazzar's shoes, do you think you would have been scared?
2) Is the Goomba or fish pond analogy helpful in understanding the potential for someone's hand to write on a wall?
3) What is the difference between "theo-magic" (see page 34) and God working in the ordnances He has established?

Hyperspace in Scripture

Chapter 4 - Seeing Through the Veil

1) Have you ever had the sense that you were surrounded by spiritual forces?
2) What was it that Elisha's servant saw and was it real or a "vision"?
3) What was it that Jacob say and why was it important to him and to us?
4) How close is the spiritual realm to us?
5) Do you think there are animals in heaven and why would God have established that?
6) Can you explain the 2D "ant farm" to 3D analogy?

Chapter 5 - Journey in Hyperspace

1) What do you think most people believe about angels?
2) Where do you think the battle between Gabriel and the Prince of Persia was fought and why was it even necessary?
3) Do you think there is a "Spiritual Texas" and a "Spiritual Israel"? What about "Mt Zion"?
4) If you are in the spiritual realm, is there distance between where you are today and Spiritual Mt. Zion?
5) What are the implications of time and length being the same in the spiritual realm as they are in the earthy realm?

Chapter 6 - The Great City in Hyperspace

1) Is Heavenly Jerusalem a real place and who is living there?
2) How can God the Father be both "outside of time" and next to Jesus on the Throne at the same time?
3) What does it mean that the earthly temple was a "shadow" of the Heavenly Temple?
4) Using Isaiah 6 and Revelation 4-5 describe what the Temple of God might be like.
5) Is God the only one/thing outside of time and space?

Chapter 7 - Hyperspace Underworld

Study Group Questions

1) When you ask people about hell, what kind of answer to you typically get?
2) What do you think about the two parts of Hades described in Luke 16?
3) Where do you think the bottomless pit is and why is the center of the earth a candidate location?
4) What do you think God's purpose is in throwing Hades into the Lake of Fire?

Chapter 8 - Hyperspace Universe

1) What are some Biblical references that imply that the universe contains higher dimensions.
2) Do you think the Big Bang parallels the Scriptures in any way?
3) What is the importance of science recognizing that time had a beginning?
4) What do you think of the consistency between the Scriptures and modern cosmological thought (see Figure 40 on page 158)?

Chapter 9 - History of Hyperspace Thought

1) Why do you think "higher dimensions" or Hyperspace type thinking was abandon in the church for so long?
2) Was it a surprise to you to discover that so much of key, modern physics is really fundamentally built around higher dimensions?
3) How solid do you think the case is that the spiritual realm is in hyperspace?

Chapter 10 - Visualizing Hyperspace

1) Have you ever tried to visualize the angels around us and how that works? How would you explain it?
2) Which if any of the techniques of cube to hypercube, wireframe shadows, flat pattern or any of the others were helpful in understanding higher dimensions?

Chapter 11 - Big Picture and Summary

Hyperspace in Scripture

1) Do you think the Biblical evidence that the spiritual real is located in hyperspace is conclusive? How strong is the case in your mind?
2) Which of the Biblical stories is most helpful for you in understanding hyperspace?
3) Which of the Biblical hyperspace discoveries in Table 1 on Page 190 was most interesting to you?
4) Is an understanding that the Spiritual Realm being located in Hyperspace helpful to you and why?
5) What has been the value in studying about Hyperspace?
6) Are you planning on spending eternity in Heaven? Why do you think that is possible?

Bibliography

Abbott, Edwin A.. *Flatland: A Romance of Many Dimensions.* 1884. Reprint, United Kingdom: Dodo Press, ND.

Alcorn, Randy. *Heaven.* Wheaton, Illinois: Tyndale House Pub., 2004.

Al-Khalili, Jim. *Black Holes, Wormholes & Time Machines.* Bristol, England: Institute of Physics Publishing, 1999.

Barnhouse. Donald Grey. *The Invisible War.* Grand Rapids: Zondervan, 1965.

Benner, Jeff A.. *The Ancient Hebrew Lexicon of the Bible.* College Station, Texas: Virtualbookworm.com Pub., 2005.

Boice, James Montgomery. *Genesis: An Expositional Commentary.* Grand Rapids: Baker Books, 1985.

Brand, Chad et. all gen. ed.. *Holman Illustrated Bible Dictionary.* Nashville: Holman Bible Pub., 2003.

Brown, Colin gen. ed.. *New International Dictionary of New Testament Theology.* Grand Rapids: Zondervan, 1967 & 1986.

Brown, F., Driver, S. and Briggs, C.. *The Brown-Driver-Briggs Hebrew and English Lexicon.* 1906. Reprint, Peabody Massachusetts: Henbrickson Pub., 2003.

Bullinger, E.W.. *A Critical Lexicon and Concordance to the English and Greek New Testament.* 1908. Reprint, Grand Rapids: Kregel Publications, 1999.

———. *Number in Scripture.* 1910. Reprint, Grand Rapids: Kregel Pub, 1967.

Davies, Paul. *It's About Time.* New York: Simon and Schuster, 1995.

Dillow, Joseph C.. *The Waters Above,* rev.ed. Chicago: Moody Press, 1982.

Dolphin, Lambert T.. *Jesus: Lord of Time and Space.* Green Forest, Arkansas: New Leaf Press., 1988.

Eastman, Mark, M.D. & Missler, Chuck. *The Creator Beyond Time and Space*. Costa Mesa, Ca.: The Word for Today Pub., 1996.

Elwell, Walter A. ed.. *Baker Theological Dictionary of the Bible*. Grand Rapids: Baker, 1996.

Fruchtenbaum, Dr. Arnold G.. *The Footsteps of the Messiah*. Tustin, Calif.: Ariel Ministries Pub., 2003.

Gaebelein, A.C.. *The Annotated Bible*. New York: Our Hope Pub., 1913

———. *Daniel*. New York: Our Hope Pub., 1911.

Geisler, Dr. Norman. *Systematic Theology*. Minneapolis: Bethany House, 2005.Vol. IV

Goldberg, Louis & Elwell, Walter A. ed., *Baker Theological Dictionary of the Bible*. Grand Rapids: Baker,1996.

Greene, Brian *The Elegant Universe*. New York: W.W. Norton & Company Ltd., 1999.

Grudem, Wayne. *Systematic Theology*. Grand Rapids: Inter-Varsity Press, 1994.

Jastrow, Robert. *God and the Astronomers*. New York: W.W. Norton & Company, Inc., 1978.

Kaku, Michio. *Hyperspace*. New York: Anchor Books, 1995.

———. *Parallel Worlds* New York: Doubleday, 2005.

———. *Physics of the Impossible*. New York: Random House, 2008.

Keil, C.F. and Delitzsch, F.. *Commentary on the Old Testament*. 1866. Reprint, Peabody, Massachusetts: Hendrickson Pub., 2006.

Klein, Judith, proj. ed.. *The Science Book*. Washington D.C.: National Geographic, 2008.

Laurie, Greg. *The Invisible World*. Santa Anna, California: FMG, 1991.

Lutzer, Erwin W.. *One Minute After You Die*. Chicago: Moody Press, 1997.

MacArthur, John F.. *The Glory of Heaven*. Wheaton, Illinois: Crossway Books, 1996.

Maimonides. *Guide of the Perplexed*. trans., Friedlander, M., New York:

Hebrew Publishing Co.,1901.

Martin, Walter *The Kingdom of the Cults*. Minneapolis: Bethany House Pub., 1965. revised – updated and expanded, 1997.

McDowell, Josh & Steward, Don. *Handbook of Today's Religions*. Nashville: Thomas Nelson Pub., 1983.

Missler, Dr. Chuck. *Cosmic Codes*. Coeur d'Alene, Idaho: Koinonia House Pub., 1999.

———. *The Book of Daniel*. Coeur d'Alene, Id: Koinonia House Pub., 2004.

———. *The Book of Genesis: Comprehensive Workbook*. Coeur d'Alene, Idaho: Koinonia House, 2004.

———. & Eastman, Mark. *Alien Encounters*. Coeur d/Alene,, Idaho: Koinonia House Pub., 1997.

Morey, Dr. Robert A.. *Death and the Afterlife*. Minneapolis: Bethany House Publishers, 1984.

Morgan, G. Campbell D.D.. *The Gospel According to Luke*. Old Tappan, New Jersey: Fleming Revell Co., 1931

Morris, Henry M.. *The Genesis Record*. Grand Rapids: Baker Book House, 1976.

Nachmanides, Ramban. *Commentary on the Torah – Genesis*, trans. Chavel, Rabbi Charles. 13th Century. Reprint, NewYork: Shilo House Pub. Inc., 1999.

Oard, Michael. *Frozen in Time*. Green Forest, AR: Master Books, 2004.

Olson, Reuben proj. chairman. *Zondervan NASB Exhaustive Concordance*. Grand Rapids: Zondervan, 2000.

Patten, Donald W., Hatch, Ronald and Steinhauer, Loren. *The Long Day of Joshua and Six other Catastrophes*. Seattle: Pacific Meridian Pub., 1973.

Payne, J. Barton. *Encyclopedia of Biblical Prophecy*. Grand Rapids: Baker Book House, 1973.

Peretti, Frank E.. *This Present Darkness*. Wheaton, Illinois: Crossway Books, 1986.

Phillips, John. *Exploring the Gospel of John.* Grand Rapids: Kregel Pub., 1989.

Pink, Arthur. *Gleanings in Genesis – Vol I & II.* Chicago: Moody Press, 1922.

Piper, Don & Murphey, Cecil. *90 Minutes in Heaven: Selections.* Grand Rapids: Revell, 2004, 2008.

Robertson, Archibald Thomas. *Word Pictures in the New Testament.* New York; Harper & Brothers Pub., 1930.

Ross, Hugh, Ph.D.. *Beyond the Cosmos.* Colorado Springs: Navpress, 1996.

Ryle, J.C.. *Heaven.* Ross-shire, UK: Christian Focus Pub., 1969.

Schofield, A.T. M.D.. *Another World.* London: Swan Sonnenschein & Co. Lim., 1888.

Schroeder, Gerald *Genesis and the Big Bang.* New York: Bantam Books, 1990.

Scofield, C.I.. *Scofield Study Bible: NAS.* 1917. Reprint, New York: Oxford University Press, 2005

Sutliff, Gary. *God Speaks Science.* Gilbert, Arizona: Hyperspace Chief Pub., 2006.

Thomas, Rev. W.H. Griffith D.D.. *Genesis: 1-XXV*, 3rd ed.. London: Religious Tract Society, 1909.

Van Flandern, Tom. *Dark Matter Missing Planets and New Comets.* Rev ed.. Berkley, Calif.: North Atlantic Books, 1993.

Vincent, Marvin R. D.D.. *Word Studies in the New Testament.* 1886. Reprint. Peabody, Massachusetts: Hendrickson Publishers, no date.

Willink, Arthur. *The World of the Unseen.* New York: Macmillan & Co., 1893.

Wiersbe, Warren. *The Bible Exposition Commentary: Vol4.* Colorado Springs: Victor, Cook Communications, 2001.

Wiese, Bill. *23 Minutes in Hell.* Lake Mary, Florida: Charisma House, 2006.

Wood, Leon. *A survey of Israel's History.* Grand Rapids: Zondervan

Publishing Huose, 1970.

Wuest, Kenneth. *Word Studies from the Greek New Testament.* 1947. Reprint, Grand Rapids: Eerdmans, 2002.

Hyperspace in Scripture

Index

Abbot 171

Abyss 124, 126, 127, 128, 129, 134

America .... v, 64, 167, 212

animals............................. 40, 111

Atbash...................................... 30

Belshazzar 26, 27, 28, 29, 30, 31, 32, 35, 182

Big Bang 137, 138, 142, 145, 146, 147, 148, 151, 152, 153, 158, 159, 161, 204

Bottomless Pit 116, 124, 125, 126, 127, 129, 132, 134, 135, 187

chariots of fire 1, 37, 39, 46, 47, 48, 53, 185, 187, 192

Christophany 59

City of the Living God 2, 3, 84, 85, 86, 95, 100, 103, 104, 110, 120, 121, 185

COBE 141

Cyrus the Great......................... 31

Einstein 140, 147, 149, 151, 152, 162, 164, 165, 166, 173

Elisha 37, 38, 39, 40, 42, 45, 46, 47, 48, 49, 51, 52, 53, 186, 192

Emmaus 9, 19, 20, 21, 22, 23, 192

Fabric of Space 138, 141, 142

fallen angels 113, 115, 116, 126, 127, 129, 134, 135

Gabriel 55, 60, 61, 62, 186, 192

gates 122, 123, 134

Golgatha.................................... 91

Goombas 15, 49, 50, 51, 66, 67, 68, 69, 70, 102, 103, 117, 122, 128

grave 8, 10, 115, 116, 117, 134, 135, 196

Greene 142, 202

Hades 78, 81, 99, 113, 115, 116, 117, 118, 119, 120, 121, 122, 123, 124, 125, 126, 127, 129, 130, 131, 132, 133, 134, 135, 187

handwriting on the wall 25, 27, 29, 30, 31, 34, 172

hell 113

209

Hell 113, 114, 121, 130, 204

horses 1, 37, 38, 39, 40, 46, 47, 53, 185, 187

hypercube 179, 180, 181, 182

Jacob 42, 43, 44, 59, 83, 121, 133, 186

Jerusalem , 20, 21, 22, 23, 26, 73, 78, 79, 81, 82, 84, 85, 86, 87, 88, 90, 91, 92, 95, 100, 101, 104, 105, 109, 110, 111, 120, 121, 127, 131, 132, 156, 178, 192

Kaku 15, 17, 33, 139, 140, 141, 147, 161, 162, 164, 165, 167, 170, 175, 202

Lake of Fire 116, 129, 130, 131, 132, 133, 134, 135, 136

Lazarus 11, 12, 14, 104, 118

length 73, 75, 154, 155, 156, 177, 179, 180, 186

living creatures 97, 98

M Theory 81

Maimonides 152, 202

Mercy Seat 90, 111

Michael 60, 62, 75, 169, 203

Mount Zion 44, 84, 85, 86, 87, 91, 95, 102, 104, 185

Nachmanides 137, 143, 144, 145, 148, 151, 152, 161, 203

Nicodemus 105

ordinances 1, 57

ordnances of heaven 190

Ornan 91

Outer darkness 133

Piper 82, 204

Prince of Persia. 62, 63, 64, 67, 75

Ramban 137, 144, 145, 152, 161, 203

resurrected body 10, 12, 13, 23, 41, 90, 95

Riemann 162, 165, 166

rolled up 138, 140, 142, 156, 158, 187, 192

Salvado Dali 182

Schofield 15, 171, 204

seraphim 97

shadow 19, 83, 92, 93, 110, 180, 186

Shechinah Glory 89

Sheol 115, 116, 117, 118, 119, 120, 121, 122

Solomon's Temple 27, 89, 90, 110

spiritual creatures 40, 46, 50, 70, 102, 107, 125, 131, 135, 177

Stephen 42, 44, 48, 109, 186

String Theory 81, 163, 167

Theo-magic 23, 34, 41

Throne of God 62, 64, 70, 71, 78, 81, 82, 95, 98, 108

time 2, 3, 4, 8, 12, 14, 15, 18, 20, 23, 24, 26, 27, 28, 29, 34, 37, 38, 40, 41, 45, 46, 52, 55, 60, 62, 63, 64, 72, 73, 78, 80, 81, 85, 89, 91, 96, 99, 100, 101, 106, 107, 108, 109, 110, 118, 119, 120, 121, 122, 127, 128, 130, 132, 133, 134, 136, 137, 138, 140, 142, 144, 145, 146, 147, 148, 149, 150, 151, 152, 153, 154, 155, 156, 157, 159, 162, 166, 168, 171, 172, 174, 177, 178, 185, 186, 187, 188, 191, 192, 193, 210

underworld 3, 113, 114, 115, 121, 122, 123, 124, 130, 131, 134, 185

unseen world 1, 12, 18, 19, 23, 24, 32, 34, 35, 40, 47, 50, 51, 61, 63, 73, 74, 79, 81, 83, 126, 142

Uphaz 71

Vanished 13

veil 2, 21, 22, 23, 24, 33, 34, 41, 43, 46, 85, 89, 94, 104, 127

visible world 11, 12, 41, 61, 66

voodoo 65

Willink 77, 139, 171, 204

WMAP satellite 141

Hyperspace in Scripture

About the Author

Raised in a loving and stable Christian family, Gary received the Lord as his personal savior and gave his life to Christ at a summer camp at the age of 13. Being born and raised in San Diego, California, he spent much of his time outdoors and at the beach, with a surfing type lifestyle typical of the 50's and 60's. At the age of 15, Gary was personally mentored by a church pastor, was one of many in the "Jesus Movement" of Southern California (of the 60's) and was very active spiritually.

At Capernwray Bible College in England, right after high school, Gary met the beautiful and talented girl who was to become his wife. They were married 4 years later, lived in San Diego and raised a family of two girls and one boy. Today, all of the children are married and Gary and his wife Kay have 6 grandsons. Spending time with family is a big part of Gary and Kay's lives, aided by the fact that all three of the families live in the local area.

Professionally, after graduation from California State Polytechnic University: San Luis Obispo (Cal Poly SLO) with a degree in Aeronautical Engineering (structures and mechanical emphasis) Gary worked as a structural design engineer at General Dynamics Convair working on the Space Shuttle mid-fuselage program, cruise missile and several classified efforts. After 6 years, Gary joined a small research and development group doing high tech classified military projects, progressing from lead engineer to engineering manager to engineering director to company chief engineer. The company was acquired by McDonnell Douglas and relocated to Arizona in 1996 and Gary assumed responsibility of a small research team of 20 people. Boeing purchased McDonnell Douglas a few years later and Gary continued in a senior manager position leading an advanced research and development group chartered to advance the technology state-of-the-art in a unique area of classified research. Gary took and early retirement from Boeing in 2012 and began working as the Executive Pastor of Ministries at Mission Community Church in Gilbert Arizona.

God has given Gary a passion to study the scriptures, which he has diligently applied over the years. Early on, Gary attended home bible studies while growing up and upon graduation from college; he began to teach the scriptures in small group settings. Gary has taught numerous bible studies and adult Sunday School classes throughout his life covering subjects from books of the bible and topical studies including science and the bible and various end times subjects. He is committed to the God given charter of the local church serving in many ministry areas over the years. Using his leadership gifts, Gary has served on elder boards for the past 30 years and has been chairman of the board for most of those. Gary has participated in 5 church building programs, leading the last two, which include a $12m church campus expansion including a new worship center seating 1,500 people.

Other current interests include woodworking, golf, backpacking and mountain climbing.

In continued pursuit of a God given passion, Gary formally studied the scriptures through Louisiana Baptist University (LBU). From LBU he received a Masters Degree in Biblical Studies and a PhD in Biblical Studies. His doctoral dissertation was *"Hyperspace and the Spiritual Realm."* He is also a teaching assistant with Dr. Chuck Missler's Kononia Institute where he continues to take on-line classes. Gary received their Silver Medallion in February 2011 and is working towards his Gold Medallion.

Gary anticipates further ministry opportunities as God enables him to do so; looking forward to new adventures God will be bringing in his life, his family and his church.

Other resources by Author:

 **God Speaks Science**: A fascinating look at a wide array of the scientific claims made in scripture. God will grow bigger and bigger in your understanding as you come to see the intricacy of His wonderful creation and how it has been revealed in the pages of Scripture.

 **Future: Plain, Simple & Scriptural**: A straight forward Biblically based look at the future of; the Earth, the universe, believers, non-believers, the United States of America and other interesting topics. Loaded with illustrations. There is much good news for those who follow the Lord Jesus.

 **End Times Logic**: A comparative look and Scriptural evaluation of Preterism, Dispensationalism, Amillennialism, Pre-Millennialism and Post-Millennialism. There are so many different views on the end times and so much controversy. This book makes a straight forward logical comparison of views and comparing them against scripture. If you are confused, this will help.

 **God's Science Quiz**: Study of the 77 science questions found in Job chapters 38-41. In what is believed to be the oldest book of Scripture God's challenges Job's understanding and reveals Himself as a God very involved in His creation. Discover 15 unique scientific claims revealed in these 4 chapters of scripture 1,000's of years prior to their scientific discovery.

Hyperspace in Scripture

Personal Recommendation:

Recommendation: If you are challenged and would like to learn more about the Bible there is a super program and group of people who are committed to helping you. These are the folks at Koinonia Institute (KI). The Institute offers on-line Biblical instruction with excellence. Offered over the internet, straight forward Biblical teaching is easily available and can be accomplished from any laptop or computer. With ease and flexibility you can listen to teachings at your convenience anywhere you can take your laptop or from the privacy of your own home. Your learning is facilitated as you are supported by an extremely capable staff and group of teacher assistants. These folks are dedicated, compassionate and passionate about the scriptures and helping others. KI offers a basic starter program, the Bronze Medallion, suited for everyone from new-believers to seasoned Bible students. In the program taught by world renowned former corporate CEO and Bible Teacher Dr. Chuck Missler's you will cover "Learn the Bible in 24 Hours" (which covers both Old Testament and New Testament); be introduced to Biblical Prophecy from Dr. Missler, a world recognized expert in Biblical Prophecy and Strategic Perspectives; and a class in Spiritual Disciplines taught by Dr. Dan Stolenbarger, head of KI and a seasoned leader and developer of small group strategies. Spiritual growth and understanding is the primary benefit of this program but the Bronze Medallion awarded upon completion will certainly grace any wall or desk.